DEBATING THE AMERICAN CONSERVATIVE MOVEMENT

Debating Twentieth-Century America
Series Editor: James T. Patterson, Brown University

DEBATING THE AMERICAN CONSERVATIVE MOVEMENT

1945 to the Present

DONALD T. CRITCHLOW AND NANCY MacLEAN

ROWMAN & LITTLEFIELD PUBLISHERS, INC.
Lanham • Boulder • New York • Toronto • Plymouth, UK

ROWMAN & LITTLEFIELD PUBLISHERS, INC.

Published in the United States of America
by Rowman & Littlefield Publishers, Inc.
A wholly owned subsidary of The Rowman & Littlefield Publishing Group, Inc.
4501 Forbes Boulevard, Suite 200, Lanham, Maryland 20706
www.rowmanlittlefield.com

Estover Road
Plymouth PL6 7PY
United Kingdom

British Library Cataloguing in Publication Information Available

Library of Congress Cataloging-in-Publication Data:

Critchlow, Donald T., 1948–
  Debating the American conservative movement : 1945 to the present / Donald
T. Critchlow and Nancy MacLean.
      p. cm. — (Debating twentieth-century America)
    Includes bibliographical references and index.
    ISBN 978-0-7425-4823-7 (cloth : alk. paper) — ISBN 978-0-7425-4824-4
(pbk. : alk. paper)
    1. Conservatism—United States—History—20th century. 2. Conservatism—
United States—History—21st century. 3. United States—Politics and
government—1945–1989. 4. United States—Politics and government—1989–
5. Conservatism—United States—History—20th century—Sources. 6.
Conservatism—United States—History—21st century—Sources. 7. United
States—Politics and government—1945–1989—Sources. 8. United States—
Politics and government—1989—Sources. I. MacLean, Nancy II. Title.
  JC573.2.U6C748 2009
  320.520973—dc22
                                                        2008048284

Printed in the United States of America

∞™ The paper used in this publication meets the minimum requirements of
American National Standard for Information Sciences—Permanence of Paper for
Printed Library Materials, ANSI/NISO Z39.48-1992.

CONTENTS

PREFACE

How did a political fringe become mainstream? In the mid-1950s most commentators dismissed American conservative movement activists as kooks. Yet by 2000, their heirs controlled the White House, both houses of Congress, and to a large extent the judiciary. How did they move from the margins to the pinnacle of power? And what have the consequences been for the country? These questions are among the most vital for understanding the last half-century of U.S. history and American political development. Exposing students to rival interpretations, each with compelling primary sources to prove its case, this book will stimulate its readers to stretch beyond their own personal inclinations and reason out conclusions based on sound evidence.

Debating the American Conservative Movement invites students to make sense of why and how a small band of conservatives in the immediate aftermath of the Second World War launched a slow-motion revolution that challenged the New Deal order, shifted American politics to the right, transformed the Republican Party into a citadel of conservatism, and set the terms of national debate on a host of policy issues as the country entered a new millennium. Our narratives offer two sharply contrasting explanations for how conservatives gained power, the first essay deeply sympathetic to the movement's goals and achievements and the second essay quite critical of them. Both interpretations are supported and illustrated by intriguing primary documents.

Donald Critchlow argues that the conservatives gained power because their commitments to individualism, free markets, limited government, traditional family values, and a strong national defense were best suited to the emerging postindustrial, Sun Belt–anchored, suburban society, and in keeping with the needs and desires of most Americans. Nancy MacLean argues, in contrast, that the conservative movement's core commitment since its founding has been to safeguard the advantages of those long privileged—whether by class, race, gender, religion, or sexual orientation—and that its leaders have systematically exploited fear and prejudice in order to acquire power. Where Critchlow sees the consequences of the conservative ascendancy as beneficial to the nation, MacLean sees them as debilitating. In short, this book presents a real debate. We offer two opposed interpretations of the central development of American political life since the late 1960s.

Still, there are some commonalities between the two perspectives that should reinforce and deepen what students in U.S. history, government, and sociology courses have learned in prior units. We both treat conservatism as a social movement—a wide-ranging, self-conscious, collective, and strategic effort to change the country's direction—rooted in some of the central developments of postwar American life. Rather than the story of a group of intellectuals, on the one side, or politicians, on the other, our approach shows how ideas, grassroots organizing, economic and social change, cultural developments, electoral politics, and institution building all interacted to produce the rise of the Right. We also identify responses to the New Deal, the Cold War, and the civil rights and feminist movements as pivotal, even while disagreeing on what exactly drove them. And we each present lively documents that will enable students to understand this movement's development in light of core contested values in the American political tradition, such as liberty, equality, and justice.

We seek to model for students how to disagree with substance and civility, a skill in woefully short supply in today's highly polarized politics. As scholars and citizens, we have watched with dismay the degeneration of American political debate into character assassination and shouting matches. As deep as the differences between us are, we share concern for how our country can meet the serious challenges it faces when our media seem to prize gladiatorial spectacle over reasoned debate based on honest identification of values and goals and rigorous assessment of appropriate evidence. We hope this book will help students learn that the strongest, most tenable positions are arrived at through careful sifting of evidence and respectful encounters with opposing points of view.

Donald T. Critchlow
Nancy MacLean

THE CONSERVATIVE ASCENDANCY

Donald T. Critchlow

INTRODUCTION

Speaking to an audience of conservatives on March 8, 1985, President Ronald Reagan, who had won reelection the year before in a landslide, noted a great change that had occurred in American politics since the end of the Second World War: Conservatism had become a respectable political point of view, accepted by millions of Americans. Noting this transformation in 1981, Reagan asked how this sea change in American politics had occurred. Why had conservatism become the mainstream? His answer was simply: "Because the other side is virtually bankrupt of ideas. It has nothing more to say, nothing to add to the debate. It has spent its intellectual capital, such as it was, and it has done its deeds. . . . We [conservatives] in this room are not simply profiting from their bankruptcy; we are where we are because we're winning the contest of ideas. In fact, in the past decade, all of a sudden, quietly, mysteriously, the Republican party has become the party of ideas."

Reagan observed that conservatism triumphed politically in these years because of an intellectual revolution of sorts. He suggested that conservatives had developed new ideas to address the needs of America in 1985, while liberals continued to maintain a philosophy based on a New Deal industrial order characterized by an economy based on manufacturing, a highly unionized workforce, and a population concentrated in the industrial Northeast and Midwest, with most people living in cities.

In 1985, when Reagan spoke, most Americans lived in the Sun Belt, the service economy had expanded at the expense of manufacturing, most workers were white collar (and many were women), and most people lived in suburbs. Furthermore, the world had changed. The economy was global

1

in 1985. In this new postindustrial world, Republicans seemed to have bold ideas about defending American liberties through less intrusive centralized government, creating equal opportunity for all social and racial groups, promoting economic prosperity for everyone through free markets, and protecting the country from foreign threats through national defense.

The election of Reagan to the White House in 1980 and 1984 marked a major transformation in American politics, characterized by a major shift in the electorate to the right. At the end of the Second World War, less than 10 percent of the electorate identified themselves as conservative. Nearly a majority of voters labeled themselves as liberals. By 1985, more American voters identified themselves as conservatives than as liberals. This pattern held into the early twenty-first century. In 2008, even with the unpopularity of the George W. Bush administration, and the decline of voters declaring themselves Republican, nearly 35 percent of voters continued to describe themselves as conservatives, while another third identified themselves as moderates, and only about 15 percent of voters identified themselves as liberals or progressives.

This volume explores the reasons for this shift. Historians are primarily interested in explaining change and continuity in history. In seeking to explain change, historians might arrive at different conclusions as to the causes of change and continuity in history, but their task is not to interject moral conclusions about their subjects. Instead, historians bring a specialized knowledge to their subjects to explain what happened and why. This does not mean that moral judgments cannot be made about history, but one does not need to be a trained historian to conclude that "Josef Stalin, the dictator of the Soviet Union in the 1930s, was evil." To explain how and why Stalin came to power in the 1920s, however, is a different matter, one left for historians to explain. This volume, *Debating the American Conservative Movement*, asks students to examine how and why conservatives became a major force in American politics in the last half of the twentieth century.

We can begin this project by reviewing the political background and the subsequent events that occurred with the conservative ascendancy.

The ascendance of the Right came through fits and starts after the Second World War. The Democratic Party coalition erected during the New Deal, based on urban voters in the North, labor unions, ethnic and racial minorities, and southern whites, remained a major political force in the immediate aftermath of the Second World War. Democrats had erected the modern welfare and regulatory state in three great waves of reform, the Progressive period in the early twentieth century, the New Deal in the 1930s, and Lyndon Johnson's Great Society in the 1960s. The modern welfare state was created to protect the unemployed, the injured, the elderly, and mothers and children living in poverty. Federal regulations protected the public from unfair and unsafe business practices. Although liberal reformers during the Progressive and New Deal eras gave little attention to black civil rights, under Lyndon Johnson civil rights and protection of voting rights were extended to blacks.

Franklin D. Roosevelt gave the people Social Security and Johnson gave the people Medicare. At the same time, Democrats enacted legislation to provide subsidies to farmers, food stamps for the poor, lunch programs for children, family planning for poor women, compensation for those injured at work, and environmental regulations.

Given these accomplishments, many liberals simply could not understand why voters began to turn away from the Democratic Party in droves in the late 1960s. Unable to explain why many voters deserted the Democratic Party for the Republican Party, liberals blamed smooth-talking Republican politicians who exploited voters' worst passions. They accused Republicans of playing on racial fears, using code words about a "color-blind" society, while seeking to maintain a racial hierarchy, mobilizing religious zealots on the Christian Right, and exploiting the patriotism shared by average Americans. Some liberals saw the evil hand of large corporations that wanted tax cuts and less government regulation, or the bigotry of reactionaries who feared racial and gender equality. There was a good deal of moralistic anger in these accusations, and often little analysis. More important, it presumed that large numbers of average Americans had been fooled and did not understand their own interests.

Conservatism in modern America is not a systematic ideology but a political perspective with a shared set of general beliefs. These political beliefs had deep roots in the American political tradition and were commonly accepted in American culture until the rise of modern liberalism in the Progressive era and New Deal era. In challenging modern liberals, conservatives returned to these older principles and beliefs embodied in the English and American concept of liberty.

Conservatives appealed to the long-standing belief in *American individualism*, distrust of centralized government, and caution about radical change. At the core of the conservative philosophy was a commitment to the axiom: "Minimum government is necessary to preserve order and defend the nation, but centralized government threatens individual liberty." American revolutionary Thomas Paine expressed this sentiment in his famous pamphlet, *Common Sense* (1776) when he wrote, "Society is produced by our wants and government by our wickedness; the former promotes our happiness positively by uniting our affections; the latter negatively by restraining our vices." He added, "Society is a blessing; government, even in its best state, is but a necessary evil; in its worst state, is an intolerable one."

This long-standing *distrust of centralized government* had prevailed in American politics and culture until the advent of Progressive reform in the early twentieth century. Conservatives sought to overturn the New Deal political order and its philosophical underpinnings.

Conservatives believed in an intimate connection between *economic freedom and political freedom*. As Nobel Prize–winning economist Milton Friedman observed in *Capitalism and Freedom* (1962), "freedom in economic arrangements is itself a component of freedom broadly understood so economic freedom is an end in itself. . . . [E]conomic freedom is also an indispensable means toward the achievement of political power." Friedman shared a fundamental belief with others on the Right that competitive capitalism promoted political freedom because it separated economic power from political power and as a result enabled one to offset the other.

A cornerstone of conservative thought was that *free markets* (competitive capitalism) created economic prosperity that benefited all classes. Capitalism was essential to maintaining political freedom because government control and too much interference in the economy translated into increased government power at the expense of individual freedom. As Frank Chodorov, a member of the *National Review* editorial board, declared in 1954, "the independence of the people is in direct proportion to the amount of wealth they can enjoy." Conservatives attacked liberal Keynesian economic policy that sought to control inflation and unemployment through the federal budget.

Conservatives called for *welfare reform*, because they believed that programs such as Aid to Dependent Children encouraged dependency and did little to relieve poverty rates.

Conservatives had long opposed the growth of the welfare state that emerged in the Progressive period at the turn of the twentieth century and expanded during the New Deal and Great Society. In *The Conscience of a Conservative* (1960), Barry Goldwater articulated the complaint against the modern welfare state when he declared, "The long range political consequences of welfarism are plain enough: as we have seen, the State that is able to deal with its citizens as wards and dependents has gathered unto itself unlimited political and economic power and is thus able to rule as absolutely as any oriental despot." Conservatives were not opposed to helping the truly needy, but the welfare state had grown immensely following the 1930s. Social science evidence from many studies in the 1970s showed that welfare abetted the growth of poverty by encouraging dependency, discouraging work, and fostering out-of-wedlock birth.

Conservatives promoted *traditional family values*. Conservatives maintained that traditional two-parent families provided the best protection for children. They drew on numerous social science studies that found a direct correlation between out-of-wedlock births and single-parent families with poverty, welfare dependency, juvenile delinquency, and adult crime.

Conservatives called for *equal opportunity*. While neither Democrats nor Republicans, liberals nor conservatives, have enjoyed a completely positive record on civil rights, the Grand Old Party (GOP), the Republican Party, has stood historically as a defender of black civil rights. In modern America, the conservatives established a strong record on civil rights for African Americans:

1922   Republicans in the House of Representatives proposed a federal antilynching law. This measure was taken up again in 1937 and 1940, only to have these bills defeated by filibusters in the U.S. Senate by southern Democrats. Conservative Hamilton Fish (R–New York) played an important role in proposing this legislation. In the First World War, Fish had volunteered to serve as an officer with the Fighting 369th, a black unit better known as the Harlem Hellfighters.

1933   Oscar De Priest (R–Illinois), the first black elected to Congress in the twentieth century and a staunch anti–New Deal conservative, successfully proposed an antidiscrimination provision for the Civilian Conservation Corps law.

1934   De Priest, who opposed federal aid to the needy, actively opposed segregation in the House of Representatives restaurant. After a three-month heated debate, the Democrats defeated integration of the House restaurant.

1947   The Republican-controlled Senate headed by Robert Taft (R–Ohio) refused to seat notorious racist Theodore Bilbo (D–Mississippi) because of intimidation of black voters in the 1946 election. The Republican report was written by Senator Styles Bridges (R–New Hampshire), a leading anti-Communist Republican.

1947   Branch Rickey, the general manager of the Brooklyn Dodgers and an anti–New Deal Republican, integrated major league baseball when he signed Jackie Robinson. Rickey described breaking the baseball color bar as a "call from heaven."

1953   President Dwight D. Eisenhower desegregated the nation's capitol, Washington, DC. At the same time he pressed ahead with the desegregation of the U.S. armed forces, which had lagged under Harry S. Truman.

1957   Eisenhower, working closely with Vice President Richard Nixon and the attorney general, submitted a "full package" civil rights bill to Congress, which would have allowed jury trials for voter intimidation cases. While Republicans backed the bill, Senate Democrats, led by majority leader Lyndon Baines Johnson, watered it down to become nearly meaningless.

1964   Congress enacted the first major civil rights legislation since Reconstruction. This legislation could not have been enacted without support from conservative and moderate Republicans, especially Senate Minority Leader Everett Dirksen (R-Illinois), a conservative. Major opposition in Congress came not from "conservatives" but from southern Democrats who generally supported Great Society welfare programs.

Conservatives called for a *strong national defense*. Conservatives maintained that a policy of "peace through strength" was the best way to protect the nation from nuclear war. Military weakness invited attack from foreign enemies. Ronald Reagan's presidency gave the highest priority to strengthening the nation's military preparedness, after nearly a decade of severe budget cuts by a Democratic-controlled Congress in the 1970s. Reagan's policies paid dividends. In the late 1980s and early 1990s, the Soviet Union and the United States signed arms control treaties that radically cut entire nuclear weapon and delivery systems for the first time in history.

Conservatives did not seek to create a perfect world; indeed, they believed this was impossible. History showed that those who sought to create a perfect world—whether it be the French revolutionaries in the eighteenth century, the Bolsheviks in the Russian Revolution, or Nazis in the 1930s—created only chaos and destruction.

In general, conservatives such as Reagan emphasize the *wisdom of history* and reject radical social change as often foolish, faddish, or willful arrogance. Conservatives respect history, its lessons, and its numerous follies. Conservatives believe in evolution (at least for the body politic, if not for the species) rather than radical change or revolution; in caution over hastiness (knowing that activist government to solve problems is often folly); in individual rights rather than collective group rights; and in liberty as a virtue necessary to provide liberty and equality, whereas a surplus of equality will so diminish liberty that there will be a tyranny of equality. Drawing from English philosopher John Locke, conservatives believe that private property is the foundation of liberty and a necessity to prevent the tyranny of an all-powerful state. As such, conservatives are suspicious of state power, except when it is exercised in the necessary external defense of the nation.

It was within this philosophical framework that conservatives such as Ronald Reagan sought new policies and a new politics as an alternative to the New Deal–Great Society welfare and regulatory state.

OUR ENEMY, THE NEW DEAL STATE

In 1935, journalist Albert Jay Nock wrote a book widely circulated by conservatives in the post–Second World War years, *Our Enemy, the State*. In the book, he outlined the conservative complaint against centralized government as a parasite that drained the productive forces from society. The state usurped individual rights in the name of the amorphous collective. For postwar conservatives such as Nock, the New Deal welfare state embodied the worst aspects of the growth of leviathan government in America.

The rise of postwar conservatism can only be understood in light of New Deal liberalism. The New Deal emerged under President Franklin D. Roosevelt in response to a worldwide crisis in industrial capitalism. The industrial revolution in the nineteenth century transformed America into the world's wealthiest economy. This industrial revolution had changed production and work itself. Factories doubled in size, hired more and more workers, and introduced more complex machinery into the workplace. Railroad lines and telegraph systems linked isolated communities into a single society. This industrial revolution brought mass-produced goods and new technology to the average American consumer, raising the nation's standard of living. This growing wealth allowed the development of the largest middle class in human history. Still, most workers were left unprotected from pay cuts, unemployment, or hazardous working conditions. Unions emerged to protect workers' rights, while some workers turned to radical third parties such as the Socialist Party to protect their interests. Social conflict between capital and labor led to violent confrontation.

Social tensions were heightened as millions of immigrants arrived in America. Many came from eastern and southern Europe. The massive influx of immigrants transformed American cities both physically and culturally, creating problems of housing, sanitation, crime, and poverty, as well as ethnic and class conflicts.

Reformers sought to address the problems created by this industrial revolution through a variety of measures. Between 1900 and the American entry into World War I in 1917, the United States experienced an outburst of reform that extended into nearly every institution and extended government powers on the local, state, and national levels. While reformers differed on methods and goals, they shared a general belief that government, especially the federal government, had a new role to play in society. This modern liberal vision found expression in the Progressive era, when government at all levels grew in size and power.

The Progressive vision informed the New Deal under President Franklin Roosevelt as government officials responded to the worst depression in American history. While New Deal economic policies failed to revive the economy—and some economists have argued they worsened matters—Roosevelt's New Deal expanded federal power and created a new political coalition that would dominate American politics for the next four decades. Under the New Deal, the modern welfare state was established through a Social Security system designed to provide via employer and employee taxes pensions for the elderly, relief for widows and single mothers with children, benefits to the blind and physically disabled, and compensation to unemployed or injured workers. The Social Security system was a federal system that provided direct federal benefits for the elderly, while providing matching funds for various programs operated through the states, including welfare, unemployment insurance, and workers' compensation. The New Deal also expanded federal regulatory powers through various agencies that oversaw Wall Street, the banking industry, food and drugs, employee labor relations, and fair prices on certain manufactured goods.

While the modern welfare state was being established and the regulatory state expanded, Roosevelt put into place a formidable political coalition composed of ethnic voters in the industrial Northeast, rural and urban African Americans, and whites in the South. The New Deal political coalition was premised on an industrial society composed of a unionized workforce earning high wages and benefits. A welfare system was designed to take care of citizens unable to work, and farmers were provided with subsidies and price supports. This political program was constrained by the southern wing of the Democratic party. As a consequence, liberals failed to enact national health insurance and failed to guarantee voting and civil rights for African Americans in the segregated South during the New Deal and Fair Deal periods.

In post–World War II America, the economy moved from an industrial basis to a postindustrial economy that undermined the New Deal liberal vision of a good society. In this economic transformation the American workforce became more white collar and less unionized. As the economy shifted to more high-tech and service jobs, employers, burdened by alarming increases in local taxes and government regulation, left eastern cities for more favorable business environments in the Sun Belt. Deteriorating conditions in the industrial East and Midwest, racial tensions, and opportunities for a better life led large numbers of people to move to the suburbs and to the Sun Belt.

In the latter half of the twentieth century, America underwent profound changes. The family was transformed as more women became college educated and developed professional careers. Marriage ages increased; family size decreased, and divorce rates went up. The suburbanization of America, changing family structures, and a service economy pulled voters toward the Republican Party's agenda of low taxes, strong national defense, and traditional social values. The New Deal's agenda based on an industrial society appeared increasingly antiquated to many voters living in the expansive Sun Belt (the South, Southwest, and California) in the post–Second World War period.

CONSERVATIVE IDEAS MATTER

For many conservatives, the New Deal overturned the long-standing American tradition that centralized government posed a threat to individual liberty. Under the Roosevelt regime, the federal government extended itself into nearly every aspect of American life—all in the guise of meeting the needs of the people. Perhaps if the New Deal had succeeded in economic recovery, it might have been tolerated by conservatives. But it did not. When war broke out in Europe in 1939, one out of five workers still remained unemployed. In an uncertain political environment, business hesitated to expand. Many in business viewed the federal government as vehemently anticorporate and enthusiastically pro–organized labor. Within the context of the rise of fascism in Germany and Communism in the Soviet Union, many conservatives saw in the New Deal another form of collectivism. They feared America was drifting toward socialism.

Before the Second World War, the American Right offered primarily a polemical attack against the New Deal. Right-wing critics of the New Deal were an odd mixture of people and views. They shared a fear that Roosevelt's policies were socialistic and individual freedom was being eroded by big government. The American Right was extremely anti-Communist, with some of the more conspiratorial minded among them equating New Dealers with Communists. A few were anti-Semitic. Most were noninterventionists who did not want the United States to become involved in another European war after Germany under Adolf Hitler and the Soviet Union under Josef Stalin invaded Poland in 1939. When Hitler betrayed his ally Stalin and invaded the Soviet Union in 1941, many American conservatives held firm to their convictions of noninterventionism in the hopes that the two nations would annihilate each other.

The war against Nazi Germany and the emergence of the Soviet Union as a world power following the war changed conservative opinion about world affairs. Most conservatives accepted a new role for the United States in the postwar world. Moreover, the rise of the totalitarian state in Nazi Germany and Communist Russia heightened fears among conservatives about whether individual freedom could be maintained in the future. In response to the totalitarian state, conservative intellectuals explored the philosophical importance of maintaining individualism, civic virtue, social morality and order, and tradition as essential to the preservation of liberty in a free society.

These ideas were explored with profound insight and through unfettered debate by a small and diverse band of intellectuals, including Jewish and Roman Catholic émigrés from Nazi or Communist Europe and a younger generation of American intellectuals. These intellectuals were joined by a large, although mostly unorganized, grassroots anti-Communist movement. The coming together of this intellectual movement and the popular anti-Communist movement laid the foundations of modern-day conservatism. Postwar anti-Communism gave coherence to the postwar Right, but underlying this sentiment was a well-articulated critique of the collectivist state, which included fascism and socialism.

Intellectual revolutions are often made by outsiders, and this was the case in the post–Second World War revolt against modern liberalism. These cultural outsiders included economist Friedrich Hayek, an Austrian economist who had fled the Nazis. He was joined by other Nazi refugees, philosophers Eric Voegelin and Leo Strauss. Novelist and social thinker Ayn Rand had fled Bolshevik Russia in the 1920s. Milton Friedman, an economist who later transformed economic thought and policy along with his colleagues at the University of Chicago, was a Jew. William F. Buckley Jr., the founder of the leading conservative magazine, *National Review*, had deep southern roots and was a Roman Catholic.

Fundamental philosophical differences separated these intellectuals, and the Cold War intensified debates over an array of questions: Should the

Right compromise its principles of small government in support of the Cold War? Did the United States have the right to intervene militarily and politically in the affairs of another country to prevent a perceived Communist takeover? Should government restrict the civil liberties of Communists in the United States? These debates were largely philosophical in nature and, until the 1960s, usually did not involve specific legislation. The Cold War intensified ideological debate within the Right. These questions gave vibrancy to the Right and appealed to a younger generation of students and activists no longer satisfied with the Freudianism or French existentialism fashionable among intellectuals (and college professors) of the day.

Although a minority voice in the 1950s, especially in American universities (where they still remain a distinct minority today), these conservative intellectuals gained immense intellectual influence in the following years. Their ideas held special attraction for many of the student generation who had grown weary of the shibboleths of their high school teachers and college professors with their overtly leftist political leanings. For many young students, their first introduction to conservatism came from reading Friedrich Hayek's *The Road to Serfdom,* published in 1944. In this short book that became a bestseller in England and the United States, Hayek warned about the dangers of centralized economic planning found in Communism, socialism, fascism, and modern-day liberalism. In its pursuit of egalitarianism, he argued, centralized government seeks to redistribute wealth, but in doing so only creates eventual scarcity. This dynamic leads to totalitarianism as people resist further redistribution when threatened by privation of goods and food. In such a system, the individual becomes only a cog in a machine. The essential point of the book was that private ownership is essential to freedom and democracy. Individualism, he maintained, lay at the core of Western civilization. When the *Reader's Digest* reprinted this book, sales shot up to more than six hundred thousand nationwide.

In 1948, Hayek joined the faculty at the University of Chicago, which had become a citadel of free market economics. Here, he joined forces with Milton Friedman, who published a decade later his influential and bestselling book, *Capitalism and Freedom* (1962).

Young students in the 1950s were also introduced to right-wing thought through the novels of Ayn Rand, although Rand was a controversial figure on the Right because of her fervent and unbending atheism. In 1943, Rand's novel *The Fountainhead* became an international bestseller. The novel held a natural appeal to student readers in her description of a young architect, Howard Roark, who lives up to his ideals against the "herd mentality" that afflicts big business, politicians, and the masses. Through her novels and nonfiction writings, Rand promoted a philosophy of "objectivism," which espoused a passionate belief in reason, individual ego, and a rejection of the altruistic ethos of the welfare state and regulated capitalism. Her major influence was on many small businessmen of the time who felt burdened by state regulation, but her appeal was to a larger audience as well. Alan Greenspan, later chairman of the Federal Reserve, became a disciple of Rand.

Historian Russell Kirk became a leading exponent of what became known as traditionalist conservatism when he published *The Conservative Mind* in 1953. In this idiosyncratic history of conservatism in America he defined a conservative as a person who is convinced that "civilized society requires orders and classes, believes that man has an evil nature and therefore must control his will and appetite." A conservative holds, he declared, that "tradition provides a check on man's anarchic impulse and maintains a belief in a divine intent that rules society as well as conscience." Kirk drew his inspiration from an eighteenth-century English author, Edmund Burke, a fierce opponent of the French Revolution.

Libertarians, or as some liked to define themselves, individualists, found Kirk's concept of tradition vague and sentimental. Instead, libertarians asked whether custom or tradition should be preserved for its own sake.

Differences between traditionalists and libertarians caused fierce debate within intellectual circles on the Right in the 1950s and early 1960s. Polemics exchanged between the two sides were heated and aroused deep personal animosity. The Cold War imparted great poignancy to these debates and raised fundamental questions that have ramifications today: Should the conservatives support a huge military-industrial complex and the huge budgetary outlays that result from a strong national defense? Should civil liberties of self-declared enemies of freedom be restricted in the United States? Should the United States intervene militarily and politically in the affairs of other nations when confronted by aggressive hostile forces?

Debate occurred in conservative magazines such as *National Review* and other periodicals with smaller circulations such as *New Individualist Review*, published at the University of Chicago, and *The Freeman*, published by the Foundation for Economic Education, founded in 1946 to promote free-market economics. William F. Buckley Jr., a recent graduate from Yale University, had gained national attention for his *God and Man at Yale*, a piercing attack on secularism and leftism at his alma mater. His magazine *National*

Review was hard-core Right in its anti-Communist and anti–New Deal and pro–Cold War perspective.

In its support of the Cold War and an interventionist foreign policy, *National Review* broke with the prewar noninterventionist Right. Within this general perspective, Buckley wanted the magazine to serve as an umbrella for traditionalist and libertarian perspectives. By the mid-1960s the magazine had reached a circulation of nearly one hundred thousand subscribers, which still hardly compared to mass-circulation magazines such as *Time* or *Newsweek*.

GRASSROOTS ANTI-COMMUNISM

Whatever their intellectual differences, conservatives agreed in their opposition to New Deal liberalism and in their anti-Communism. This anti-Communist movement emerged following shocking revelations in the immediate aftermath of the Second World War in 1945 that Communist spy rings had infiltrated the highest levels of the American government in the 1930s and 1940s. (Evidence later found in the Soviet Archives and in the U.S. National Security Agency revealed that more than three hundred Soviet agents had infiltrated every branch of government.)

Beginning in 1945, spy case after spy case broke that showed that Communist agents, working on the behalf of Soviet intelligence agencies, had penetrated agency after agency in the federal government, including Roosevelt's White House, the State Department, the Treasury Department, the Labor Department, the Agriculture Department, the Federal Bureau of Investigation, the National Security Agency, and the Office of Strategic Services (the forerunner of the Central Intelligence Agency). The Manhattan Project, which had developed the atomic bomb, was penetrated by multiple spies working independently from one another. In 1948, former Communist and Soviet agent Whittaker Chambers appeared before Congress to testify that Alger Hiss, a formerly top-level State Department official in the Roosevelt administration, was a Communist.

As the Hiss investigation proceeded, Chambers led FBI investigators to hidden State Department documents that he said had been given to him by Hiss as part of a Soviet espionage ring operating in Washington, DC, in the 1930s. Hiss's testimony under oath that he had not given any government information to Chambers led a grand jury to indict him on two perjury counts in December 1948. In January 1950 a former Soviet spy, Hede Massing, testified how she had taken over Chambers's spy ring after he broke

with the party in 1938. Her testimony, as well as an abundance of other cir-
cumstantial evidence, led to Hiss receiving a stiff five-year prison term, although many liberals continued to defend Hiss well into the 1990s.

On September 23, 1949, President Harry Truman announced to a
stunned nation that the Soviets had exploded an atomic bomb. The following month Mao Tse Tung proclaimed a Communist takeover of China.
Seven months later the Cold War turned hot in Korea.

These events heightened concerns within America of a genuine Communist threat. Americans had never liked Communists, even at the height
of the Depression in the 1930s. The events in the late 1940s, however, intensified anti-Communist feelings among the American electorate.

Republicans were genuinely concerned about the threat of Communism at home and abroad. Republicans rallied voters who were anxious
about the revelations of Communist spies in government, as well as Communist infiltration into labor unions, the film industry, and progressive political organizations. Republicans believed that both the Roosevelt and Truman administrations had been too ready to ignore Communist influence in
"progressive" causes and government in the 1930s and Second World War
years. Leading the charge against the Democrats after 1950 was Republican
senator from Wisconsin Joseph R. McCarthy, who gained national attention for his charge in 1950 before a women's club in Wheeling, West Virginia, that Communists were still being employed in the State Department.
The outbreak of the Korean War in June 1950 heightened popular anti-
Communist feelings in America, and McCarthy rode this sentiment to gain
popularity. Not all conservatives liked McCarthy or his tactics. For some,
he represented an irresponsible form of demagoguery that threatened individual rights. Senator McCarthy's influence in the Senate declined after he
was condemned in a Senate resolution in December 1954 for not cooper-
ating with the Senate Subcommittee on Rules and Regulations, which was
investigating McCarthy's conduct in that body, but he continued to remain
popular with a segment of the American Right.

Conservatives believed that Communist subversion at home and Soviet expansionism abroad were the most important questions facing America. Opposition to Communism swamped all other issues, including civil
rights for blacks, high taxes, and organized crime. Conservatives believed
that Communism was a direct threat to the United States, and if America
did not survive as a nation, and was not willing to defend itself against an
overtly hostile power like the Soviet Union, other issues would be meaningless. The survival of the United States—indeed, Western civilization—

was at stake. Conservatives had a fear of Communism shared by most Americans.

During this time a popular anti-Communist culture emerged in America, evident in movies, television programs, community activities, and grassroots organizations. This popular anti-Communist culture generated patriotic rallies, parades, city resolutions, and an array of anti-Communist groups concerned about Communist influence in the schools, textbooks, churches, labor unions, industry, and universities. Although numbering at its height in World War II no more than eighty thousand members, the Communist Party in the United States had gained considerable influence in some areas of public life in America, especially during the 1940s during the Popular Front period, so called when Communists formed alliances with liberals within the Democratic Party in the war against fascism.

As postwar tensions between the United States and the Soviet Union intensified, many liberals turned against the Communist Party. Indeed, anti-Communist liberals led efforts to expel Communists from leadership positions in labor unions, student groups, civil rights organizations, and political organizations, including some associated with local and state Democratic parties.

Revelations about Communist infiltration into government led some anti-Communist leaders and organizations to walk down the path of conspiracy theories. Some anti-Communists charged Communists as promoting fluoridation of public water, promoting progressive education programs, or being behind the United Nations. Anti-Communist conspiracy theorists were easily parodied by their opponents and allowed genuine concerns about the Soviet Union and domestic Communist influence (even though it was dwindling in the 1950s) to be tar brushed as "loony tunes." And, at times, some of these conspiracy-minded activists were off the deep end, as when they warned that fluoridation in water was part of a Communist conspiracy to weaken the health of Americans, or that rock 'n' roll was part of a Soviet plan to hypnotize American children, or that the federal government was under the control of Soviet agents.

Liberal opponents of conservatism picked out examples of what they characterized as the Far Right to portray the entire conservative movement as a fringe movement (a technique employed later by the Left to associate the conservative movement with segregation and racial backlash). Nonetheless, liberals remained generally on the defensive throughout most of the 1950s, forced to react to Dwight D. Eisenhower's Republican administration that spanned from 1953 to 1961.

The founding of the anti-Communist John Birch Society (JBS) in 1958, however, provided liberals with what appeared to be a ready-made target. Named after an American soldier who had been killed by Chinese Communists during the Second World War, the John Birch Society emerged as a national organization.

Founded by Boston candy manufacturer Robert Welch, the JBS grew by leaps and bounds in its first years, although its membership never reached more than one hundred thousand. The JBS held that an organized Communist conspiracy threatened every value of American life. Welch claimed that the real threat of Soviet Communism was not a military attack from the Soviet Union, but the gradual encirclement of the United States by Communist nations. Welch saw encirclement fast approaching. He tended to equate European democratic socialism with Communism, so many of the socialist Scandinavian nations were placed in the Communist camp. He warned that the Communists were rapidly acquiring control of Syria, Lebanon, Egypt, Libya, Tunisia, Algeria, and Morocco. And, for all practical purposes, Finland, Iceland, and Norway were under Communist control.

Liberals seized upon these hysterical claims by painting the entire conservative movement as extremist. Liberal magazines and newspapers were full of stories about how the JBS and other conservative organizations were a threat to democracy.

Fearing that the JBS was hurting the entire conservative movement, William F. Buckley Jr. in the early 1960s moved to isolate the JBS. Establishment conservatives such as Buckley believed that Welch encouraged wild conspiracy theories among JBS members. As conservative Clare Boothe Luce, wife of the owner of *Time* magazine, wrote Buckley, "Birchers refuse to believe that sheer stupidity and ignorance of history have an enormous amount to do with our foreign policy, and that the increasing secularization of a pluralistic society naturally favors the Left."

Buckley had become increasingly upset with Welch, observing that "by silliness and injustice of utterance" Welch had become the "kiss of death" for any conservative organization. Other conservatives joined in distancing themselves from Welch. The so-called expulsion of the John Birch Society leads historians to ask obvious questions: Was the JBS an actual threat to democracy? Were anti-Communists entirely of the same mind about the nature of the Communist threat? Why did liberals use the JBS to paint the entire conservative movement as kooky?

CONSERVATIVES AND THE
EISENHOWER ADMINISTRATION

Buckley's denunciation of Robert Welch was intended to protect the conservative movement from liberal attacks that might persuade the average American that conservatives were extremists. Such accusations, Buckley feared, would hurt efforts by conservatives to move the nation back on track toward smaller government and a forceful foreign policy that did not seek accommodation with the Soviet Union, in the hope that Kremlin leaders would voluntarily withdraw from Eastern Europe, end their arms buildup, and stop their efforts to spread revolution abroad. Conservatives believed winning control of the Republican Party was critical to their efforts.

To achieve this goal, conservatives knew they had to win average voters to their cause. It also meant that the western and southern regions of the party needed to take control of party leadership away from the dominant eastern wing of the party, represented by the liberal governor of New York, Nelson Rockefeller, the grandson of oil tycoon John D. Rockefeller. Furthermore, conservatives were especially interested in mobilizing young students to the conservative cause. Students represented the future of the conservative cause and winning eventual control of the GOP.

With this objective in mind, Buckley joined with *National Review* publisher William Rusher to organize the Young Americans for Freedom (YAF), a conservative youth group. Founded in 1960, YAF became, as one historian observed, "cadres for conservatism." YAF provided a pool of talent to the conservative cause for the next two decades. The first step in organizing YAF came when Buckley invited ninety young conservatives to his estate in Sharon, Connecticut. Out of this meeting came the Sharon Statement, the founding document of YAF. The statement opened, "In this time of moral and political crisis, it is the responsibility of the youth of America to affirm certain eternal truths." One of the most important of these truths, the document declared, is the "individual's use of his God-given free will, whence derives his right to be free from restrictions of arbitrary force."

Three years after its founding YAF had grown large enough to hold its first national convention. Hundreds of chapters had been organized across the country. YAF members shared a belief in individual freedom and American democracy. This was apparent when the convention hotel in Florida where the first national conference was to be held refused a room to Jay Parker, an African American and member of the YAF national board. YAF delegates threatened to leave the hotel unless the management changed its segregationist policy. The hotel relented.

Protest came easily to YAF. During these years, YAF launched a national crusade against American corporations trading with the Soviet Union. IBM, Mack Trucks, and Firestone Tire and Rubber came under YAF criticism because of their investment in and trade with the Soviet Union and other Communist bloc countries. When YAF threatened to distribute a half-million pamphlets at the Indianapolis 500 race denouncing Firestone for proposing to build a synthetic rubber plant in Romania, the corporation withdrew its plans. YAF boycotts were conducted against stores selling Communist-produced clothing, foodstuffs, and wine. These activities suggested that the YAF was hardly a shill for American big business. Indeed, this distrust of American corporate business as placing its interest above the national interest remained a persistent strain in the conservative movement.

In addition, YAF members held mixed feelings about the Republican Party. This ambiguity toward the GOP was found among others on the Right, especially libertarians. Most conservatives believed, however, that the major fight lay within the Republican Party. The first step in overthrowing the modern liberal regime was to transform the Republican Party into a voice of conservatives.

GOP conservatives generally agreed on a range of domestic and foreign policy issues: They opposed foreign aid and the United Nations; they believed that welfare payments and government should be reduced. They feared that government bureaucracy and government regulation had created unnecessary burdens on business and the American people through unprecedented and unchecked power and bureaucratic aggrandizement. They believed labor unions, while useful at one time, had become instruments for serving the interests of a few overpaid union officials (some of them corrupt) and the Democratic Party. Conservatives feared national health insurance as another power grab by government that would only lead to an inefficient, expensive, and perhaps even a harmful program. GOP conservatives wanted low taxes and a balanced budget. They believed in a strong national defense and were patriotic Americans in their sentiment and expression.

Many conservatives were not enthusiastic about Dwight D. Eisenhower during his presidency, 1953–1961. Eisenhower was too moderate for their taste, although they appreciated his efforts to maintain a balanced budget. They believed that Eisenhower had turned back the further advance of the New Deal, but he had allowed the Social Security system, federal public housing, and social welfare programs to grow. They were most concerned, however, about foreign affairs in the last years of Eisenhower's presidency when he appeared to reach out to Soviet leader Nikita Khrushchev.

Khrushchev, who had succeeded Stalin, called for peaceful coexistence with the United States, but conservatives remembered Khrushchev as Stalin's henchman. Khrushchev had served as Stalin's viceroy in Ukraine and Byelorussia in the 1930s, where he had directed a massive campaign of repression in which 1.25 million people, or 10 percent of the population, were deported and another half million were imprisoned. Some fifty thousand people were executed or tortured in prison, and three hundred thousand died in exile. Conservatives pointed out that Khrushchev had ordered tanks into Budapest, Hungary, in 1956 when Hungarian freedom fighters had tried to throw off the Soviet yoke.

The Republican Right was especially upset when the Eisenhower administration voluntarily banned atmospheric nuclear testing without requiring the Soviet Union to undertake its own ban in 1958. The Right took it as an article of faith that the Soviet Union would fail to live up to any arms control agreement unless such an agreement included on-site inspection. Similarly, they abhorred the concept of unilateral disarmament by the United States. As one right-wing activist wrote, "An agreement with the Russians will not stop Red aggression any more than disarming our local police will stop murder, theft, and rape."

The American Right warned that the Soviet Union had undertaken a massive arms buildup, including its nuclear arsenal. (By 1980, even after a series of arms control treaties, many defense experts believed that the Soviet Union had gained or was extremely close to having nuclear superiority over the United States.) Under Khrushchev, the Soviet Union pursued an adventurist foreign policy, including support for the Cuban revolution under Fidel Castro, who soon after he came into office imposed a Communist dictatorship on this island just ninety miles off America's coast.

Conservatives believed adamantly that Soviet Communists could not be trusted to live up to any arms control treaty, unless it could be verified through on-site inspection. As a consequence, conservatives believed in a strong national defense and demanded nuclear superiority. Only nuclear superiority, they reasoned, had prevented war with the Soviet Union. Titles of conservative publications captured the hawkish sentiment: Fred Schwarz, *You Can Trust the Communists (to Be Communists)* (1962), Robert Morris, *Disarmament: Weapon of Conquest* (1963), Admiral C. Turner Joy, *How Communists Negotiate* (1955).

The Right found proof of the Soviet Union's expansionist impulse in the Communist takeover of Cuba in 1959 led by revolutionary Fidel Castro, who within a year of coming to power had imposed a dictatorship and formed an alliance with the Soviet Union. While liberals maintained that Castro was driven into the arms of the Soviet Union by America's unwillingness to support the revolution, later historical evidence suggests that Castro began preparing for a Communist takeover of government immediately after he came into power, if not before. Anti-Communists saw in the Cuban revolution Soviet plans to encircle the United States, and many conservatives began warning as early as 1960 that the Soviet Union would try to place missiles in Cuba. Right-wing radio commentator Clarence Manion declared, "the Communists in Cuba mean business. . . . Either the government of the United States acts now to dissolve the menace of Communism in Cuba, or we—the people of the United States—must prepare ourselves for the same kind of conquest of Communism that overtook Czechoslovakia and Eastern Europe."

Conservatives also warned that Castro would try to take control of the Panama Canal. Castro was a revolutionary who never hid his hatred of America, so conservatives were not surprised when Castro established a Communist dictatorship in Cuba and spread Communist revolution throughout the Western Hemisphere. If conservatives had known at the time that one of Castro's first acts had been to send money to a left-wing Chilean senator, who later became president, Salvador Allende, they would have had further cause for anxiety.

Right-wingers worried about growing liberalism—collectivism—at home that was undermining the ability and the will of Americans to fight against a deadly foe. American principles of freedom were being eroded through the extension of federal power and judicial power. Conservatives expressed particular complaints about the Supreme Court under Chief Justice Earl Warren, an Eisenhower appointee to the court. The Right disliked what they saw as Warren's judicial activism on the court. Some liberal critics later accused conservatives of being upset with the Supreme Court decision *Brown v. Board of Education of Topeka* (1954), which declared state laws creating separate black and white schools unconstitutional. Major opposition to this decision, however, came from southern Democrats, who denounced the decision in Congress. In early 1956, nineteen senators and seventy-seven members of the House of Representatives, including the entire delegations of the states of Alabama, Georgia, Louisiana, Mississippi, South Carolina, and Virginia, signed the "Southern Manifesto" denouncing the *Brown* decision and school integration. Every one of the senators was a Democrat and seventy-five, all but two, of the House members signing the manifesto that accused the Supreme Court of "clear abuse of judicial power" were Democrats.

In the North, a few conservative intellectuals such as Brent Bozell Sr., the brother-in-law to William F. Buckley Jr., took issue with the legal reasoning of the Warren Court in the *Brown* decision. Bozell criticized the decision not because it overturned racial segregation but because the Warren Court overturned "the organic process of the fluid constitution." Bozell maintained that the court had imposed through judicial fiat a uniform solution on the country that precluded the possibility of "consensual adjustment and accommodation." Prior to the decision, he maintained, great progress was being made in racial relations in this country. He wrote, "the country's practices by and large had kept abreast of the country's attitudes: the progress that had been made toward improving race relations was thus progress in depth, progress bound to endure because it was rooted in the consent and behavior of those directly concerned."

Bozell's views did not reflect general Republican or conservative opinion in the North, either in Congress or among Republican voters. Bozell's complaint against the Warren Court, however, became part of a larger critique of liberal courts and judicial activism.

A series of decisions by the Warren Court in the 1950s and 1960s created further consternation among the Republican Right, including the overturning of restrictive legislation against Communists, the banning of prayer in public schools, the liberalization of criminal procedure, and reapportionment of state legislatures.

Moreover, the Republican Party remained steadfast in its support of black civil rights. As president, Dwight D. Eisenhower completed the desegregation of the armed forces, desegregated the federal government in the District of Columbia, and appointed pro–civil rights judges to the federal courts. The Eisenhower administration pushed through Congress the first major civil rights bill for African Americans since 1875. In the Senate the bill ran into strong opposition from southern Democrats but won overwhelming support from Republicans. Throughout the 1950s (and early 1960s), conservative Senate Republicans including Everett Dirksen (Illinois) and William Knowland (California) took the lead in supporting equal rights for all Americans. The Civil Rights Act of 1957 proved largely ineffectual in its enforcement, in large part because Democratic Senate Majority Leader Lyndon Johnson from Texas pulled the teeth out of the bill in the Senate.

Eisenhower's commitment to civil rights was also evidenced when he sent troops to Little Rock, Arkansas, to enforce school integration in 1957. The sending of federal troops by Eisenhower drew heavy criticism from southern Democrats, including the governor of Texas, a Democrat who called the use of the military "undemocratic." In defending his action in his radio address, Eisenhower pointed to the human rights provision of the United Nations Charter.

While northern Republicans supported civil rights for African Americans and abhorred violence toward blacks in the South, most conservative activists remained focused on the struggle against Communism. These anti-Communists perceived the Soviet Union as a deadly threat to the United States and they gave primary attention to this threat, in much the same way that liberals had placed black civil rights on the back burner in order to win the war against fascism during the Second World War.

CONSERVATISM IN AN AGE OF RAGE

With the approach of the 1960 election, most conservatives within the Republican Party saw Vice President Richard Nixon as the front-runner. A few rallied behind the conservative senator from Arizona, Barry Goldwater, but there was a general sense that it was Nixon's time. Nixon had made a reputation for himself as a young Congressman by pursuing the investigation of Alger Hiss. He had loyally served as Eisenhower's vice president for eight years and his knowledge of domestic politics and foreign policy were unrivaled in the Republican Party. Most conservatives were not thrilled about Nixon, but in spite of their mixed feelings about him, they despised his major rival for the nomination, Nelson Rockefeller, who symbolized for them all the faults of the eastern, internationalist-minded establishment. When Nixon won the nomination, they went to work for him.

The Democrats gave the presidential nomination to John F. Kennedy, the young U.S. senator from Massachusetts. Kennedy selected fellow senator Lyndon Johnson as his running mate, a clear signal to the southern wing of the Democratic Party that he recognized the importance of the South in winning the election and the influence this wing exerted on the party. Johnson proved critical in winning the South for Kennedy in one of the tightest elections in American history. When Kennedy was assassinated in November 1963, Johnson stepped into the White House, pledging to fulfill the Kennedy legislative agenda and to expand it.

The Republican Right turned to Goldwater as their candidate to challenge Johnson in 1964. Following Kennedy's assassination, Goldwater's eagerness for the presidential race had vanished, however. He had looked forward to running against Kennedy, whom he had known in the Senate and personally liked. He had talked with Kennedy about running an old-fashioned cross-country debate on issues of the day, he said, "without Madison Avenue, without any makeup or phoniness, just the two of us traveling around on the same airplane, but when he was assassinated that ended that dream." In the end, Goldwater decided that he was obligated to his supporters to enter the race, but he understood that the sympathy vote for the Democrats would be decisive in giving the election to Lyndon Johnson.

The GOP Right adored Goldwater. Goldwater's *Conscience of a Conservative* became a national bestseller after it was published in 1960. The publication of the book had been organized by a group of conservative supporters to bolster Goldwater's national visibility. The group commissioned William F. Buckley Jr.'s brother-in-law Brent Bozell to ghostwrite this manifesto against modern liberalism. *Conscience of a Conservative* introduced many Americans, especially many young students, to the conservative philosophy. The book defined conservatism as a philosophy that upheld "the dignity of the individual human being" and was counterposed to "dictators who rule by terror, and equally those gentler collectivists who ask our permission to play God with the human race."

Goldwater articulated conservative principles of individualism, small government, private enterprise, and the foibles of modern liberalism to a popular audience. In this 150-page book, written in a simple, easy-to-read style, Goldwater discussed why he believed federalism was being subverted by power-hungry politicians in Washington, DC, his support for racial integration, his opposition to federal subsidies for farms, his opposition to forcing employees to join unions through closed shops, and his support for employment over welfare. He outlined his views on low taxes and his idea that the federal government was taking over public education. Conservatives shared Goldwater's views, but his greatest appeal was his call for winning the Cold War against the Soviet Union through an aggressive policy that began with military superiority.

He wrote, "And still the awful truth remains: We can establish the domestic conditions for maximizing freedom, along the lines I have indicated, and yet become slaves. We can do this by losing the Cold War to the Soviet Union." Here, in a nutshell, Goldwater went to the core of conservative anxieties about the state of the world. All the domestic reforms at home would not mean a thing in the face of a militarily superior Soviet Union able to intimidate and blackmail the United States. He accused liberals of ignoring the "central political fact of our time: the Soviet aim to conquer the world." He declared that America's goal in the Cold War should be victory. He wrote that America's goal is "not to wage a struggle against Communism but to win it." To accomplish this, America needed "to achieve and maintain military superiority." In addition, America must remain economically strong by releasing business from "government strangulation."

In foreign affairs America needed to act as a great power, reflecting "strength and confidence and purpose, as well as good will," but never letting any nation believe that American rights can be "violated with impunity." Foreign aid should only be given to anti-Communist governments. We should aid our allies militarily. He warned that America faced two futures: one in which the Communists would remain on the offensive, inviting local crisis after local crisis, ultimately forcing us to choose "all out war and limited retreat"; or, he declared, "America will summon the will and the means for taking the initiative, and wage a war of attrition against them—and hope, thereby, to bring about the internal disintegration of the Communist empire."

Goldwater's warning proved prescient. By the late 1970s, America did seem to be in retreat. Local crises had followed one another with swift rapidity in Southeast Asia, Africa, Central America, and the Middle East. Many spoke of America becoming a second-rate power, a nation in decline. In 1980, Americans went to the polls to choose a former Goldwater supporter in 1964, Ronald Reagan.

Still, Goldwater's chances of winning the election in 1964 were slim to nil after Kennedy's assassination in 1963. Shocked by the assassination, most Americans sympathized with and admired Johnson's leadership during this crisis. Goldwater understood this and saw his candidacy doomed from the outset, but he believed he had an obligation to his supporters in the party to accept the nomination.

Goldwater supporters were wildly enthusiastic about their candidate and certain in their faith that if Americans were given "a choice, not an echo"—as conservative author Phyllis Schlafly put it in her bestselling book of that title—they would choose the conservative. The only thing that stood between Goldwater and the Republican nomination was Nelson Rockefeller, who also threw his hat in the ring. Throughout the summer Goldwater and Rockefeller battled through the primaries. When Goldwater won the California primary in June, his nomination was assured.

Throughout the primary battle, Rockefeller portrayed Goldwater as an extremist who should not be near the hydrogen bomb. This depiction of Goldwater was carried into the GOP convention by Rockefeller and other liberal Republicans and was extended by the mass media, which caricatured Goldwater as a warmonger, racist, and potential führer.

CBS correspondent Daniel Schorr reported that as soon as the Republican convention ended Goldwater planned to travel to Bavaria, a former stronghold of Hitler's Nazi Party, to meet with Germany's right wing and to visit Berchtesgaden, "once Hitler's stomping ground." Schorr reported that this "pilgrimage" was Goldwater's way of appealing to right-wing elements in the United States and abroad. The report did not mention that Goldwater was of Jewish ancestry and hated Nazism and everything it stood for. Nevertheless, other mainstream newspapers and magazines picked up the charge. Nationally syndicated columnist Drew Pearson wrote that "the smell of fascism has been in the air at this convention." Civil rights leader Reverend Martin Luther King Jr. told the press, "We see dangerous signs of Hitlerism in the Goldwater campaign." Innuendo served in place of substantive debate on issues.

Goldwater tried to take the offensive against the charge that he was an extremist. In his acceptance speech, televised before millions of viewers, Goldwater tried to impart a positive meaning to the word *extremism* when

Anti-Goldwater protesters dressed in fake KKK hoods demonstrate against Goldwater supporters at the 1964 Republican convention. Note the African American Goldwater supporter. (Courtesy of the Library of Congress)

he declared, "Extremism in the defense of liberty is no vice. Moderation in the pursuit of justice is no virtue." Goldwater's defense of extremism back-fired. He came under severe and immediate criticism from the media, moderate Republicans, and the Democrats. Americans did not like extremism in any guise and Goldwater's words continued to haunt him throughout the campaign.

Goldwater's vote against the historic Civil Rights Act of 1964 further weakened his campaign. Critics charged that he voted against the legislation as a ploy to win the South, but Goldwater understood that his opposition to the most important civil rights legislation in American history would damage him in his bid for the presidency. Goldwater took issue with two parts of the civil rights bill when it came before Congress in June 1964. Goldwater based his opposition to the bill on constitutional grounds. He declared that government had a responsibility to protect civil rights, but he did not support Titles II and VII of the bill, which allowed federal regulation of public accommodations and private employment. Goldwater believed these two sections of the bill represented an undue and unconstitutional interference in private enterprise, warning that enforcement of these sections would require, in effect, "the creation of a federal police force of mammoth proportions." He concluded, "If my vote is misconstrued, let it be, and let me suffer the consequences."

Goldwater was a strong supporter of racial integration, but he believed that racial integration should not be forced through federal action. He was a member of the National Association for the Advancement for Colored People (NAACP). He implemented racial integration in his business in Phoenix, Arizona, and he had supported racial integration of the Air National Guard to which he belonged. Furthermore, he had voted for the Civil Rights Act of 1957 and later civil rights legislation.

Goldwater, in voting against the bill, broke ranks with the leadership of his party, including Republican Minority Leader Everett Dirksen, a conservative representing the state of Illinois. Clearly Goldwater represented a minority voice within the Republican Party. When the bill came to a vote in the Senate, it overwhelmingly won the endorsement of northern Republicans, who voted twenty-seven to five for the bill. Twenty-one Democrats, nearly half of the Democratic caucus, voted against the bill. Twenty of these oppositional votes came from southern Senators. In the House a similar pattern followed.

Goldwater's opposition to the Civil Rights Act of 1964 hurt him during the general campaign, but his opposition to the Civil Rights Act was echoed by the editors of the *National Review.* Since its inception in 1955, the editors of the *National Review* had opposed federal involvement in enforcing racial integration of public accommodations and protecting black voting rights in the South. At times, their rhetoric overstepped the bounds of civility, as in the case of a 1960 unsigned editorial that declared, "In the Deep South the Negroes are, by comparison with Whites, retarded. . . . Leadership in the South, then quite properly, rests in White hands. Upon the White population this fact imposes moral obligations of paternalism, patience, protection, devotion, and sacrifice." The editorial was probably written by William F. Buckley Jr. Although Buckley apologized many decades later for his opposition to federally enforced racial integration, his rhetoric in 1960 appealed not to common sense but to racial prejudice. It remains unclear, however, whether he spoke for the large majority of rank-and-file northern conservatives, who after all voted for those Republicans in Congress who voted for the Civil Rights Act of 1964. And, while the *National Review*'s language is unforgivable, the racial demagoguery on the part of southern Democrats was equally offensive and carried more political weight than Buckley's magazine.

During the general campaign, Goldwater tried to pursue a moderate campaign, downplaying issues of race and the war in Vietnam, which was just beginning to heat up. His refusal to play the "race card" during the summer of 1964 speaks to Goldwater's principles. That summer in 1964 major race riots broke out in Harlem, Brooklyn, and Rochester, New York; Jersey City and Elizabeth, New Jersey; Toledo, Ohio; Kansas City and St. Louis, Missouri; and Philadelphia, Pennsylvania. Goldwater refused to take political advantage of these riots by linking them to Johnson's Great Society. Instead, when Goldwater met privately with Johnson in late July following the Republican and Democratic conventions, Goldwater told Johnson that he would not bring up the issue of racial riots or Vietnam because he feared raising racial tensions or undermining the war effort in Vietnam.

Johnson was not one to fight with one hand tied behind his back, however. Through his legislative aide, Bill Moyers, who later joined the Public Broadcasting System as a broadcaster and producer, Johnson produced one of the most devastating negative television spots in campaign history. The ad focused on a young girl picking petals off a daisy, when suddenly in the background an atomic bomb explodes. Silence follows as an image appears: "Vote for President Lyndon Johnson on November 3rd. The stakes are too high to stay home." The Johnson campaign aired the "Daisy" spot only once, but it appeared many times as newscasts discussed what became a notorious political commercial.

Johnson won forty-three million votes to Goldwater's twenty-seven million. This vote was not surprising given that more than twice as many voters described themselves as Democrats than as Republicans. The Goldwater debacle was costly to the Republican Party and the conservative movement.

Johnson's landslide victory marked a high point for modern liberalism. The election gave Johnson the go-ahead to expand the welfare and regulatory state through his Great Society program. He sent to Congress proposals for Medicare and Medicaid, a host of antipoverty programs, public housing legislation, family planning programs, and substantial cash infusions into public education from preschool through graduate school. He created the National Endowment for the Humanities and the National Endowment for the Arts. He promised to end poverty in American in a generation. American cities would be rebuilt, highways beautified, people given meaningful jobs, and race relations improved. He promised to defeat Communism in South Vietnam.

Racial riots following the election did irreparable damage to Johnson's domestic programs. Only five days after Johnson signed the Voting Rights Act of 1965, a racial riot in the Watts section of Los Angeles erupted. The Watts riot lasted a full week and left 34 people dead, 1,110 injured, and an estimated $40 million in property damage. The following year, there were thirty-eight riots that resulted in seven deaths and five hundred injuries. In the first nine months of 1967, there were 164 riots. Public disturbances in Newark and Detroit lasted for a week each and left a total of sixty-four people dead. These riots undermined white blue-collar and white middle-class support for the Great Society.

Surveys before and after the riots consistently showed improving attitudes by whites toward blacks in both the North and the South, including a growing acceptance of school integration. Racial riots following Johnson's election did not derail improving racial attitudes, but they did raise apprehension among whites about social order and lessened support for Johnson's Great Society programs.

Johnson's escalation of American involvement in Vietnam following the 1964 election further eroded support for his Great Society. By 1965, there were 184,000 American troops in Vietnam, eventually increasing to nearly 500,000 troops by 1967. As the United States found itself in a quagmire, unable to force the North Vietnamese to negotiate or to extricate itself from Vietnam, a massive antiwar movement developed, leading to campus protest and violence. At the same time, the Democratic Party split between hawks and doves who wanted to withdraw American troops from Vietnam, either gradually through negotiation or immediately by executive order.

The March on the Pentagon in 1967 reflected anti–Vietnam War sentiment in college campuses, but angered many Americans who would elect Richard Nixon to the presidency in 1968. (Courtesy of the Lyndon Baines Johnson Library; photo by Frank Wolfe)

College campuses, especially elite universities on the East and West coasts, became centers of anti–Vietnam War protest and revolutionary actions. Antiwar activists burned draft cards, protested war-related corporate recruiting efforts, and seized campus buildings in protest of the war and in support of third-world liberation movements. Most college students were not radicals; the number of students who identified themselves as conservatives, members of such organizations as Young Americans for Freedom, nearly equaled the number of radicals on campus. Yet the general perception among the public was that left-wing anarchy was prevailing on many campuses across the country.

Young radicals identifying themselves as New Leftists reinforced this image of campuses as hotbeds of anti-American leftism. Actually these New Leftists were not liberals. Indeed, they distrusted what they decried as the liberal establishment. New Left critics charged that Progressive and New Deal liberal reforms had been designed to preserve capitalism by benefiting large corporations. As part of this critique they alleged that Johnson's War on Poverty was really a war on the poor, an instrument to keep the poor in a state of dependency and a surplus workforce in a cyclical capitalist economy. As a result, New Left campus activists saw liberal reform as an instrument to preserve a regulated capitalist system that prevented a socialist transformation into a genuinely egalitarian society. They accused the Johnson administration of waging a racist and imperialist war in Vietnam.

Conservatives shared much of this critique of liberal domestic reform, but they found themselves in an unusual position with the war in Vietnam. For twenty years conservatives had called for a tougher stand against Communist expansion, but they also saw Vietnam as Johnson's war. While some on the isolationist and libertarian right denounced the Vietnam War, the majority of conservatives were hawks. Conservatives believed that having gotten involved in the war in the first place, the United States should seek military victory and not a settlement with the North Vietnamese. They called for the administration to take off the gloves by unleashing America's military power through the mining of North Vietnamese ports, bombing Hanoi, and sending American troops into the north if necessary. At the same time, the Right believed that Johnson's war distracted the United States from the continued nuclear arms buildup by the Soviet Union. Conservatives warned that not only was Johnson's conduct of the war ensuring a disaster there, under his leadership the United States was falling behind the Soviet Union in the nuclear arms race.

While conservatives criticized Johnson's conduct of the war, divisions within the Democratic Party over Vietnam split the party, leading Senator

Eugene McCarthy (no relation to Joe McCarthy), a little-known Democrat from Minnesota, to enter the Democratic presidential primary in New Hampshire in 1968. When McCarthy, relying heavily on youth volunteers, won a surprising 42 percent of the primary vote, Robert Kennedy, the younger brother of the late president, threw his hat into the ring as well. On March 31, Johnson announced he would not seek the nomination of his party for another term. Johnson's announcement left the Democrats severely divided.

On April 4, two days after McCarthy won the Wisconsin primary, civil rights leader Martin Luther King Jr. was gunned down by a lone assassin in Memphis. Rioting broke out in dozens of cities. In the nation's capital, the skies were lit by dozens of fires across the city. In April and May, students at Columbia University went on strike, taking over the president's office and demanding that the university stop its proposed expansion into the surrounding urban area.

For many conservatives, the war at home, racial riots, campus protest, and rising crime rates were all linked to the failure of modern liberalism. Republicans began calling for law and order, an issue of major concern to the American public anxious about rising street crime, campus protest, and urban riots. Too often, liberals did appear soft on crime. Following racial rioting in the summer of 1968, Vice President Hubert Humphrey told the press that if he had been born in a ghetto he might have staged a good riot himself, to which his Democratic challenger George Wallace, the pro-segregation governor of Alabama, answered that he had grown up in a house without running water but he had never started a riot.

Democrats attempted to respond to the law-and-order issue by taking a tougher stand on crime. Johnson's administration successfully pushed through the Safe Streets Act of 1968, which sought to alleviate the economic and social conditions that they believed cause crime. Many liberals in Congress, however, refused to back the measure because of its provision for wiretapping, which only reinforced their image as being soft on the issue. Democratic candidate Robert Kennedy sought to bolster his image as a crime fighter by emphasizing that as attorney general of the United States he had prosecuted corrupt labor leader Jimmy Hoffa, head of the Teamsters Union. Kennedy understood the importance of the law-and-order issue to American voters, but his campaign came to a tragic end when he was assassinated by a twenty-four-year-old Christian-born Palestinian who had immigrated to America with his family as a child. Vice President Humphrey won the nomination of a party severely damaged by bloody riots between radical antiwar protesters and the Chicago police outside the convention.

The nomination of Hubert Humphrey to head the Democratic Party ticket in 1968 split the party. Humphrey, a well-known liberal, was not Left enough for many in the Democratic Party. For some voters, he was too liberal. Pro-segregationist Alabama Governor George Wallace, a Democrat, took advantage of the disarray to form an American Independent Party, which attacked black militants, radical students, welfare mothers, and drug-taking youth. The Wallace campaign drew little support from conservative Republicans in the North or the South, but attracted white blue-collar workers disgruntled with the Democratic Party.

At the Republican National Convention some conservatives tried to nominate the recently elected Republican governor of California, Ronald Reagan. Reagan had won the 1966 governor's race against a liberal Democrat by more than one million votes in part by focusing on student protest at the state's premier university, the University of California at Berkeley.

Reagan had become a hero to the conservative movement following his televised speech for Goldwater in 1964. His language in the speech was direct and simple to understand, as when he declared,

> "[T]he full power of centralized government"—this was the very thing the Founding Fathers sought to minimize. They knew that governments don't control things. A government can't control the economy without controlling people. And they know when a government sets out to do that, it must use force and coercion to achieve its purpose. They also knew, those Founding Fathers, that outside of its legitimate functions, government does nothing as well or as economically as the private sector of the economy.

The GOP right looked upon Reagan as an up-and-coming star, but in 1968 most conservatives turned to Richard Nixon, after he promised to restore American nuclear superiority. In the general election, Nixon ran on a platform of ending the war in Vietnam, reforming welfare, and quelling violent protest on college campuses and riots in the inner cities. His opponents accused Nixon's law-and-order campaign of using code words for attacking racial minorities. Whatever Nixon's intentions, he identified antiwar and student protesters as easy symbols to rally supporters.

Nixon understood that voters were growing tougher on law-and-order issues, including street crime, campus violence, and inner-city riots. Nixon intuited voters' concerns, but no doubt law and order had racial associations. As *Time* magazine observed shortly before the 1968 presidential election, "For millions of voters who are understandably and legitimately dismayed by random crime, burning ghettos, disrupted universities and violent demonstrations in downtown streets, law and order is a rallying cry that evokes quieter days. To some, it is also a shorthand message promising repression of the black community. To the Negro, already the most frequent victim of violence, it is a bleak warning that worse times may be coming." Public opinion surveys over the next decade revealed that both white and black attitudes toward crime and criminals hardened. Moreover, in 1968 when Nixon was running for the White House, public opinion surveys showed that blacks took an exceptionally tough line toward inner city rioters, although they believed the riots were caused by bad social conditions. Nixon did not expect to win the African American vote, but law and order was on the mind of many voters in 1968.

Nixon's appeal on the law-and-order issue went directly to the heart of the conservative movement's complaint against liberalism in the 1960s. Prior to the 1960s, the GOP Right had battered liberals on the issues of Communism and big government. With social discord apparent in campuses and inner cities across America, conservatives added a third prong, cultural disarray, to their attacks on modern liberalism. Conservatives believed that the crisis of modern American life was largely moral and cultural. This position was contrary to the premises of Great Society liberals who concentrated on materialism and physical well-being. Moreover, as conservative philosopher Leo Strauss argued, the measure of a healthy society was not just material freedom, but how virtuous its citizens were. While 1960s liberals called for more individual freedom around cultural issues, the Right believed that the emerging crisis in America was not the absence of individual liberty, but the destruction of individual virtue, replaced by dependency on government, an inability of people to take responsibility for their actions, and a culture that emphasized materialism over transcendence, immediate gratification over temperance, and the experimental over tradition. Conservatives claimed that the liberal attack on traditional values and institutions such as patriotism and religion through the courts, protest movements, the media, and liberal spokesmen subverted the very foundations of American society.

The 1968 election proved extremely close. On Election Day, Nixon barely won by getting 43.5 percent of the vote to Humphrey's 42.7 percent and Wallace's 13.5 percent. Even though Nixon made heavy inroads into the white ethnic vote in the Northeast and Midwest, he failed to have a major breakthrough in the South. In large part this was because of George Wallace's attraction in the Deep South. Until Republicans won the South, any political realignment would be thwarted. Nixon won only North Carolina, South Carolina, Tennessee, Florida, Virginia, and Kentucky. Increasingly, many voters once aligned with the Democratic Party began to see the party and its liberal agenda as hostile to their interests. Their allegiance had been substantially shaken, as evidenced in the Wallace vote.

Yet, once in office, Nixon alienated the right wing of his party by expanding the the welfare and regulatory state and pursuing arms reduction with the Soviet Union. Nixon appointed some conservatives to his administration, but he believed the key to political success rested in usurping the liberal Democratic program. Moreover, Nixon faced a Democrat-controlled Congress that had become increasingly liberal. As a result, Nixon pursued a zigzag policy. Vice President Spiro Agnew attacked the liberal media, student protesters, and militant black nationalists, while Nixon proposed new initiatives in welfare, health care, federal aid to states, and executive reform. He proposed a guaranteed income program through the Family Assistance Plan, and when it failed to win support among liberals because it did not go far enough, or among conservatives because it expanded government, Nixon proposed a food stamp program and the Supplemental Security Income Act, which led the federal government to assume responsibility for aid to the aged, the blind, and the disabled. He extended subsidized housing and the Job Corps program.

Nixon's record on civil rights proved mixed. His administration challenged forced busing in which black and white children were transported out of their neighborhood school districts to achieve racial integration. Under federal court order, however, the Nixon Justice Department quietly presided over desegregation of southern schools, which cut the percentage of black children attending all-black schools from 68 percent in 1968 to 8 percent in 1972. In 1972, Nixon signed the Equal Employment Opportunity Act. Through the Equal Employment Opportunity Commission, Nixon imposed targets for hiring minorities and women on federal projects. Nixon also endorsed, although not with great enthusiasm, the Equal Rights Amendment (ERA) passed by Congress in 1972 and sent to the states for ratification. He instituted and expanded federal family planning programs and international programs for population control.

He also supported the National Environmental Policy Act, which required every federal construction project to have an environmental impact study before beginning work. This led him to establish the Environmental Protection Agency. He signed the Clean Air Act, which established emission standards for automobiles, and created the Occupational Safety and Health Administration. Unable to forestall rising inflation and economic stagnation, Nixon imposed wage and price controls in 1971. He removed the United States from the international gold standard and let the dollar float on world currency exchanges. Under Nixon the federal budget continued to grow.

Speaking from a conservative perspective, the recently elected Republican senator from North Carolina Jesse Helms observed in 1974, "It pains me to say this, but the [Nixon] administration cannot escape a large measure of blame for the current easy acceptance of Leviathan-like government expansion. This expansion has, if anything, become even faster under the current administration."

Nixon escalated the bombing in Vietnam to bring North Vietnam to the negotiating table. Finally, in 1972, Nixon announced the Paris Peace Accords, which appeared to bring peace to Vietnam. In 1973, American military forces withdrew from Vietnam. The Communist North Vietnamese did not live up to the agreement, and with significant Soviet military aid, North Vietnam captured Saigon in April 1975, renaming it Ho Chi Minh City, after the brutal Communist dictator of North Vietnam. In 1975, Cambodia also fell to the Communists. Once in control, Communist regimes in Vietnam and Cambodia massacred hundreds of thousands of opponents. In Cambodia, an estimated one to three million people died under the abominations of a Communist regime. Liberals blamed the United States for creating this mass killing, but most Americans felt that this tragedy was typical of Communist dictatorships.

In the spring of 1971, while the Vietnam War continued, Nixon and Secretary of State Henry Kissinger announced that the United States had opened relations with mainland China. The conservative movement exploded in anger. For decades conservatives had called for the defense of the island of Taiwan, where the anti-Communist Nationalists had fled in 1949, and insisted on the isolation of mainland China. By opening diplomatic relations with mainland China, Richard Nixon reversed this policy. As one right-wing activist wrote, "This is madness, of course, but it reveals that Nixon is a politician first, statesman second, and 'anti-communist' also ran." Shortly after this announcement of opening relations with China, the Nixon administration announced in the summer of 1972 that Nixon and Soviet leader Leonid Brezhnev had signed the Strategic Arms Limitation Treaty (SALT). Conservatives were convinced that, arms treaty or no arms treaty, the Soviet Union posed a serious military threat and that it was intent on achieving first-strike nuclear superiority with the aim of either intimidating the United States or launching a surprise attack. Recognition of Communist China and the signing of SALT symbolized for the GOP Right

Nixon's broken 1968 promises to them to strengthen American nuclear forces and confront what they saw as Soviet adventurism in Asia, Africa, and Latin America.

Nixon easily won reelection in 1972 against a left-wing antiwar Democratic presidential candidate, Senator George McGovern from South Dakota. Nixon's downfall came shortly afterward when he was forced to resign from the presidency in 1974 following revelations in 1972 that he had tried to cover up a break-in of the Democratic Party national campaign headquarters in Washington, DC, at the Watergate apartment complex. Shortly before Nixon's resignation, in a separate investigation, Vice President Spiro Agnew was forced to resign his office in late 1973 in a plea bargain after being charged with accepting bribes as governor of Maryland. Nixon appointed well-liked moderate congressman Gerald Ford (R-Michigan) to become vice president. With Nixon's resignation, Ford became the president of the United States.

THE REVIVAL OF THE RIGHT

Following Nixon's resignation, the Republican Party stood in complete disarray. In 1974, Democrats made significant gains in the congressional elections. Most of these "Watergate Democrats" were liberal and not given to bipartisan compromise. Polls revealed that in 1974 only 18 percent of voters identified themselves as Republicans. Conservatives within the Republican Party stood as an isolated minority within a minority party.

Over the next five years, however, conservatives rebounded, as a broad-based movement and as a political force within the Republican Party. This resurgence began on the institutional level when conservatives began to establish new research institutes (think tanks) and new activist organizations. At the same time, the conservative revival was characterized by a backlash against the liberal agenda on social issues, including banning prayer in school, legalizing abortion, and the ERA, a proposed constitutional amendment passed by Congress in 1972 that guaranteed equal rights under the constitution regardless of sex. The ERA needed ratification by three quarters of the states (thirty-eight) to become a constitutional amendment.

Foreign policy also played a major role in revitalizing the conservative movement in the post–Vietnam War era. In 1980, conservative Republican Ronald Reagan was elected president of the United States, marking a major shift in the electorate and in the balance of power between the Left and the Right.

Signs of liberal erosion within their own ranks became apparent in the late 1960s when a group of New York Jewish intellectuals, later called neoconservatives, began to drift away from the Democratic Party, largely over defense issues. The Democrats began moving leftward with George McGovern's nomination in 1972. McGovern won the nomination as an anti–Vietnam War candidate, but his nomination also reflected a quota system of proportional representation of women, ethnic minorities, homosexuals, and activists among convention delegates. As these proportional requirements were implemented, delegates to the Democratic Party became increasingly left-wing ideologically and secular-progressive in their religious outlooks. These activists brought to the party a politics that was anti-imperialist, antiracist, profeminist, proabortion, and pro–homosexual rights.

This shift within the party upset New York intellectuals such as Norman Podhoretz, editor of the Jewish magazine *Commentary*, and book editor Irving Kristol. Podhoretz and Kristol, operating independently from one another, deserted liberalism by expressing their disillusionment with the McGovernite Democratic Party over its support for the expanded welfare state, affirmative action, anti–Vietnam War sentiment, and downsizing of the military and significant arms reduction. Other intellectuals rallied to this criticism of liberalism, which often found expression in expertly crafted social science assessments of liberal programs. Labeled neoconservatives by their opponents, these intellectuals did not constitute an organized movement, but an intellectual orientation that included intellectuals and academics who expressed disenchantment with the prevailing liberal orthodoxy. These neoconservative intellectuals brought a policy expertise to the conservative movement that had generally been missing in the 1950s. Although many older conservatives—traditionalists and libertarians—disliked these late arrivals to conservatism, the "neocons" brought new intellectual energy to the conservative movement.

This turn toward public policy was encouraged by the growth of conservative policy institutes, or think tanks, in the 1960s and 1970s. The American Enterprise Institute (AEI), founded in 1943, grew rapidly and emerged as a powerful force in Washington in the late 1960s. Its influence was found in a number of policy areas, especially in its call for deregulation of the economy. Deregulation was promoted by conservatives as well as some liberals. In the mid-1970s, President Jimmy Carter and Senator Ted Kennedy (D-Massachusetts) joined conservatives in calling for deregulation of a number of industries, including the airline industry. Deregulation relieved corporations of pricing oversight by federal regulatory agencies. The AEI also undertook an extensive public outreach program to promote its economic, defense, and foreign policy studies. By 1977, AEI was spending $1.6 million in its public outreach programs, which included 118 publications received by four hundred universities. Its public affairs programs reached seven hundred television stations across the country.

In 1973, the Heritage Foundation was founded by two former congressional aides, Edward Feulner and Paul Weyrich. Backed by money from beer magnate Joseph Coors and Pittsburgh millionaire Richard Scaife, the Heritage Foundation sought to influence Republican legislators and stem the tide of what they considered anticorporate attitudes in Congress. Five years later in 1977, Edward H. Crane, the former national chairman of the Libertarian Party, organized the Cato Institute to promote a libertarian perspective of limited government, individual liberty, and free-market economics in the policy arena. Major funding for this policy institute came from Kansas businessman Charles G. Koch. The institute considered itself classically liberal and not conservative. It opposed the military-industrial complex and American involvement abroad. On domestic matters it called for cutting government, reducing spending, and legalizing marijuana, and it supported abortion rights. While a minority voice on the Right, libertarians exerted considerable intellectual influence on conservative policy discussions. The libertarian influence revealed the protean nature of conservatism—its rich diversity in ideas, policy prescriptions, and arguments.

While the Right was finding intellectual rejuvenation, the grassroots were revived through the mobilization of traditional Christian voters who felt that their religious values and beliefs were under assault by the secular Left in the 1960s and 1970s. The Democratic Party reflected these secular values by aggressively supporting abortion, feminism, gay rights, and a strong separation of church and state. These issues awakened a sleeping giant: the traditional Christian vote, composed of evangelical Christians, traditional Roman Catholics, and Mormons. Postwar conservatives had expressed great anxiety about the decline of traditional values and Christian morality in America, and these concerns gained poignancy when the Supreme Court banned school prayer in 1962. In 1973, the Supreme Court in *Roe v. Wade* ruled that abortion was a constitutional right of women.

Traditionally, the First Amendment clauses concerning the separation of church and state and the free exercise of religion had been interpreted narrowly to prohibit the federal government from favoring one Christian denomination over the other. Following the ban on school prayer, the Court issued decisions that banned the reading of the Bible and recitation of the Lord's Prayer in school. These rulings shocked and angered many

Christian Americans. Even more offensive, especially at first to Roman Catholic voters, was the *Roe* decision.

Prior to *Roe*, abortion had been legal, but restricted primarily to save the life of the mother. The decision took the issue of abortion and any regulation of this medical procedure out of control of the state legislatures—the democratic process—and put it in the hands of the courts. In the course of the next three and a half decades, the battle between the proabortion and antiabortion forces took place in the federal courts. The debate inevitably spilled into controversies over Supreme Court appointments. Conservatives argued that *Roe v. Wade* was a legally weak decision in its argument that the Fourteenth Amendment implied a "penumbra" of understood rights, and they contended that the abortion issue should be returned to the states for public discussion and debate. Conservatives advocated letting the people decide such issues through the democratic process.

Opposition to abortion led religious groups to mobilize on the state level. During the fight to extend legalized abortion in California in 1967, a measure backed by then-governor Ronald Reagan, antiabortion activists organized the Right to Life League and Mothers Outraged at the Murder of Innocents. Other groups formed in other states on the grassroots level. The establishment of the National Right to Life Committee imparted a national focus to this movement. It was mirrored by the proabortion National Association for the Repeal of Abortion Laws. Both groups drew largely from white, suburban, middle-aged, college-educated women.

Paralleling the abortion debate, controversy arose over the Equal Rights Amendment approved by Congress in 1972. Supported by the newly formed National Organization for Women (1966), a feminist organization headed by author Betty Friedan, ERA passed Congress with surprisingly little controversy. The amendment simply declared, "Equality of rights under the law shall not be denied or abridged by the United States or by any State on account of sex." Bipartisan support was easily found for this broadly worded amendment, which appeared on the surface only to promote equality under the law. The amendment needed approval by three-fourths of the states for ratification. At first the amendment looked as though it was going to sail through, but a conservative activist and homemaker, Phyllis Schlafly, started a grassroots organization called STOP ERA that soon had chapters throughout the country. She warned that ratification of ERA would result in women being drafted into the military, abortion on demand, same-sex marriage, and loss of legal protections for wives, mothers, and female workers. She also claimed that the amendment was unnecessary because Congress had already enacted the Equal Pay Act (1962),

Title VII of the Civil Rights Act (1964), equal opportunity through the Equal Employment Opportunity Act (1972), Title IX of the Education Amendments (1972), and credit protection through legislation enacted in 1974. She maintained that if further inequalities or discrimination existed, it should be remedied through specific legislation. The ERA was so loosely worded, she asserted, that it would necessitate further court interpretation, and given the recent record of the court, homemakers and average women should not trust the courts to uphold their interests.

By 1976, momentum for ERA ratification had been halted. In organizing against ERA, Schlafly tapped into a reservoir of Roman Catholic, Mormon, and evangelical Christian opposition to the ERA. These evangelical Christian women became critical to the anti-ERA movement. In fighting ERA, many of these women became involved in politics for the first time. Looking at Schlafly's success in mobilizing Christian women, especially in key southern states, conservative Republican strategists became convinced that evangelical Christians, traditional Roman Catholics, and Mormons could be brought into the Republican Party.

Schlafly's activism coincided with the formation of other conservative organizations aimed at mobilizing the grassroots. Labeled the New Right by the media, the leaders of these groups included fund-raiser Richard Viguerie, former Nixon administration official Howard Phillips, activist Paul Weyrich, and campaign strategist Terry Dolan. Most of these people were certainly not new to conservative causes. Schlafly had been involved in conservative Republican politics since the late 1940s; Viguerie and Phillips had been young conservative activists in the 1960s. These activists expanded on traditional conservative issues, anti-Communism, big government, defense, and low taxes, while tapping into grassroots discontent over social and moral issues such as abortion, prayer in school, ERA, and national defense. They also pioneered the use of new technologies such as computer mailing lists. The mobilization of the New Right and grassroots conservatism caught both liberals and the Republican establishment off guard.

By 1980, the GOP Right had been revitalized through the formation of think tanks, the antiabortion and anti-ERA movements, and the New Right political organizations. This revitalized conservative movement had roots in the early Cold War period, but conservatives had broadened their base, established a network of research institutes, and expanded their program to include social issues such as prayer in school, the Equal Rights Amendment, and abortion.

Conservatism was set to enter into a new phase in its history.

Protesters for the Equal Rights Amendment are depicted demonstrating on Women's Suffrage Day. The call for zero population growth combined environmentalism with feminism. (Courtesy of the Environmental Protection Agency, National Archives)

RONALD REAGAN WINS ELECTION

The emergence of social and moral issues, and the unwillingness of many within the Republican establishment to engage these issues, frustrated many conservative activists. They turned to Ronald Reagan as a leader who could transform the GOP into a voice of conservatism, a voice of the people. These frustrations were personified in the presidency of Gerald R. Ford, Nixon's successor.

Ford, confronted by a heavily Democratic Congress and a weak Republican base, tried to pursue a moderate political course. As a moderate, he believed, in principle, in balanced budgets and free enterprise. He tried to avoid the abortion issue and supported the ERA. In foreign policy, Ford at first followed the advice of his secretary of state, Henry Kissinger, who counseled him to endorse SALT II negotiations and détente with the Soviet Union.

Conservatives adamantly opposed further arms control negotiations with the Soviet Union without stricter verification that arms were being reduced. Conservatives feared that America was losing power to the Soviet Union in Asia, Africa, and Central America, and they warned that the Soviet Union was quickly surpassing—some said it had already surpassed—the United States in conventional and nuclear weapons. In 1975, the Soviet Union had five hundred more intercontinental ballistic missiles than the United States, an equal number of submarine-launched missiles, five times as many tanks, and an army twice the size of the U.S. army. Conservative Republicans and increasing numbers of hawks within Democratic Party intellectual circles warned that the United States appeared to be headed toward disaster. Most experts agreed that the Soviet Union's massive arms buildup had followed the signing of SALT I in 1972. Ford seemed oblivious of these criticisms of SALT I when he met with Soviet leader Leonid Brezhnev in November 1974 and agreed to further arms reductions, setting the foundations for a SALT II treaty. A year later Ford met with Brezhnev again and signed the Helsinki Accords, which gave de facto recognition of Soviet control of Eastern Europe and called for the protection of human rights. For conservative critics of the language, this was an unconscionable reversal of thirty years of American bipartisan foreign policy.

While Ford tacked to the center, he often appeared to ignore the wind blowing from his starboard. Indeed, Ford did nothing to reach out to the favorite of the Right, Ronald Reagan. In 1975, Reagan announced that he would challenge Ford for the GOP presidential nomination. He declared, "The Republican party is in serious danger of extinction because it has ceased to represent anything more than a broad based pragmatism." He promised a resurgence of conservatism if he won the GOP nomination.

Most of the liberal media dismissed Reagan's challenge. The *New York Times* mockingly described Reagan as engaging in "frivolous fantasy," while the liberal *New Republic* caricatured Reagan as an "essentially mindless and totally unconvincing candy man." He was portrayed as nothing more than a Hollywood actor put up by corporate interests desiring low taxes and other benefits.

Actually, Reagan was a highly intelligent man who had carefully studied conservative classics from Plato to Hayek. He was an eloquent writer and speaker, but his easygoing manner and Hollywood background made it easy for critics to dismiss him as a lightweight. His opponents tended to underestimate him, and Gerald Ford was no exception. In the end, Ford barely won the nomination at the convention, leaving the GOP divided.

The Democrats selected Jimmy Carter, a former governor of Georgia, as their candidate. Carter had won the Democratic nomination running as an outsider, and he carried this role into the general election. The election proved exceptionally close, with both Ford and Carter stumbling in their campaigns. (Ford hurt himself badly during a televised debate when he astounded the audience by declaring that the Soviet Union did not dominate Eastern Europe.) When the votes were tallied in the early morning hours, Carter won by only 2 percentage points, 50.8 to Ford's 48.02. A change of a little more than twenty-three thousand votes in Ohio and Wisconsin would have given the election to Ford. A born-again Christian, Carter swept the South, winning evangelical Christians to the Democratic Party.

Carter came to the White House with a promise to restore people's faith in government. Democrats controlled the House and the Senate, so for the first time since Johnson government appeared unified. In the House, Democrats held a majority of nearly two to one, 291–144. In the Senate, Democrats held sixty-two seats and Republicans thirty-eight seats. Yet even with a clear majority, Carter ran head-on into a Congress that had swung considerably to the Left. While his legislative program bogged down in Congress, inflation and unemployment rates soared, fueled by a hike in gasoline prices by Arab oil producers. This triggered a recession in 1974–1975, the most serious downturn in the economy since the Great Depression of the 1930s. The stock market and the gross domestic product fell. New York City, after years of financial mismanagement, stood on the edge of bankruptcy. By the spring of 1975, unemployment stood at 9 percent and inflation reached double digits. Carter was unable to convince Congress or the American public that he had a solution to the problem. He prevailed upon Congress to ratify two treaties for the eventual returning of the Panama Canal to the Panamanians, and he brokered a peace treaty between Israel and Egypt in 1979. This marked the high points in his foreign policy achievements.

One of his greatest failures was with a new SALT II treaty. He brought to Congress a new treaty, but after intense criticism from Republicans and Democrats—and the Soviet invasion of Afghanistan in 1979—Carter was forced to withdraw it. A further crisis came when militant revolutionary Islamic students in Iran seized the American embassy in Tehran and held more than fifty Americans hostage for the next 444 days.

As the 1980 election approached, many people believed that the world had come apart and could not be put back together again. During a 1980 debate, Ronald Reagan, having won the GOP nomination, poignantly asked the American voter, "Are you better off today than you were four years ago?" Most believed that they were not. They turned to Reagan, the first avowed conservative to win the White House.

On Election Day, voters rejected Carter. Reagan received almost 51 percent of the popular vote to Carter's 42 percent. (Representative John Anderson from Illinois, running as an independent, received 7 percent of the vote. Reagan received 489 electoral votes to Carter's 49.)

President Jimmy Carter delivered a televised address on energy in April 1977 asking Americans to lower their thermostats. His inability to address the energy crisis helped cost him the election in 1980. (Courtesy of the Jimmy Carter Library)

Surveys suggested that the electorate voted as much against Carter's ineptness as president than for Reagan's conservative message. Nonetheless, Reagan had won election running as an avowed conservative, and over the course of the following years more and more voters began to identify themselves as conservatives. Reagan expressed an optimistic faith in America's future, individuals' ability within a democracy to achieve their goals through hard work and character, and a deep patriotic faith in the United States as an example of freedom to the rest of the world, "a shining light on a hill."

In winning election, Reagan sliced through traditional Democratic support, winning union workers in the Northeast and Midwestern industrial cities. He won evangelical Christians who had earlier voted for Carter in 1976. And Reagan took the South, the first step in transforming the South into a bastion of the Republican Party.

The takeover of the South by Republicans led some scholars to claim that white voters in the South turned to the Republican Party as a reaction to desegregation and the growing power of African Americans within the Democratic Party, but this "racial backlash" hypothesis has not stood up well under more detailed studies.

The movement of southern voters to the Republican Party began on the presidential level in the 1950s, when many southerners voted for Eisenhower. This voting pattern worked its way to the suburbs, but the change came gradually. Republican candidates appealed to these voters through their call for low taxes, probusiness policies, national defense, and family values. The burgeoning suburban middle class went Republican in 1980 and continued to go Republican. Rural southern whites, whose resistance to racial integration was most pronounced, continued to vote Democratic.

This pattern was evident among southern white voters who voted for segregationist George Wallace in 1968 and later for Jimmy Carter in 1976 and 1980. In Carter's first race for the presidency, 79 percent of the districts in the South (the eleven states of the old Confederacy) that had voted for Wallace in 1968 went for Carter in 1976. Carter won only 59 percent of the districts that had voted for Nixon in 1968. Even more revealing was what happened four years later in the Carter versus Reagan race. In the 1980 election, Reagan swept the South, but the majority of the districts that voted for Carter were those that had voted for Wallace in 1968. In other words, racial backlash translated into Democratic votes, not Republican votes. Middle-class suburbanites in the South might have moved to the suburbs to avoid problems of the inner city, but they also moved to the suburbs, as had most Americans, to find better homes, better schools, safer conditions for their families, and lower taxes. These voters reflected a new postindustrial America. For many, it was natural that they went Republican in 1980.

Reagan accomplished much in his eight years in office. During his administration the economy boomed and the Cold War waned. Reagan often did not pay close attention to the details of policy, especially in those areas that did not interest him, but he restored confidence in the presidency after the disastrous Carter years. Reagan had a superb ability to communicate his ideas to the larger public and provide a realistic sense of what was possible. His critics at the time accused Reagan of just being an actor who memorized lines from his speechwriters. They said he was not aware of the world around him, that he was sleepwalking through history. Historians who have studied Reagan through his archives later concluded that Reagan was a superb president, a man of strong conviction, and a leader willing to pursue new directions, even when those around him warned him of the political dangers. His personal letters are eloquent testimony to how his opponents, and many academic historians, let their personal biases color their assessments.

Reagan proved to be a consummate politician. In 1984, he easily defeated a liberal Democratic ticket, Walter Mondale and Representative Geraldine Ferraro (D-New York), a feminist. During the campaign, Reagan's optimism contrasted sharply with Mondale's pessimistic picture of a nation in decline. Reagan swept through the Electoral College and the popular vote, receiving 54.4 million votes to win 525 electoral votes. Liberals such as Mondale and Ferraro misunderstood that most Americans refused to see their country as being in decline. Instead, most voters shared Reagan's optimistic realism: Sure the country had problems, but the people of the United States were problem solvers. Reagan captured a sentiment that the United States was the best place in the world to live and worth defending.

The Economic Recovery Act—for which Reagan personally lobbied when he was recuperating from a failed assassination attempt—reduced income taxes, lowered capital gains taxes, and indexed tax rates for inflation. This was the largest tax cut in American history. Reagan also made deregulation another part of his economic program. While Reagan's policies were not the sole cause of economic revival, the economy boomed during his eight years in office. During the Reagan years, real incomes rose nearly twice as fast and consumption increased as much as one-third faster than original projections made by Reagan's critics in the first years of his presidency. Contrary to critics at the time who maintained the rich were getting richer and the poor poorer, the American people moved up in wealth during the Reagan presidency, although the number of people at the very bottom also increased. Americans went on a buying spree. Low mortgage rates led Americans to buy new homes that were larger and better equipped.

Throughout Reagan's presidency, reports in newspapers and on network television charged that homelessness was on the increase. From November 1986 through 1989, ABC, CBS, and NBC evening newscasts devoted 103 television stories to the homelessness problem in the America. The *New York Times* published hundreds of articles and books abounded on the homeless problem. Critics claimed that Reagan's cuts in social programs and welfare increased the problem. Later, social scientists such as sociologist Christopher Jencks, undertaking more precise studies of the homeless problem, found that homelessness was not as widespread as reported. Contrary to liberal activists who claimed ten million homeless, Jencks concluded there were fewer than four hundred thousand homeless in America and that homelessness was due to a complex set of social problems related to the breakdown of family, drug and alcohol dependency, and sexual mores among the poor. Jencks found that cuts in mental health facilities and the release of mentally ill patients were major contributing causes of homelessness.

Liberals and gay activists also accused the Reagan administration of not doing enough to tackle the human immunodeficiency virus (HIV) and acquired immune deficiency syndrome (AIDS). AIDS reached epidemic levels, primarily among gay men and drug users, in the 1980s and found its way into the medical supply, infecting those in need of blood transfusions. The spread of AIDS caught many public health officials off guard, but once the scale of the disease became apparent, local, state, and federal officials undertook extensive public health, research, and education efforts. Activists claimed that the Reagan administration was not doing enough because of a fear of a backlash from the Christian Right, some of whose leaders asserted that HIV/AIDS was God's punishment for unnatural and sinful behavior. While Reagan himself showed little understanding of HIV/AIDS, his administration reacted to the AIDS epidemic as a public health issue and beginning in 1983 budgeted $26.5 million for research. This was increased to $500 million in 1985, with levels continuing to increase until Reagan left office in 1988. While these sums pale in comparison with later levels of spending, the full extent of the AIDS epidemic was not known in the early 1980s.

At the same time, the Reagan administration began a massive arms buildup. The president urged Americans to "speak out against those who would place the United States in a position of military and moral inferiority." In the face of worldwide public demonstrations calling for the United States to undertake a "nuclear freeze" and stop building missiles, Reagan pursued a policy of massive military increases. His administration spent $2.7 trillion for defense over his eight years in office. He believed that the United States should be protected, but he also believed in "peace through strength." He hoped that the leaders in the Kremlin would see the will of the United States to remain strong, and this would force them to undertake serious and verifiable arms reduction negotiations. This is exactly what did occur in Reagan's second term, when Reagan and Soviet leader Mikhail Gorbachev met in Reykjavik, Iceland, to set the stage for the START I Treaty, which dramatically reduced America's strategic arsenal by 25 percent and the Soviet Union's by 35 percent. The following year, under George H. W. Bush, the START II Treaty was concluded, which reduced nuclear arsenals by another 50 percent and abolished an entire class of land-based missiles.

Furthermore, by encouraging Gorbachev's reform policies within the Soviet Union, Reagan helped in the eventual dismantling of the Soviet empire in Eastern Europe. By 1989, Communist regimes in nearly every Soviet bloc country except Albania had collapsed. For millions of people in Eastern and Central Europe, the oppressive yoke of Communism was lifted from their shoulders. And, contrary to those leftist critics today who note with some relish stories of economic and social hardship in Eastern and Central Europe and the Soviet Union after the collapse of Communism, the great majority of people in these nations believe they are better off.

Reagan's presidency was not without its missteps and errors, however. Even conservative critics pointed to the high budget deficits that the administration ran up during its eight years in office. (Reagan's defenders noted that Democrats controlled Congress throughout most of Reagan's presidency, making it impossible to undertake budget cuts in social spending.) Reagan made other mistakes as well. His administration violated the spirit of Congressional restrictions in helping to fund counterrevolutionary forces operating against the pro-Cuban Sandinista government in Nicaragua. Congress had prohibited such aid through legislation. Instead the administration sought to circumvent the intent of Congress by using the National Security Council to raise private and foreign funds for the anti-Sandinista Contras. Although Saudis provided most of the funds for this covert operation, financial support was also provided by private American citizens. As part of this operation, the United States secretly sold missiles to the radical Islamic regime in Iran. The Iran-Contra scandal in 1986 consumed the administration and Congress the last two years of the Reagan administration and was carried into the subsequent Bush administration for the next four years.

Some conservative movement leaders criticized Reagan's administration for being too pragmatic in pursuit of its agenda by placing social issues on the back burner in order to pursue economic issues. Attempts by conservative Senator Jesse Helms (R–North Carolina) to pass an antiabortion amendment and voluntary school prayer legislation failed in Congress. Social conservative movement activists were not pleased by the appointment of Sandra Day O'Connor to the Supreme Court because they felt she was proabortion. Conservatives also pointed out that much of the liberal welfare and regulatory state erected in the New Deal and expanded during the Great Society survived the Reagan Revolution.

The Reagan presidency united the various strains and factions within the conservative movement during his eight years in office. Tensions between these factions flared up periodically during his administration, but the GOP Right remained unified around Reagan, an avowed conservative. The strains between social and economic conservatives, however, intensified in the later Republican presidencies of George H. W. Bush and George W. Bush.

President Ronald Reagan sharing a joke with conservative leader William F. Buckley at a birthday party for the president on February 7, 1986. These two men played key roles in shaping the conservative movement. (Courtesy of the Ronald Reagan Library)

AFTER THE REAGAN REVOLUTION

When Reagan left office, he had become an icon for conservatives. He had shown that a conservative running as a conservative could win the White House. The House and Senate, however, remained under Democratic control through 1994. Reagan's popularity as president enabled his vice president, George H. W. Bush, to succeed him. During the campaign against Democrat Michael Dukakis, Bush ran as a conservative promising never to raise taxes in his famous line at the Republican National Convention, "Read my lips. No new taxes." Once in office, however, Bush moved to the center. His greatest success as president came during the Gulf War in 1991, when a U.S.-led army expelled Iraqi forces from neighboring, oil-rich Kuwait. Bush's popularity fell dramatically when, under pressure from a Democrat-controlled Congress, he backed raising taxes, with the promise that Democrats would cut domestic spending. The Democrats did not live up to their bargain by cutting spending.

By breaking his pledge, Bush lost his base of support among conservatives, while a downturn in the economy beginning in late 1991 led to a sharp decline in his popularity among the general electorate. Bush tried to maintain his conservative base, while reassuring the general public that the economy was coming out of its recession. As conservatives looked at the Bush record, it seemed mixed. He appointed black conservative Clarence Thomas to the Supreme Court in 1991, over the protests of outraged liberals and feminists who maintained that he had sexually harassed an employee when he was chair of the Equal Employment Opportunity Commission. Bush's actions were insufficient to maintain conservative support, and this contributed to his losing reelection in 1992 against a centrist Arkansas governor, Bill Clinton.

Clinton came into office as a centrist who often came across as more conservative than his rivals in the Democratic Party and sometimes more conservative than conservatives. Clinton's new Democratic agenda faced strong opposition within his own party, both among grassroots activist constituencies and in Congress. Clinton ran into problems even before he stepped into the White House when he announced that he was going to fulfill a campaign promise by lifting the ban on homosexuals in the military. Under pressure from the military, he reversed course and accepted a policy of "don't ask, don't tell," which allowed gays in the military provided they did not announce they were homosexual. Once in office, Clinton encountered further problems when he proposed an elaborate and bureaucratic national health insurance scheme that had been drafted by his wife, Hillary Clinton, and an ad hoc committee. The proposal failed in the face of opposition from Republicans and Democrats, as well as from the insurance industry and conservative grassroots activists. By 1994, Clinton faced resistance from both the GOP Right and the Democratic Left, which was well represented in Congress. The Democratic Left wanted Clinton to push policies to expand abortion rights and government programs to address the social problems of the country.

Clinton also faced a well-organized conservative grassroots, aroused by the flood of talk radio programs that had followed Reagan's deregulation of broadcasting and the ending of the Fairness Doctrine, which had forced television and radio to allot time to differing political perspectives. The king of conservative talk radio was the sharp-witted natural entertainer Rush Limbaugh, whose radio program became nationally syndicated in the summer of 1988. His daily radio program soared to twenty million listeners, who heard Limbaugh refer to feminists as "feminazis," liberal professors as "pinheads," and his followers as "dittoheads." His success gave rise to other conservative talk shows that became a staple of AM radio.

Talk radio played an important role in winning the House for the Republicans in 1994. That year a group of conservative Republicans—Newt Gingrich (Georgia), Dick Armey (Texas), Vin Weber (Minnesota), and Tom DeLay (Texas)—announced a "Contract with America," a pledge by House Republicans, if they won control of the House, to pass ten specific pieces of legislation. The contract called for welfare reform, anticrime measures, a line-item veto, regulatory reform, and tax reduction. Hot-button issues such as abortion, pornography, and school prayer were not included in the plan in order to avoid the charge that the Republican Right represented only the Religious Right. The exclusion of these issues, however, was noted by social conservatives at the time, who nonetheless continued to vote Republican.

On Election Day, Republicans captured the House. For the next one hundred days the new Republican-controlled House focused on passing the Contract with America. Bills were introduced on crime, congressional term limits, welfare reform, a balanced budget, Social Security, defense, illegal drugs, and taxation. All but two pieces of Republican legislation were passed, a term limit bill and a space-based missile defense bill, but the program met resistance in the Senate. In the end, only two pieces of legislation from the contract were enacted into law, one that mandated federal employment law be applied to Congress and another one prohibiting unfunded federal mandates.

Under pressure from a Republican-controlled Congress, Clinton tacked to the Right politically in order to win reelection. Clinton incorporated many

Republican issues into his own agenda. Nonetheless, he refused to undertake severe budget cuts in federal spending that House Republicans called for. This led House Republicans to shut down the federal government when they refused to pass a budget bill in 1995. The Republican ploy backfired and bolstered Clinton politically. At the same time Clinton deftly called for a balanced budget and he accepted Republican calls for welfare reform. The Personal Responsibility Act (1996) barred mothers under the age of eighteen from receiving welfare aid, food stamps, or public housing. Liberal opponents to the measure, such as Senator Daniel Moynihan (D-New York), warned that tens of thousands of people would be left homeless under the act. However, the Personal Responsibility Act proved successful in reducing welfare rolls and encouraging job training and employment programs for poor people. Some two million women left welfare for jobs. Later studies from the Congressional Budget Office found that from 1991 to 2005 real incomes doubled for female-headed households. Low-wage households with children had incomes after inflation one-third higher in 2005 than in 1991, a 78 percent increase in earnings, the highest growth of any income group.

Calls for the legalization of same-sex marriages and civil unions for gay and lesbian couples met with intense opposition from traditional conservatives worried about the cultural, legal, and financial consequences of overturning long-established tradition. In 1996, Clinton signed the Defense of Marriage Act, defining a family as a union between a man and a woman. In moving to the center, Clinton sought to position himself within an American culture that tended toward social conservatism on issues such as the family.

Clinton's strategy of tacking to the center worked and he won reelection in 1996 against a weak Republican candidate, Senator Robert Dole (R-Kansas), who failed to generate much enthusiasm from the conservative movement. (Newt Gingrich had called Dole the "tax collector for the welfare state.") Whatever success Clinton might have enjoyed in his second term was prevented by a series of political and personal scandals within his administration that allowed Republicans to revive the character issue in the 2000 election.

George W. Bush's election to the White House in 2000 marked a triumph for conservatives in a struggle that had begun a half century earlier. The 2000 election proved exceptionally close. Democratic candidate Albert Gore Jr. won the popular vote 48.4 percent to 47.8 percent, but lost the Electoral College 271 to 255. Gore lost every southern and border state that the Clinton-Gore ticket had carried in 1996, including Gore's home state of Tennessee. A change of 537 votes in Florida would have given Gore the presidency. A 5–4 Supreme Court decision (*Bush v. Gore*) ruled that Bush had won Florida, letting the original count stand and overturning two Florida state supreme court rulings that ordered more recounts of the ballots. Both conservative and legal scholars found reasons to criticize the majority decision, but generally conservatives were supportive of the view that the state court had violated article II, section 1, of the Constitution by invading the authority of the state legislature to set election standards and procedures. The intervention of the Supreme Court became a rallying cry for Democrats who claimed that Bush was "president-select."

Bush's presidency was shaped by a terrorist attack on the United States on September 11, 2001. National security reemerged as a major political issue for the first time since the end of the Cold War. His leadership in this crisis strengthened him politically in his first six years in office. In 2002 Republicans won a majority in Congress for the first time since 1994. Bush put his own stamp on conservatism by proclaiming himself a "compassionate conservative."

This identity allowed Bush to combine traditional conservative principles of individual responsibility and free enterprise, while acknowledging the important role that government had come to play in American life. Bush sought to use activist government to allow more individual choice in programs. His faith-based initiative allowed faith-based charitable organizations to provide social services to the poor. Under his leadership, Congress enacted legislation to make public schools more accountable by linking federal aid to testing standards set by state governments. The Bush administration supported the expansion of federal health insurance to the elderly through a drug prescription program, and a measure allowing Americans to set up health savings accounts that provided more individual choice and incentives to contain costs. He called for reform of Social Security through limited privatization, but this call for reform failed to gain political traction among the electorate or politicians. Bush's greatest contribution to extending the Reagan Revolution was through new appointments to the Supreme Court and the federal judiciary.

Bush came into the White House with the economy in a recession because of the collapse of the late 1990s technology bubble. Less than nine months later the events of 9/11 became a defining moment for national security, but also had severe economic consequences. The attacks were aimed at our country's financial sector and led to the suspension of stock trading, the closing of stores and shopping malls, cancelled airplane flights, and the loss of nearly a million jobs in the following three months.

In response to the deepening recession, Bush called successfully on Congress to enact tax cuts. In the following six years, the American economy boomed with uninterrupted growth. More than eight million jobs were added after August 2003—more than in all the other major industrial countries combined. Federal tax receipts increased. At the same time, Bush began to rebuild the military after budget cuts in the 1990s. Support for intelligence, law enforcement, and homeland security also increased. A war in Iraq and Afghanistan radically increased federal expenditures, but by 2007, the projected national debt as a percentage of the gross domestic product had reached historical lows, until the economic meltdown in October 2008.

Bush's decision to invade Afghanistan and Iraq placed his entire administration on the line politically. Initially, Bush's decision won strong approval from the electorate. In the 2004 election against Democratic presidential nominee Senator John Kerry (D-Massachusetts), the Bush campaign developed an extensive grassroots organization based on nearly 71.5 million e-mail addresses of supporters and 1.5 million volunteers. These volunteers ran "virtual precincts" using the Web to register voters and organize family and friends. This grassroots base proved important in Bush's winning the 2004 election. (In 2008, Senator Barack Obama drew a page from the Bush-Cheney playbook in mobilizing grassroots support for his candidacy.)

As the war in Iraq intensified with sectarian and foreign terrorists, the American public lost confidence in the war effort and by 2006, Bush's public approval rating had fallen nearly as low as had Carter's during the Iranian hostage crisis. This allowed Democrats to regain control of Congress in 2006.

This downturn in Republican fortunes caused fissures within the ranks of conservatives, reminiscent of divisions during the Cold War. Old Right conservatives such as Patrick Buchanan and libertarians associated with *Reason* magazine and the Cato Institute denounced the war in Iraq as arrogant and ill conceived. By 2006, other conservatives were criticizing the war, including William F. Buckley Jr., who came out against the war shortly before his death in 2008, and former Bush speechwriter David Frum. They accused the Bush administration of holding Wilsonian aspirations to spread democracy to the world. Conservative opposition to the Iraq war lessened with the apparent success of the military "surge" when Bush committed an additional thirty thousand American troops in Iraq.

Still, many conservatives on the grassroots level branded the Bush administration as "Big Government Republicanism" because of its support for drug prescriptions for the elderly, expanding the federal government's role in education through the No Child Left Behind Act (2002), and its faith-based initiative program. Moreover, grassroots conservatives broke ranks with the Bush administration over its support of an immigration bill that promised to tighten security along the border between the United States and Mexico but also to establish a guest worker program and a path to citizenship for illegal immigrants.

During the Bush presidency, partisanship in Congress and the electorate sharpened. At the same time, the war in Iraq intensified public distrust in government. Surveys showed that distrust in government, political leaders, and Congress had begun to rise in the late 1960s. With the war in Iraq, this distrust reached all-time high levels, especially among the young. Within this polarized environment, neither political party was given to easy compromise. Debate often proved shrill and reconciliation seemed impossible. This discord reflected the vibrancy of a mature democracy.

CONSERVATIVES: CREATORS OF THE FUTURE?

Conservatism has been a dynamic political movement in the twentieth century, influenced by new ideas and ideological tensions. Before World War II it consisted mainly of a defense of the cultural traditions of Western civilization and of a vehement defense of laissez-faire and free markets. Pre–World War II conservatives staunchly defended localism, a strict adherence to the Constitution, and distrust of strong executive power in the face of profound technological and political change.

The Cold War altered conservatism profoundly. Most conservatives accepted the tenets of Cold War containment and extended the fear of Communism into the domestic sphere of American politics. In order to combat liberalism at home and Communism abroad, it was necessary for conservatives to enter politics, not just plead for their views in the intellectual realm. From the 1950s to the election of Ronald Reagan in 1980, and beyond to the end of the Cold War, conservatives constructed a political movement based upon the idea of firmly opposing state-building tendencies at home while combating Communism abroad. There were inherent contradictions in such a policy, but conservatives kept their focus on policies and programs designed to fulfill these two goals. The end of the Cold War deprived conservatives of an enemy and left those critical of Cold War conservatism, such as journalist Patrick Buchanan, to help awaken old Right isolationism when it came to the post-9/11 world.

Modern liberalism proved to be a formidable opponent and even with Republican victories, the modern welfare and regulatory state was not easily dismantled. Still, the conservative ascendancy within the Republican Party and in the electorate in the last half of the twentieth century led to significant political and policy changes. Politically, conservatives were able to mobilize large numbers of voters to their cause. More important, while conservatives acting through the Republican Party were not able to scale back federal involvement in Social Security, Medicare-Medicaid, education, or environmental protection, conservatives won notable victories in strengthening national defense, reforming welfare policy, restricting reproductive rights, reinvigorating monetary policy, deregulating major industries, and appointing conservative-minded federal judges.

A broad historical perspective of the last half of the twentieth century suggests that conservatives accomplished much of significance. Conservatives claimed to have strengthened American defense; helped dismantle an oppressive Soviet regime in Eastern Europe; revived the economy in the 1980s when many liberal pundits declared the United States in decline; and had played critical, indeed essential, roles in passing civil rights legislation and reforming a welfare system that many experts, as well as centrist Democrats, believed kept millions in a state of dependency. For these reasons, Ronald Reagan and others on the Republican Right claimed that conservatives were the creators of the future, befitting a dynamic nation that looked with optimism to the future.

Barack Obama's election to the White House and the Democratic control of Congress, following the 2008 election, called into question GOP optimism. Although Obama only won 1.5 percent more of the popular vote than George W. Bush had in 2004, Republicans were soundly defeated in 2008. Especially disturbing for Republicans was the defection of nearly 20 percent of those Republicans who had voted for Bush in 2004. Moreover, Obama won among independents, women, and the young. White males, white Catholics, and seniors barely went for Republican presidential candidate, Senator John McCain (R-Arizona). No longer were the Republicans a majority party.

As conservatives sought to regroup, they could take little consolation in the historical reminder that Republican success often followed Democratic mistakes in office. Given the severity, however, of the 2008 financial meltdown, and the ongoing international threats of rogue nations, oil shortages, nuclear proliferation, and military involvement in the Middle East and Afghanistan, even the most partisan-minded Republicans hoped that their return to office would not be built on a failed Obama presidency.

While partisan differences would not be ignored, Democrats and Republicans, progressive and conservatives alike, understood that above all else, Abraham Lincoln's words in 1858 remained valid: "A house divided against itself cannot stand."

DOCUMENTS

1

CONSERVATIVES DEBATE THE COLD WAR: EXCERPT FROM RONALD HAMOWY AND WILLIAM F. BUCKLEY JR., "CONSERVATISM AND THE *NATIONAL REVIEW*: CRITICISM AND REPLY" (NOVEMBER 1961)

In 1961, libertarian Ronald Hamowy and the founding editor of the conservative weekly *National Review*, William F. Buckley Jr., debated the meaning of conservatism and the Cold War. What were Hamowy's criticisms of Buckley's conservatism? Why did Hamowy not support the Cold War? How does the debate inform us about the concerns of the Right in these years?

Since its inception in 1955, *National Review* has gradually assumed the leadership of the Right in America until today it stands practically unopposed as the intellectual spokesman of conservatism throughout the country. It boasts a staff of sophisticated and witty editors, the chief of whom is William F. Buckley, who has, in fact, achieved the status of national celebrity. Well-educated and self-assured, he has, in his countless appearances on television, at public lectures, and on dozens of college campuses including his own beloved Yale, impressed the general public with the fact that conservatives do not fall into the category of what H. L. Mencken used to call "yahoos."

So much is Mr. Buckley identified with everything intelligent on the Right that if in the common image of modern conservatism Senator Goldwater can justly be portrayed as the sword, William Buckley is, without doubt, the pen. Given this phenomenon of Buckley as one of the directors of the Right, it becomes incumbent on all those who would attach themselves to this movement to carefully investigate the policies which he and his group espouse and to answer the crucial question of just where they are leading us. Nor should we be drawn away from this task by loud cries for "unity." It is the duty of all thinking men to reflect and examine before falling into step behind any leader. Indeed, it has always been an unfortunate disposition of most Right-wingers uncritically to follow the man and not the principle.

It is the contention of this article that William Buckley and *National Review* are, in fact, leading true believers in freedom and individual liberty down a disastrous path and that in so doing they are causing the Right increasingly to betray its own traditions and principles.

Better to see how far the Conservative movement has been straying under *National Review* guidance, let us briefly examine its genesis. The modern American "Right," was, in essence, a much-needed and healthy reaction against the New Deal, that revolution in domestic and foreign affairs wrought by Franklin D. Roosevelt which aimed at the radical transformation of the role of the State in American life and whose goal was the aggrandizement of government power at the expense of the individual. This modern Right represented the emerging opposition to such a shift and was, therefore, a movement stressing individual freedom. Domestically, the corollary of individual liberty was a call for free enterprise as against the socialist tendencies of the State; in foreign affairs, it stood for peace, neutrality, and isolationism as opposed to the Rooseveltian drive towards collective security, foreign entanglement, and war.

At a time when the Left had a virtual monopoly on all intellectual activity, during the early 40's, a small but ever-growing libertarian movement began to emerge. Its leaders were such eminent publicists and political thinkers as Isabel Paterson, Rose Wilder Lane, Garet Garrett, Albert Jay Nock, and Frank Chodorov. Philosophically, it was firmly dedicated to individual liberty, and consequently embraced free enterprise in economics, a strict adherence to the civil liberties of the individual, and peace. Historically, it ranked among its heroes Jefferson, Tom Paine, Thoreau, and Herbert Spencer.

Six years ago, however, a revolution took place "within the form," as Garet Garrett once wrote of the New Deal. The articulate publicists of *National Review*, founded at that time, have succeeded in remoulding the American Right until it travesties the intent of its original founders. Mr. Buckley and his staff have been able to achieve this transformation with such apparent ease simply because there has been no journal of opinion to oppose it, or even to call attention to the surgery that has been committed on the American Conservative movement.

How far this revolution within the form has gone may be gauged, for example, by the current conservative attitude towards Mr. Justice Frankfurter. Fifteen years ago, Justice Frankfurter was generally regarded by the

Right as the personification of collectivist jurisprudence, as a destroyer of the Constitutional guarantees of liberty against the State. Today, he is considered to have become part of the Conservative movement and his name has actually been cheered by groups of conservative youth. To those who would take the trouble of investigating the judicial philosophy of Mr. Frankfurter, however, it immediately becomes apparent that his position remains unchanged. He is guided solely by the principle that the courts must legitimize nearly every power the government decides to exercise. He is, and has always been, a thorough Statist. But now he is hailed by the Right because his most publicized decisions, especially in the Wilkinson and Uphaus cases, show him trampling upon the civil liberties of Leftists. His continued willingness to compromise with property rights is totally ignored by those who now reserve their zeal for the coercing of as many Communists and Communist sympathizers as they can lay their hands on. It is not Justice Frankfurter's position which has shifted, but that of the American Right.

And in this shift the lead has been taken by Mr. Buckley and his colleagues. *National Review* has time and again exerted its considerable intellectual influence *against* individual liberty. Through issue after issue of the journal we read of the "rights of the community," of five thousand years of conservative tradition, of authority and order, of the duty of the West to uplift the Negro with Bible and bullwhip, of the sacred obligation all free men have to coerce Communists at home and slaughter them abroad. Where once the Right was fervently devoted to the freedoms propounded in the Bill of Rights, it now believes that civil liberties are the work of Russian agents. Where once it stood for the strict separation of Church and State, it now speaks of the obligation of the community to preserve a Christian America through a variety of Blue Laws and other schemes for integrating government and religion. Where once the Right was, above all, dedicated to peace and opposed to foreign entanglements, it now is concerned with preparing for war and giving all-out aid to any dictator, Socialist or otherwise, who proclaims his unbending "anti-Communism." Where once the Right wanted America to exert its moral effect upon the world by being a beacon-light of freedom, it now wants to turn America into an armed camp to crush Communism wherever it appears. Can it be less than fifteen years ago that the right-wing members of Congress voted against NATO and aid to Greece and Turkey? Can it be only a decade ago when Joseph Kennedy and Herbert Hoover were calling for withdrawal of our armies to our shores and when Howard Buffett, Taft's mid-west campaign manager, denounced this country's military bases abroad and the growing militarism in America?

It is not only on the Communist issue that the Right has abandoned its libertarian principles. All foreign policy questions are considered solely from the point of view of "historic traditions" or "American national interest." *National Review*'s applause for the British-French-Israeli invasion of Suez is typical: for here was a situation where it could blend its fanatical opposition to anyone considered pro-Communist with its contempt for non-European and non-Christian peoples. The foreign policy position of the libertarian Right was essentially that held by Cobden and Bright in the nineteenth century: opposition to aggression, to imperialism, and to war. The foreign policy position of the new Right is that of Colonel Blimp and Rudyard Kipling, the pseudo-aristocratic outlook of "cane the bloody wogs" and "send the marines," coupled with the ever-present background mutterings of retired Generals and Admirals of "what they need is a whiff of grape."

These differences concerning foreign policy are of much greater importance than might first be realized, for they call into question the philosophic problem of moral principle. One of the outstanding features of *National Review* is its pretension of moral superiority, its insistence that it alone represents the conservator of two thousand years of Western Civilization and Christianity. But surely one who believes in natural law must hold that it be eternal and fixed, and that the natural rights of the individual apply at any time, for any place. Yet the position that *National Review* holds grants rights only, and then begrudgingly, to Anglo-Saxons. Spain must respect its heritage of the dictatorial *Caudillo*; Central Europe must revert to the divinely-inspired Crown of St. Stephen; British colonies must be subjugated to the Mother Country; France's historical role is to be governed by a clique of fascist generals whose function it must be to hurl still more conscripts into the sacred task of crushing Moslems in Algeria. Surely there is no appreciable difference between this system of double morality and the contention often heard on the Left, when asked how they can reconcile a demand for civil liberties at home with support of such dictators as Nkrumah and Toure in modern Africa. . . .

The great moral principle of individual liberty has been superseded by the arrogance of the pseudo-aristocrat who preserves his civilized airs by exploiting the serf labor of "inferior" people; the libertarian principle of peace and non-intervention has been replaced by the heroics of a barroom drunk who proudly boasts that "he can lick anybody in the room." This posture is rendered tragic by the fact that the *National Review* group who proclaim "give me liberty or give me death" are willing to cremate countless millions of innocent persons whom they give no opportunity to make a choice.

Another touchstone of how far the Right has traveled is its position on conscription. Before and after World War II it fought the draft as unconstitutional, as slavery, and as the ultimate aggrandizement of the State. To the current conservative, anyone who dares to raise a principled voice against conscription is labeled a Communist or Communist dupe. The same libertarians who during the Second World War were accused by the Left of being "mouthpieces of the Goebbels line," are now accused, this time by the Right, of "doing the work of the Communists." One would expect libertarians to be reviled and slandered by the apologists of the State. It is, in fact, both noble and honorable to have such enemies. But that *National Review* should take the lead in this slander can mean only one thing: that the Right, under the aegis of *National Review* has itself become a leading minion of the State. From an advocate of individual liberty against the State, the Conservative movement has now become a champion of the State against individual liberty. The entire concept of "right-winger," as it has been understood in America since the 1930's, has been taken by the Buckley group and, like the old word "liberal" at the hands of the Left, has been transformed into its very opposite.

We are left with one significant area: the economic. And even here, modern conservatism fares no better. It is true that there is still much talk about the free market, but a careful study of the literature of the Right today makes it quite clear that it is engaged in beating a steady, persistent retreat from libertarianism even in the economic sphere. One searches in vain, for example, in the concrete political programs of the Young Americans for Freedom, whose organizational meeting was held at Mr. Buckley's estate in Sharon, Conn., for any clear statement on the reduction of the economic intervention of the State. Nowhere, any longer, does a rollback or repeal of the New Deal seem to be seriously contemplated. The only real goal of the *National Review* Right is to keep the Federal government from advancing much further down the socialist road—a goal in itself contradicted by the war economy that it desires. And one is at a loss to find any genuine attempt on its part to examine the relationship between an ever-increasing military establishment and government interference in the economic affairs of the country. At no time has a disarmament agreement with Russia been given as serious consideration as it deserves nor has it been viewed as a welcome possibility. Rather, editors of *National Review* proceed to look on increased government spending not only as permissible but as desirable if it is earmarked for the production of bombs and other paraphernalia of death. On such questions the libertarian is almost forced to stand with the Leftists. If government spending is to be kept at such a high level, better that it be used to build roads, schools, playgrounds, and other things which have some value, no matter how small, rather than be employed to manufacture a new and better type of H-bomb or rocket-launching satellite or used to finance some new inquisitorial government investigatory committee. A return to the free market is indeed hardly a burning issue on the Right today.

The new American Right would seem to reserve its real passion for such causes as giving Khrushchev bi-weekly ultimatums and suppressing civil liberties at home. Mr. Buckley himself has begun, of late, to show increasing asperity towards those misguided souls who still cling to individual liberty as their main political preoccupation by chiding us that social security is, after all, here to stay and really isn't so bad and by denouncing those libertarian "extremists" for cleaving to consistency and truth in speaking against government monopoly control of the roads and post-office. It seems that the desired unity behind our self-appointed leaders is being threatened by the tiny minority who have remained true to those very ideals of individual freedom which led them to become Right-wingers in the first place.

Just what is the direction in which *National Review* is leading the Right and would lead America? There is, of course, an inevitable diversity among the luminaries of that august journal. Willmoore Kendall believes that the Greek "community" had the duty, *a fortiori* the right, to murder Socrates. Frank S. Meyer finds the vision of a total nuclear holocaust not entirely unappealing. Garry Wills finds his pet peeve in capitalism. Frederick Wilhelmsen desires above all other earthly things that we venerate the Crown of St. Stephen. Hugh Kenner finds solace not only in the poetry but in the economics of Ezra Pound. But underneath this collection of attitudes there are manifested certain features that generally characterize them all. They may be summed up as: (1) a belligerent foreign policy likely to result in war; (2) a suppression of civil liberties at home; (3) a devotion to imperialism and to a polite form of white supremacy; (4) a tendency towards the union of Church and State; (5) the conviction that the community is superior to the individual and that historic tradition is a far better guide than reason; and (6) a rather lukewarm support of the free economy. They wish, in gist, to substitute one group of masters (themselves) for another. They do not desire so much to limit the State as to control it. One would tend to describe this devotion to a hierarchial, warlike statism and this fundamental opposition to human reason and individual liberty as a species of corporativism suggestive of Mussolini or Franco, but let us be content with calling it "old-time conservatism," the conservatism not of the heroic band of libertarians who founded the anti-New-Deal Right, but the traditional conservatism that has always been the enemy of true liberalism;★ the conservatism of Pharonic Egypt, of Medieval Europe, of the Inquisition; the conservatism of Metternich and the Tsar, of James II and Louis XVI, of the rack, the thumbscrew, the whip, and the firing squad. I, for one, do not very much mind that a philosophy which has for centuries dedicated itself to trampling upon the rights of the individual and glorifying the State should have its old name back.

—Ronald Hamowy

THREE DRAFTS OF AN ANSWER TO MR. HAMOWY

First Draft

Dear me, thumbscrews, whips, firing squads, war, colonialism, repression, white supremacy, fascism—what a lot of things for *National Review* to have foisted upon the Right in a mere six years! There was a time when Associate Imperialist Henry Hazlitt, who appears on our masthead, was interested in personal liberty: now he wants war and white supremacy. Associate Torturer Erik von Kuehnelt-Leddihn, a founder of the neo-Liberal movement in Europe, and author of *Liberty or Equality*, has abandoned his views, to go authoritarian, along with *National Review*. "[What] a tremendous relief to read your periodical at a moment when we can only say, with Frederick the Great, 'Toute la boutique va au diable'." wrote Wilhelm Roepke, author of *Civitas Humana*, teacher of Ludwig Erhard, president of Mt. Pelerin Society, in a letter to *National Review* a week ago—how sad, to turn one's back on freedom, after so noble a lifetime spent in pursuit of it. (Contributing Torturer Kirk—what would you expect?—writes admiringly about Roepke in the current issue of *National Review*†.) Senior Warmonger Frank Meyer argues that freedom is the meaning of life, that without freedom there is no life, that indeed that is why he would rather be dead than Red. He does not know that to be a true libertarian you must love freedom, but not that much—you must prefer to be Red than dead, or you cannot be in the libertarian tradition. Sad, is it not, to see Contributing Executioner John Chamberlain, who opposes the income tax, become a part of a statist movement; and Senior Suppressor James Burnham, who has written that the government has no business regulating the use of fireworks,

---

★I use the term "liberalism" as it was employed in the 19th century in the hope that the dedicated libertarian might one day have his historic name again.

†October 21, 1961.

end up trampling upon the rights of the individual and glorifying the State. And Associate Colonialist Frank Chodorov cracking the whip: "Call me Massa Frank," he growls at all black men, yellow men, and non-Christians, from the poop-deck of *National Review*. "Six of the best for the next man who says Uhuru," echoes Associate Racist Morrie Ryskind . . .

Pity the people whom
NR has led askew . . .

Second Draft

1. The editorial section of the current issue of *National Review* includes: a) an analysis of the inflationary policies of the Federal Reserve, deploring the state's bureaucratic impositions on business; b) a joyful rundown on the accomplishments of the European Common Market, made possible by the dissipation of statist-enforced economic boundaries; c) a pat on the back for the government of Portugal for its phased increase of self-government in Angola and Mozambique, including extended programs for multi-racial integration (a traditional Portuguese policy); d) an account of a poll by the Council for the Advancement of Small Colleges, yielding the happy news that two-thirds of the student leaders of the small colleges are unsympathetic to "the current trend of the federal government to increase its influence in all areas"; e) an analysis of the shifty legwork of the National Labor Relations Board which has the effect of circumventing the state right-to-work laws by the evasion of the agency shop, which requires a non-union member to contribute to the union's kitty; f) a report on the creeping sanity of Professor Paul Samuelson, who in the last five editions of his famous book on economics has reduced from 5 per cent to 1 per cent the tolerable annual inflation; g) an appreciative obituary account for two men who had battled the overweening state for years; and h) renewed support for Editor William F. Rickenbacker's refusal to sign the Census Department's prurient questionnaire . . .

2. The Sharon (Charter) Statement of the Young Americans for Freedom includes the following asseverations: "political freedom cannot long exist without economic freedom . . . the purposes of government are to protect . . . freedoms through the preservation of internal order, the provision of national defense, and the administration of justice . . . when government ventures beyond these rightful functions, it accumulates power which tends to diminish order and liberty . . . the market economy, allocating resources by the free play of supply and demand, is the single economic system compatible with the requirements of personal freedom . . .

when government interferes with the work of the market economy, it tends to reduce the moral and physical strength of the nation; when it takes from one man to bestow on another, it diminishes the incentive of the first, the integrity of the second, and the moral autonomy of both . . ."

3. The last paragraph of the most recent address I have delivered is (in part): ". . . the direct problems that face the world are the making of governments in action; for only government can exercise the leverage necessary to transform individual vices into universal afflictions. It took government to translate *Mein Kampf* into concentration camps; it takes positive action by government to preserve many of the imbalances in our economic system; only government, with its monopoly of force, can perpetuate injustice that individuals, given the freedom to do so, might redress. It was long ago understood, in the evolution of political theory, that just about the only *intolerable* answer to big government is *no* government. Government there must be, this side of paradise, so that the challenge is, and always will be, how to restrain and direct that government without which we cannot get on. The facile answer of the 19th century, when the body of the world's progressive social theorists seized intoxicatingly upon literacy and self-rule as the solvents of the enlightened and domesticated state, has proved naive. The insufficiency of democracy as a sole guarantor of enlightened public action is now perceptible. The only defense against the shortcomings and abuses of collective action by the state is concerted resistance by individuals. That resistance can only issue from an undamaged critical faculty and moral sense. If the entire thinking class indulges itself in the suppression of the intellect and the conscience, anything can happen: wars that should not be fought, are fought; and wars that should be fought are not fought; and human impulses that should be restrained are not restrained, and human impulses that should not be restrained, are restrained; and great nations are humbled."

Third Draft

Dear Mr. Hamowy:

Your article contains a number of factual errors (when on earth did *National Review* ever celebrate the existence of Felix Frankfurter? We have merely applauded his position on certain issues, as we applaud the position on certain issues of Sidney Hook or Paul Douglas or Lucifer); and, of course, your article seeks to make its points by caricature, which is okay by me, although by so doing, you impose upon me the responsibility of deciding where you are being merely playful, and where you mean to be taken seriously.

Putting aside the thumbscrews, I judge that your criticisms revolve around two central assumptions of *National Review*, which I herewith state, and attempt briefly to show why I judge that they come naturally to American conservatives. The first assumption is that freedom can only be defended in our time by the active use of one's strategic intelligence; and this calls for understanding the Position of the Soviet Union in world affairs.

Among the corollaries of this assumption are: 1) it becomes necessary to forfeit a part of the freedom one might ideally exercise, in order to secure the greater part of our freedom; and corollary 2) our nation's role in world affairs, to the extent it is the state's responsibility to enact it, should turn on and be confined to the question of the national security.

The national security is a proper concern for the libertarian because without it he stands to lose—in this case—all his freedom. The conservative, who is a libertarian but other things, too, supports the large national effort that aims at neutralizing the Communist threat, because a conservative must be prepared to face reality. A conservative is not one of those pure and seraphic intellectualists Bishop Parker spoke about who, forsooth, despise all sensible knowledge as too gross and material for their nice and curious faculties. We conservatives are all for paradigmatic self-examinations from time to time, that aim at drawing attention to all those freedoms we do not have: but we never lose sight of the value of what we do have, and the reason why we have it, namely, because we have a formidable military machine which keeps the Soviet Union from doing to us what it did to the Hungarians, and the Cubans. There is room in any society for those whose only concern is for tablet-keeping; but let them realize that it is only because of the conservatives' disposition to sacrifice in order to withstand the enemy, that they are able to enjoy their monasticism, and pursue their busy little seminars on whether or not to demunicipalize the garbage collectors.

★ ★ ★ ★

And the second assumption shared by the editors of *National Review* is that an approach to any human problem that calls for the ruthless imposition of any social schematic, whether Marxist or Benthamite, is self-defeating, for the reason that ideology can never replace philosophy. While it is true that freedom is good, it is not true that freedom can be promulgated in any given country simply by saying, Ready, Set, Be Free. The count-down is much longer. Sometimes it takes centuries. A conservative will argue for that system in a given country which will *maximize* freedom. But that system is not necessarily one that is based on one man, one vote;

or even, necessarily, on the right of self-rule. We cannot, merely by re-nouncing colonialism instantly, write a script that will bring eudemonia to Upper Volta.

The American conservative needs to proceed within the knowledge of history and anthropology and psychology; we must live in our time. We must indeed continue to cherish our resentments against such institutional-ized impositions upon our prerogatives (see my books) as social security. But we must not, if we are to pass for sane in this tormented world, equate as problems of equal urgency, the repeal of the social security law, and the containment of the Soviet threat. The problem of assigning priorities to the two objectives is not merely a problem of intellectual discrimination, but of moral balance. Mr. Hamowy should examine the processes of thought even among his associates on the Committee for a Sane Nuclear Policy, which I am informed he has recently joined. I hope he will find there still is a dif-ference between him and the moral and intellectual emasculates among whom he mingles; I hope the difference is still discernible; I, and I am sure all conservatives, hope that.

—**William F. Buckley, Jr.**

A REJOINDER TO MR. BUCKLEY IN ONE DRAFT

It is always enjoyable to hear from Mr. Buckley; his style and wit make for relaxing reading. However, it is a fact of life which Mr. Buckley appears to ignore, that an abundance of charm coupled with good intentions is an in-adequate substitute for cogency of thought. Had he dealt with my argu-ments, my task in defending them would have been simpler. As it stands, I can find few points worthy of serious reply. Therefore, I dismiss Mr. Buck-ley's First Draft with the admission that all those whose names appear on *National Review*'s masthead are not, in any sense, consistent conservatives in the Buckley tradition and that, in particular, Henry Hazlitt and Frank Chodorov share few, if any, of the sentiments with which my article deals. Just one point more. Pray, of what neo-Liberal movement in Europe is Mr. Kuehnelt-Leddihn a founder? Does Mr. Buckley regard an intellectual at-tachment to enlightened despotism in Central Europe as in the tradition of Cobden and Bright?

Concerning the Second Draft. (1) The current issue of *National Re-view* also contains: (a) plaudits for the Supreme Court ruling on the regis-tration of the Communist Party with the Justice Department. We are told that this is "a bright day for freedom." Someone or something (it is not indicated who or what) is "resourceful enough to bear down upon the unassimilable political minority for whom the normal rules cannot apply"; (b) an essay by James Burnham to the effect that one can either be for peace or against Communism but that to hold strongly to both positions is "a source of trouble"; (c) a defense of Franco Spain by Lev Ladnek. Mr. Ladnek feels that it is unrealistic to suppose that when idealists call for freedom they are not confining that freedom to just one group in Spanish society at the expense of another. He goes on to say that to champion freedom of expression and free elections is to invite civil war; (d) a report on the Mt. Pelerin Society by Russell Kirk in which he gleefully reports that Liberalism is slowly passing out of fashion as the new Conservatism sweeps all before it. We are informed that some old 19th-century individualists detracted from Kirk's enjoyment of the meeting but that on careful consideration "the moral and political doctrines of Bentham 'the great subversive' are fallen from favor nowadays, except in their *reductio ad absurdum*, Marxism."

(2) Despite the high-sounding phrases of the Sharon Statement, *no concrete political program* of the Young Americans for Freedom has concerned itself with a call for the reduction of the economic intervention of the State. Instead, they have devoted their time and energy to picketing in support of the House Committee on Un-American Activities and the American government's invasion of Cuba and against negotiations on Berlin. A charter member of this organization informs me that its Policy Committee has voted to decline to take a stand against the John Birch Society and State segregation laws. That they pay lip-service to freedom indicates nothing.

(3) Mr. Buckley's speech indeed expresses a noble sentiment. However, it bears no relevance to the arguments I present in my article.

The Third Draft presents 2 arguments, the first, that the external threat of Communism is of such magnitude that internal freedom becomes of minor importance. To this is added a sub-argument that it is only thanks to people like Buckley sacrificing themselves "in order to withstand the enemy," that "tablet-keepers" like me might "enjoy their monasticism and pursue their busy little seminars on whether or not to demunicipalize the garbage collectors."

It might appear ungrateful of me but I must decline to thank Mr. Buckley for saving my life. It is, further, my belief that if his view-point prevails and that if he persists in his unsolicited aid the result will almost certainly be either my death (and that of tens of millions of others) in nuclear war or my imminent imprisonment as an "un-American."

Mr. Buckley would seem to imply that my position rests on a personal fear of death, and if this is the case, it indicates a total misreading of the facts. I hold strongly to my personal liberty and it is precisely because of this that I insist that no one has the right to force his decisions on another. Mr. Buckley chooses to be dead rather than Red. So do I. But I insist that all men be allowed to make that decision for themselves. A nuclear holocaust will make it for them.

The second argument has as its underlying premise that "freedom cannot be promulgated . . . by saying, Ready, Set, Be Free," that it is something which is earned and often takes centuries to achieve. Promulgated by whom? Earned? Who is the paymaster? No one *gives* anyone else his freedom nor is anyone indebted to others for it. Mr. Buckley either rejects or is unfamiliar with the premises of political philosophy upon which our nation was founded. Namely, that freedom is, in fact, not earned, but the *right* of each human being. Mr. Buckley, I hold these truths to be self-evident, that all men are created equal, that they are endowed by their Creator with certain unalienable Rights, that among these are Life, Liberty, and the Pursuit of Happiness.

—Ronald Hamowy

Source: Excerpt, Ronald Hamowy and William F. Buckley Jr., "Conservatism and the *National Review*: Criticism and Reply," *New Individualist Review*, November 1961, I:3, 5–11. (Courtesy of Liberty Fund Inc.)

2

YOUNG CONSERVATIVES ORGANIZE: THE SHARON STATEMENT (SEPTEMBER 11, 1960)

In the fall of 1960, William F. Buckley Jr. hosted a meeting at his home in Sharon, Connecticut, for young conservatives from across the country to form the Young Americans for Freedom. The Sharon Statement embodied the principles of this organization that appeared on many college campuses. What views did this organization express toward transcendent values? The purpose of government? The free market? How did these beliefs differ from those of modern-day liberals?

In this time of moral and political crises, it is the responsibility of the youth of America to affirm certain eternal truths.

We, as young conservatives, believe:

That foremost among the transcendent values is the individual's use of his God-given free will, whence derives his right to be free from the restrictions of arbitrary force;

That liberty is indivisible, and that political freedom cannot long exist without economic freedom;

That the purpose of government is to protect those freedoms through the preservation of internal order, the provision of national defense, and the administration of justice;

That when government ventures beyond these rightful functions, it accumulates power, which tends to diminish order and liberty;

That the Constitution of the United States is the best arrangement yet devised for empowering government to fulfill its proper role, while restraining it from the concentration and abuse of power;

That the genius of the Constitution—the division of powers—is summed up in the clause that reserves primacy to the several states, or to the people, in those spheres not specifically delegated to the Federal government;

That the market economy, allocating resources by the free play of supply and demand, is the single economic system compatible with the requirements of personal freedom and constitutional government, and that it is at the same time the most productive supplier of human needs;

That when government interferes with the work of the market economy, it tends to reduce the moral and physical strength of the nation; that when it takes from one man to bestow on another, it diminishes the incentive of the first, the integrity of the second, and the moral autonomy of both;

That we will be free only so long as the national sovereignty of the United States is secure; that history shows periods of freedom are rare, and can exist only when free citizens concertedly defend their rights against all enemies;

That the forces of international Communism are, at present, the greatest single threat to these liberties;

That the United States should stress victory over, rather than coexistance with, this menace; and

That American foreign policy must be judged by this criterion: does it serve the just interests of the United States?

Source: Young Americans for Freedom, *The Sharon Statement*, adopted in a conference at Sharon, Connecticut, September 11, 1960. (© 1960 by National Review, Inc., 215 Lexington Avenue; New York, NY 10016. Reprinted by permission)

3

A CONSERVATIVE SPEAKS IN FAVOR OF CIVIL RIGHTS: SENATOR EVERETT DIRKSEN, *CONGRESSIONAL RECORD* (JUNE 1964)

Senator Everett Dirksen, Republican minority leader in the Senate, played a critical role in the passage of the Civil Rights Act of 1964, which met major opposition from southern Democrats. What is Dirksen's argument in favor of this bill? Does Dirksen's support of civil rights legislation appear idealistic or pragmatic? Why would Republicans support civil rights legislation, even though the majority of African Americans voted Democratic?

Mr. DIRKSEN. Mr. President, we are on the threshold of what I suppose everyone will consider a historic vote. I am deeply grateful to the majority leader [Mr. Mansfield] Senator Mansfield for his patience, his tolerance, and his sense of self-effacement in all the tedious struggle that has gone on for nearly 100 days; and I am truly grateful to the deputy majority leader [HUMPHREY], because of the attributes he has brought to this struggle. He has been fair, tolerant, and just, and always has brought to this problem an understanding heart.

To my revered assistant, the distinguished whip on the minority side [Mr. Kuchel] I say with equal accolade how grateful I am for the way he stood by under every circumstance and for the rare patience he has displayed in all this difficult time.

Mr. President, it has been a tedious matter. It has been a long labor, indeed. On looking back, I think a little of the rather popular television program called "That Was the Week That Was." I think tonight we can say, "That was the year that was," because it was a year ago this June that we first started coming to grips with this very challenging controversy on civil rights.

On the 5th of June, my own party, after 2 days of labor and conference, came forward with a consensus to express its views on the subject. That consensus is printed in the Congressional Record. I shall read only a portion of what we said in the course of that statement. Before I do so, I wish to say that prior to the conference I had worked out on a portable typewriter what I thought was a general and acceptable statement of principle. In the course of the conference, a word was removed, and then it was restored; a phrase was removed, and then it was restored. Finally, we came up with a declaration of which I think we can all be proud, for among other things, the statement included the following:

It is the consensus of the Senate Republican conference that: "The Federal Government, including the legislative, executive, and judicial branches, has a solemn duty to preserve the rights, privileges, and immunities of citizens of the United States in conformity with the Constitution, which makes every native-born and naturalized person a citizen of the United States, as well as the State in which he resides. Equality of rights and opportunities has not been fully achieved in the long period since the 14th and 15th amendments to the Constitution were adopted, and this inequality and lack of opportunity and the racial tensions which they engender are out of character with the spirit of a nation pledged to justice and freedom."

I recite one other paragraph from that statement of principle:

The Republican Members of the U.S. Senate, in this 88th Congress, reaffirm and reassert the basic principles of the party with respect to civil rights, and further affirm that the President, with the support of Congress, consistent with its duties as defined in the Constitution, must protect the rights of all U.S. citizens regardless of race, creed, color, or national origin.

Mr. President, that conference took place on June 5, 1963, and this is June of 1964. So with a sense of propriety I can say for the bone pickers who will be setting it down on the history books that "this is the year that was."

After this statement of principle came the conferences at the White House. Those also occurred in the month of June. I remember how patient the late President of the United States was when he met first with the joint leadership, and then with individual Members, and then with the minority Members in the hope that his message and his bill to be presented to both branches of the Congress could be scheduled for early action.

I recited once before that I and my party had chided the late President of the United States for his dereliction in the matter, and said that there was a promise and a pledge that when a new Congress began in 1961 there would be early action on the civil rights issue.

When that action was not forthcoming, we were unsparing, of course, in our criticism, until at long last that bill was submitted.

Then came the grinding of the legislative mill. That mill grinds slowly but it grinds exceedingly fine. What has happened in "the year that was" is a tribute to the patience and understanding of the country, to the Senate, and generally the people of this Republic. It was marked, of course, by demonstrations and marches, and on occasion by some outbursts of violence. But the mills have ground before, Mr. President, where a moral issue was involved, and it is not too far from fact and reason to assert that they will continue to grind in the history of this blessed and continuing Republic. . . .

I reemphasize the fact that it required no constitutional change to bring this about, because it appeared there was latitude enough in that document, the oldest written constitution on the face of the earth, to embrace within its four corners these advances for human brotherhood.

It leads us—it leads me, certainly—to the conclusion that in the history of mankind there is an inexorable moral force that carries us forward.

No matter what statements may be made on the floor, no matter how tart the editorials in every section of the country, no matter what the resistance of people who do not wish to change, it will not be denied. Mankind ever forward goes. There have been fulminations to impede, but they have never stopped that thrust. As I think of it, it is slow. It is undramatic. Somebody once said that progress is the intelligent, undramatic application of life on what is here.

It is a good definition. When I think of the word dramatic, I think of what Woodrow Wilson said in World War I. I was in uniform on the Western Front. There was a movement in this country to send Theodore Roosevelt there to head a division. That suggestion had great appeal. Letters by the hundred of thousands moved into the White House. Woodrow Wilson settled the issue with a single sentence. He said, "The answer is 'No' because the business in hand is undramatic."

This is not dramatic business. Here we are dealing with a moral force that carries us along.

Argue and fuss and utter all the extreme opinions one will, Mr. President—our people still go forward, and we will not be worthy of our trust if we do not give heed to the great, mobile force that carries humankind along its path. . . .

I remember the day when I sat with General Eisenhower in his office. I saw a picture on the wall. I said, "That looks like Marshall Zhukov to me." He said, "It is. I want to tell you a story about him and when they gave me my decoration"—I forget whether it was the Red Star, or the Order of Lenin. He said, "You know, he is a great general, and he is an intriguing fellow, but he is very cynical. He has little regard for human life on the battlefield. When I told him of one of our forays and I told him we sent a minesweeper into the area so our soldiers could proceed, Zhukov said, 'Oh, you sent in your minesweepers? We do not do that. One life—what is it? One thousand lives—what are they? Ten thousand lives—what are they? Poof.'" That shows a disregard for human life and for all the attributes that go with it.

So today we come to grips finally with a bill that advances the enjoyment of living; but, more than that, it advances the equality of opportunity.

I do not emphasize the word "equality" standing by itself. It means equality of opportunity in the field of education. It means equality of opportunity in the field of employment. It means equality of opportunity in the field of participation in the affairs of government, and the day in the life of a citizen when he can go to the polls, under a representative system, to select the person for whom to vote, who is going to stay in that position for a period of years, whether it is at the local, State, or National level?

That is it.

Equality of opportunity, if we are going to talk about conscience, is the mass conscience of mankind that speaks in every generation, and it will continue to speak long after we are dead and gone.

Every generation, of course, must march up to the unfinished tasks of the generation that has gone before. . . .

They will also be found in the domain of freedom. They will be found in the pursuit of happiness as the Declaration of Independence asserts. They will be found in expanded living for people, for that is one of the goals of mankind. They will be found in the field of equal opportunity. They will be the unfinished work of every generation.

Mr. President, I must add a personal note, because on occasion a number of the "boys" up in the gallery have asked me, "How have you become a crusader in this cause?"

It is a fair question, and it deserves a fair answer.

That question was asked me once before. It was many years ago. I was then in the House of Representatives [and] went to a meeting, and I listened to a Chinese doctor from the front at the time of the Japanese invasion of China come in and plead for money, for bandages, for medicine, in order to carry on. There was one line he used in his plea that seared itself indelibly into my memory.

He said, "They scream, but they live." I carried those words with me for days and weeks, and when finally I was requested to go into the country for a number of speeches in the interest of Chinese relief, I did so.

A friend said to me, "Why do you waste your time on so remote a project? After all they are people with yellow skins, 12,000 miles from home. You are wasting time which you might well devote to your own constituents."

I said, "My friend, as an answer, there occurs to me a line from an English poet, whose name was John Donne. He left what I believe was a precious legacy on the parchments of history. He said, 'Any man's death diminishes me, because I am involved in mankind.'"

I am involved in mankind, and whatever the skin, we are all involved in mankind. Equality of opportunity must prevail if we are to complete the covenant that we have made with the people, and if we are to honor the pledges we made when we held up our hands to take an oath to defend the laws and to carry out the Constitution of the United States.

Eight times I did it in the House of Representatives.

Three times—God willing—my people have permitted me to do it in the Senate of the United States.

There is involved here the citizenship of people under the Constitution who, by the 14th amendment, are made not only citizens of the State where they reside, but also citizens of the United States of America.

That is what we deal with here. We are confronted with the challenge, and we must reckon with it.

Mr. President, in line with the sentiment offered by the poet, "Any man's death diminishes me, because I am involved in mankind," so every denial of freedom, every denial of equal opportunity for a livelihood, for an education, for a right to participate in representative government diminishes me.

There is the moral basis for our case. It has been long and tedious; but the mills will continue to grind, and, whatever we do here tonight as we stand on the threshold of a historic rollcall, those mills will not stop grinding.

So, Mr. President, I commend this bill to the Senate, and in its wisdom I trust that in bountiful measure it will prevail.

I close by expressing once more my gratitude to the distinguished majority leader for the tolerance that he has shown all through this long period of nearly 100 days.

But standing on the pinnacle of this night, looking back, looking around, looking forward, as an anniversary occasion requires, this is "the year that was," and it will be so recorded by the bone pickers who somehow put together all the items that portray man's journey through time that is history. I am prepared for the vote.

The ACTING PRESIDENT pro tempore. The bill having been read the third time, the question is, Shall it pass? The yeas and nays have been ordered, and the clerk will call the roll.

The legislative clerk called the roll.

The result was announced—yeas 73, nays 27 . . .

Source: *Congressional Record*, Vol. 103: Pt. 6, June 17–26, 1964 (Washington, DC, 1964), 14509–11.

4

A CONSERVATIVE OPPOSES
THE CIVIL RIGHTS ACT OF 1964:
SENATOR BARRY GOLDWATER,
CONGRESSIONAL RECORD
(JUNE 1964)

> Senator Barry Goldwater from Arizona was one of the few
> Republicans to vote against the Civil Rights Act of 1964,
> even though he had presidential ambitions. Why does Gold-
> water say he is in favor of black civil rights, but is voting
> against this legislation? What role does he see for government
> in the civil rights issue? Why does he believe that the federal
> government should not be involved in overseeing employ-
> ment policy? Why did some conservatives see Goldwater's
> stance as principled, while others saw it as fatal to his 1964
> campaign?

Mr. GOLDWATER. Mr. President, there have been few, if any, occa-
sions when the searching of my conscience and the reexamination of
my views of our constitutional system have played a greater part in the determination of my vote than they have on this occasion.

I am unalterably opposed to discrimination or segregation on the basis of race, color, or creed, or on any other basis; not only my words, but
more importantly my actions through the years have repeatedly demonstrated the sincerity of my feeling in this regard.

This is fundamentally a matter of the heart. The problems of discrimination can never be cured by laws alone; but I would be the first to agree
that laws can help—laws carefully considered and weighed in an atmosphere
of dispassion, in the absence of political demagoguery, and in the light of
fundamental constitutional principles.

For example, throughout my 12 years as a member of the Senate Labor and Public Welfare Committee, I have repeatedly offered amendments
to bills pertaining to labor that would end discrimination in unions, and

repeatedly those amendments have been turned down by the very members of both parties who now so vociferously support the present approach to the solution of our problem. Talk is one thing, action is another, and until the Members of this body and the people of this country realize this, there will be no real solution to the problem we face.

To be sure, a calm environment for the consideration of any law dealing with human relationships is not easily attained—emotions run high, political pressures become great, and objectivity is at a premium. Nevertheless, deliberation and calmness are indispensable to success.

It was in this context that I maintained high hopes for this current legislation—high hopes that, notwithstanding the glaring defects of the measure as it reached us from the other body and the sledge-hammer political tactics which produced it, this legislation, through the actions of what was once considered to be the greatest deliberative body on earth, would emerge in a form both effective for its lofty purposes and acceptable to all freedom-loving people.

It is with great sadness that I realize the nonfulfillment of these high hopes. My hopes were shattered when it became apparent that emotion and political pressures—not persuasion, not commonsense, not deliberation—had become the rule of the day and of the processes of this great body.

One has only to review the defeat of commonsense amendments to this bill—amendments that would in no way harm it but would, in fact, improve it—to realize that political pressure, not persuasion or commonsense, has come to rule the consideration of this measure.

I realize fully that the Federal Government has a responsibility in the field of civil rights. I supported the civil rights bills which were enacted in 1957 and 1960, and my public utterances during the debates on those measures and since reveal clearly the areas in which responsibility lies and Federal legislation on this subject can be effective and appropriate. Many areas are encompassed in this bill and to that extent, I favor it.

I wish to make myself perfectly clear. The two portions of this bill to which I have constantly and consistently voiced objections and which are of such over-riding significance that they are determinative of my vote on the entire measure, are those which would embark the Federal Government on a regulatory course of action with regard to private enterprise in the area of so-called public accommodations and in the area of employment—to be more specific, titles II and VII of the bill. I find no constitutional basis for the exercise of Federal regulatory authority in either of these areas; and I believe the attempted usurpation of such power to be a grave threat to the very essence of our basic system of government; namely, that of a constitutional republic in which 50 sovereign States have reserved to themselves and to the people those powers not specifically granted to the Central or Federal Government.

If it is the wish of the American people that the Federal Government should be granted the power to regulate in these two areas and in the manner contemplated by this bill, then I say that the Constitution should be so amended by the people as to authorize such action in accordance with the procedures for amending the Constitution which that great document itself prescribes. I say further that for this great legislative body to ignore the Constitution and the fundamental concepts of our governmental system is to act in a manner which could ultimately destroy the freedom of all American citizens, including the freedoms of the very persons whose feelings and whose liberties are the major subject of this legislation.

My basic objection to this measure is, therefore, constitutional. But, in addition, I would like to point out to my colleagues in the Senate and to the people of America, regardless of their race, color, or creed, the implications involved in the enforcement of regulatory legislation of this sort. To give genuine effect to the prohibitions of this bill will require the creation of a Federal police force of mammoth proportions. It also bids fair to result in the development of an "informer" psychology in great areas of our national life—neighbors spying on neighbors, workers spying on workers, business spying on businessmen—where those who would harass their fellow citizens for selfish and narrow purposes will have ample inducement to do so. These, the Federal police force and an "informer" psychology, are the hallmarks of the police state and landmarks in the destruction of a free society.

I repeat again: I am unalterably opposed to discrimination of any sort and I believe that though the problem is fundamentally one of the heart, some law can help—but not law that embodies features like these, provisions which fly in the face of the Constitution and which require for their effective execution the creation of a police state. And so, because I am unalterably opposed to any threats to our great system of government and the loss of our God-given liberties, I shall vote "no" on this bill.

This vote will be reluctantly cast, because I had hoped to be able to vote "yea" on this measure as I have on the civil rights bills which have preceded it; but I cannot in good conscience to the oath that I took when assuming office, cast my vote in the affirmative. With the exception of titles II and VII, I could whole heartedly support this bill; but with their inclusion, not measurably improved by the compromise version we have been working on, my vote must be "no."

If my vote is misconstrued, let it be, and let me suffer its consequences. Just let me be judged in this by the real concern I have voiced here and not by words that others may speak or by what others may say about what I think.

My concern extends beyond this single legislative moment. My concern extends beyond any single group in our society. My concern is for the entire Nation, for the freedom of all who live in it and for all who will be born into it.

It is the general welfare that must be considered now, not just the special appeals for special welfare. This is the time to attend to the liberties of all.

This is my concern. And this is where I stand.

Source: *Congressional Record*, Vol. 103: Pt. 6, June 17–26, 1964 (Washington, DC, 1964), 13421.

5

THE COLD WAR AND THE ARMS RACE: EXCERPT FROM MEMORANDUM TO DONALD RUMSFELD FROM PAUL H. NITZE (DECEMBER 19, 1974)

By the mid-1970s, many defense experts warned that the Soviet Union had not lived up to the SALT I arms control agreements signed during the Nixon administration. For this reason, conservative Republicans opposed signing a SALT II agreement proposed by the Ford administration. Conservatives found support in arguments made by Paul Nitze, a Democrat who had helped negotiate SALT I, who in this 1974 memorandum outlined complaints about the Soviet Union. How does Nitze describe Soviet foreign policy? Why does he argue that the Soviet Union has broken SALT I? Why does he not believe that the world has become more unstable since SALT I? How does nuclear deterrence help prevent nuclear war?

I

After the Summit meeting in Moscow last June, Dr. Kissinger called for a national debate on the issue of strategic arms and arms control. No such debate has taken place. It has been overtaken by the more immediate issues of inflation, the liquidity of the international banking system, and the extent to which Arab oil profits can be reduced, offset or recycled. But these more immediate issues are, in turn, dependent on what happens in the Middle East with its triple problem of the unresolved Arab-Israeli conflict, the oil weapon, and Soviet ambitions to control the world's economic jugular, the Eastern Mediterranean, the Red Sea and the Persian Gulf. The ability of the United States favorably to influence the resolution of these issues depends upon the strength of its ties with other countries with similar interests and its economic and military potential. Thus, we are once more brought face to face with the interdependence of our economic and our national security policies.

The October 1973 Middle East crisis marked a watershed. For a decade, important elements of the basic strength of the American position at home and abroad had been in a negative trend. But these adverse trends were obscured by what appeared to be offsetting factors. Growing budgetary deficits, adverse balance of payments, and increases in the price index at home were offset by the economic miracles of Western Europe and Japan. It was hoped that Europe and Japan would become independent centers of power, strong enough to relieve us of many responsibilities which in the past the United States had had to shoulder more or less alone. The growth in the relative military power and political influence of the Soviet Union seemed to be offset by the development of detente and a special relationship between the U.S. and the USSR, by the Sino-Soviet conflict and by the breakthrough in improved Chinese Communist-American relations. In the Middle East it was assumed that the military strength of Israel was such as to deter an Egyptian-Syrian attack, that divisions of interest among the OPEC countries were such as to make it unlikely that they could agree on an aggressive and unified plan of action, and that the Soviet Union would not risk detente by an attempt to change the balance of power in the Middle East in a manner adverse to Western interests.

In a period of just two weeks in October of last year, these hopeful assumptions were found to be unwarranted. Egypt and Syria launched their surprise attack. The Soviet Union, with advance knowledge of the attack, did not advise us of its imminence. The OPEC countries stood together, embargoed oil shipments to the United States and quadrupled the price of oil. The Soviet Union threatened to introduce its own military forces into the area when the Israelis recovered the military initiative. Our European allies and Japan, with greater economic interests in the Middle East than our own, were almost totally without influence in the situation. The combination of U.S. military capabilities, conventional and strategic, Arab concern about ever greater Soviet presence in the area, and hard diplomatic negotiations by Dr. [Henry] Kissinger [Secretary of State under Ford] produced a partial Israeli withdrawal and a temporary ceasefire. But the risk of a renewal of the crisis is still very much with us.

To the very real problems revealed by the Middle East crisis, there are no easy solutions. The first element of wisdom would seem to be a realization of the seriousness of the situation we face. To my mind, it is more serious than any since the announcement of the Stalin-Hitler Pact of 1939.

Realization that the situation is serious is rapidly taking place. The more difficult problem is that of what to do about it. Obviously SALT is only one piece of the puzzle; it is, however, an important piece.

II

Before dealing with SALT in the context of today's issues, I believe it would be helpful to recall a few of the basic historical points. It was in the late fifties, even before Sputnik, that many of us became concerned with the stability of the nuclear relationship between the Soviet Union and ourselves. Our nuclear strategic capability, and that of the Soviet Union, were then largely concentrated in our heavy bomber forces; those forces were concentrated on a small number of fields, early warning systems had substantial gaps and could be evaded; a well executed surprise attack could have the prospect of emasculating the strategic forces of the other side. Sputnik and the possibility that the Soviets might attain a threatening ICBM force, before we could deploy an adequate counter-deterrent, further exacerbated the problem. The result was an enormous U.S. R&D and deployment effort to avoid those risks. U.S. obligational authority for Program I, the strategic program, during the six years from 1956 to 1962 averaged some 18 billions a year, expressed in constant 1974 dollars. The result was that from 1962 to the present day the strategic relationship between the U.S. and the Soviet Union has been such that neither side could have hoped to gain from a surprise attack or from preempting in a time of crisis.

In the mid-sixties, however, the United States decided to go down one line in its strategic program while the Soviet side went down a quite different line. I was one of those who participated with Bob McNamara in the decisions of those years. Under a stable nuclear umbrella, what counted as the cutting edge of policy were, in addition to a strong political and economic posture, conventional forces adequate to deter other forms of pressure against our allies. Economic and budgetary considerations made it wise to cut the percentage of our GNP and defense budgets going to Program I. By and large, it is cheaper, at least in the short run, to make technological improvements than to increase force size. We decided to halt the Minuteman program at 1,000, to halt the Polaris/Poseidon program at 41 boats and to substantially reduce the size of heavy bomber and air defense force levels. Instead emphasis was put on improved reliability, command and control, accuracy, and penetration capability, including pen aids and MIRVs. In 1967 the decision was made to go forward with the Sentinel/Safeguard technology despite McNamara's doubts as to its cost effectiveness. As a result of these decisions it became possible to reduce Program I's real annual expenditures by almost two-thirds; it 1974 they were approximately seven billion dollars.

The Soviet Union made quite different decisions. They decided first of all to equal and then to exceed us in the number of strategic missile launchers and greatly to exceed us in the average throw-weight of the missiles these launchers could launch. This left them with the option subsequently technologically to improve the capabilities of this large force size. Their program has required an increase, rather than permitting a reduction, in their annual expenditures on what we would call Program I.

Many people today emphasize the potentially destabilizing nature of technological progress. To me, the lesson of the last twenty years is quite different. Technology is inherently neutral; whether it is good or bad depends on the uses it is put to and whose ox is being gored. Without an enormous technological effort it would not have been possible for the U.S. to restore crisis stability by its efforts of the late fifties and sixties. Whether we will need to make, and be able to make, a comparable effort in the late seventies and eighties is at the heart of the SALT TWO problem.

III

This brings me to what I consider to be the central issue of the SALT TWO negotiations. After the SALT ONE agreements were signed in Moscow in May 1972, the U.S. Delegation had one interpretation of the meaning of the Interim Agreement, the Soviet side seems to have come away with quite a different interpretation.

The U.S. Delegation testified before the Congress in support of the ratification of the SALT ONE agreements that the Interim Agreement was, in essence, a short term freeze on new strategic missile launcher starts beyond the number then assumed to be operational and under construction. Both sides had agreed promptly to negotiate a more complete agreement to replace the Interim Agreement. The Interim Agreement specifically provided that its provisions were not to prejudice the scope or terms of such a replacement agreement. The ABM Treaty which embodied the principles of equality, stability, and in the case of the United States, of actual destruction of a facility under construction, together with the short term freeze on new offensive missile launcher starts, should provide a favorable climate for negotiating such a long term treaty limiting offensive arms to serve as a complement to the ABM Treaty. It was hoped that such a replacement agreement could be negotiated in far less than the five year term of the Interim Agreement. At the Washington Summit of 1973, the year 1974 was agreed as the target date for the completion of the negotiation of such a replacement agreement.

When the SALT TWO negotiations began at Geneva it became evident that the Soviet side had come away from the Moscow 1972 Summit with quite a different view of the meaning of the Interim Agreement. It was their interpretation that the Interim Agreement was not just a temporary freeze. It was their view that the unequal missile launcher numbers and the unequal throw-weight permitted by other provisions of the Interim Agreement had been agreed at the highest level to compensate the Soviets for other inequalities in the positions of the two sides. The phrase they used was "geographic and other considerations." Their conclusion was that the Interim Agreement missile limitations, having been settled at [the] highest level, should be carried over unchanged into the replacement agreement. The remaining task was to work out limitations on all other strategic offensive arms including bombers and their armaments, new weapon systems, including our B-1 and Trident, and so-called forward based systems. It was their contention that their new family of weapon systems were merely replacements involving technical modernization and therefore not subject to limitation.

Up until April of this year the U.S. Delegation held to its position that the terms of the Interim Agreement were not to prejudice the terms of the replacement agreement, and that the replacement agreement should be based on the principles of equality—or essential equivalence—enhanced stability, and hopefully reductions. And the Soviet side held to its quite different position. The negotiations at the Delegation level thus appeared to be deadlocked.

At this point, Dr. Kissinger attempted to achieve a conceptual breakthrough to undeadlock the negotiations. The most time sensitive matter was that of the Soviet deployment of MIRVs. Kissinger first tried to get them to agree to limit the deployment of MIRVs to an equal missile throw-weight on both sides in return for a two or three year extension of the Interim Agreement. This they refused to accept. He then modified the proposal so that the U.S. would be permitted a larger number of MIRVed missiles but the Soviet side a larger aggregate throw-weight of MIRVed missiles with the same two or three year extension of the Interim Agreement. This the Soviet side also refused to accept. At the Summit President Nixon made a further attempt with no greater success. Finally, at the last minute the two sides agreed to change the target of the negotiations. Instead of trying to achieve either a long term comprehensive agreement, or a short term extension of the Interim Agreement with a MIRV add-on to give more time for the negotiation of a long term agreement, the two sides would attempt to negotiate a new ten year agreement.

The question is where this leaves the negotiating situation. It would seem to me that this framework tends to divert the negotiations from a long term solution based on the principles we have been insisting upon, to a negotiation about the add-ons each side will be permitted to make over the next ten years in relationship to some assumed base line. If that base line is assumed to be the current programs of the two sides, we would basically be trading a stretchout of our B-1 and Trident programs for some limit on the rate at which the Soviet side deploys their broad family of weapon systems now under test, together with a ban on certain new systems now in R&D, not now programmed for deployment. I have a hard time seeing how it would be possible to negotiate, in this framework, limitations which would not end up in strategic superiority for the Soviets, and a decrease in crisis stability.

IV

In talk to various audiences in the last few months, I have often been asked whether I was optimistic or pessimistic about the prospects for a new SALT agreement. In reply I have said there are really two questions to be answered. The first is "what are the prospects for a SALT agreement?" The second is "how useful an agreement can we expect, if one is possible?"

As to the first question there are some grounds for optimism. I would expect the Soviet leaders to be more anxious to make progress, and to be more flexible in their approach, than they have been in the last two years, and in particular, more so than during the Nixon/Brezhnev summit early this summer. At that time, they were fully aware of the President's crumbling domestic support and the possibility that he might be impeached. There were no pressing reasons why they should at that time fall off their previous hard line and show flexibility on the important issues.

Today things are different. Mr. Ford can be expected to be President until at least January 20th, 1977. The Interim Agreement expires in 1977. If I were in the Soviet shoes I would try to get some kind of agreement to replace or extend the Interim Agreement before the election year of 1976. Secondly, Soviet doctrine calls on them to pay careful attention to the correlation of forces—the trend of political, social, economic and military factors on a global scale. As they look at what is happening to the economic and political foundations of Western Europe, Japan, the non-oil producing parts of the third world—and even in the United States—they cannot but judge that new opportunities are opening up for them. Furthermore, I believe they see their relative military position improving as they deploy the new family of weapons which they have been developing and testing during recent years.

Under those circumstances, if I were they, I would not wish to rock the boat too much. I would try to maintain "detente" and the special relationship with the United States. Some form of extension or replacement of the Interim Agreement would fit in with such a strategy.

On the second part of the question—how useful an agreement might we expect if one is possible—I believe the answer must be much less hopeful.

The Soviets in the past have taken an extremely one-sided position with multiple built in possible fallbacks. Even if they show considerable new flexibility, I do not believe they could justify to themselves giving up the superior position they see virtually within their grasp. They believe we too must recognize that the correlation of forces is moving against us. They believe that positions that may now look unequal to us we will later accept as being realistically the best we can hope to obtain. With a three hundred billion budget ceiling and continuing inflationary and balance of payments problems, they must see little prospect of our adding to our strategic programs sufficient additional real resources to change the present relative trends. I therefore do not see how, under present circumstances, we can expect to achieve an agreement which will significantly unstress our growing defense problems, particularly an anticipated shift from parity to Soviet superiority and from assured, to significantly less assured, crisis stability.

V

It is my impression that what I have said up to this point is not really that controversial among those in the Executive Branch who have been dealing with SALT issues; although each participant would undoubtedly summarize the current negotiating situation and the crucial developments which have led up to it somewhat differently. The difficult and truly controversial question is, "what should we now do?"

In order to get at the central issues involved in that question, it may be useful to summarize one hypothetical line of argument and see where that leads us. That line of argument asks three questions about the principles of essential equivalence and of crisis stability—the principles which have, in the past, been central to the U.S. SALT position. These questions are; first, are essential equivalence and crisis stability measurable; second, if measurable, are they meaningful; and, third, if measurable and meaningful, is there anything we can do to maintain them? I believe it to be important to discuss each of these questions in turn.

In comparing two disparate strategic forces, one is always faced with the problem of finding meaningful common denominators; otherwise one finds oneself equating doubtful apples with very good oranges. An SS-11 is not the same thing as a Minuteman III or an SS-18. An SLBM is not the same as an ICBM. A heavy bomber has quite different characteristics from an offensive missile. Much work has gone into finding such common denominators. The most useful approach that the U.S. SALT community has come up with to date is the throw-weight of missile boosters as a common denominator for the potential effectiveness of missiles and the missile throw-weight equivalent of a heavy bomber for heavy bombers. But it can be argued that it is wrong to equate ICBM throw-weight with SLBM throw-weight, and that any attempt to find a rational basis for settling on a missile throw-weight equivalent for a heavy bomber involves a large uncertainty factor. Even more difficult is the question of defining what bombers are to be included in the definition of a heavy bomber. Is the Backfire bomber, which I am told is a more competent plane than the Bison, to be included or not included? At the present time, the Soviets do not have an adequate tanker capability to refuel the Backfire. But it is not proposed to limit tankers and I am told the Soviets have an appropriate plane under conversion for such a tanker role. I think the answer must be that no mathematically precise and verifiable criteria for measuring essential equivalence or for measuring crisis stability are possible.

But I believe it is possible to have an overall gross view as to whether strategically significant changes in parity and crisis stability have taken place. To my mind there is little doubt that the United States enjoyed nuclear superiority until the early seventies and that from that time to the present rough parity or essential equivalence has been maintained. I also believe there is little doubt that in the late fifties the nuclear relationship had a dangerous and growing risk of being or becoming unstable. During the period from 1962 to the present, that relationship has appeared to me to be inherently stable in the sense of crisis stability, if not in the sense of dynamic stability. Furthermore, it seems to me these judgments were widely shared not only in the United States, but generally in the world.

In summary, I would answer the first question by saying that the criteria of parity or essential equivalence and of crisis stability, while not precisely measurable in detail, are susceptible to judgment in gross.

The second question was, are the criteria of essential equivalence and crisis stability, even if judgment can be made about them, meaningful? I would suggest that this question be examined at three levels of analysis. The first is at the military level, the second at the level of the central decision makers, the President and his closest advisors on our side and the Politburo and its advisors on the Soviet side, the third at the level of the general climate of significant political opinion in the world.

The popular viewpoint is that the present inventories of nuclear weapons are so large that, no matter what we or the Soviets do, the outcome of a nuclear war would be essentially indistinguishable between the two sides. This rests, in essence, on the usual overkill argument which deals with weapons in inventory, not with alert, reliable, survivable, penetrating weapons subject to proper command and control. Furthermore, it deals with today's situation rather than with the potentially critical period five, ten, fifteen years from now.

It is my view that it is possible to think of highly plausible scenarios, assuming a position of Soviet strategic superiority and a deterioration of crisis stability, in which, should the balloon go up, the outcome would be highly one-sided.

Would a situation of significant inequality and erosion of crisis stability affect the way in which the central decision makers on both sides make their decisions? During the Berlin crisis of 1961 and the Cuban missile crisis of 1962, the possibility that nuclear war might result was directly faced by the central decision makers on both sides. In the Cuban missile case we had decisive local conventional military superiority. In the Berlin case the situation was reversed. I know that President Kennedy was determined never again to face anything analogous to the Berlin crisis because it was clear that we would never again enjoy the degree of strategic superiority which we then enjoyed. On the Soviet side, Khrushchev decided not to test Kennedy's determination in regard to Berlin; in Cuba he decided to withdraw when his bluff was called. I doubt whether he would have made those decisions, particularly the Berlin decision, if the relationship of strategic superiority had been reversed.

This brings me to the level of significant public opinion in the world. In large measure, public opinion in the non-Communist world follows our own evaluation. If we firmly believe we have essential equivalence and have maintained crisis stability, most people are prepared to accept that judgment.

But in our open society it is not possible long to kid ourselves, and thereby be persuasive to others, on a position widely differing from observable facts. Should the Soviet Union be perceived to enjoy significant superiority and should there be serious doubt as to the quality of crisis stability, it is probable that third countries would move toward increased accommodation to Soviet views. In the case of certain countries, such a situation could increase incentives to have nuclear capabilities of their own, and thus lead to further nuclear proliferation.

The most difficult of the three questions I posed is the third; if essential equivalence and crisis stability are roughly measurable and meaningful, is there anything we can do about it? If not, why shouldn't we accept the best SALT deal which is negotiable and hope that detente will become irreversible.

This brings to mind an episode in the days when Dean Acheson was Secretary of State and I was Director of the State Department Policy Planning Staff. Acheson called me into his office and said he wished to get one point clear. He wanted the Policy Planning Staff to work out its analyses and recommendations as to what the U. S. should do in the national security and foreign policy fields without considering the acceptability of those recommendations to Congressional or public opinion. He and President Truman would very much have to take those considerations into mind and make the compromises they thought necessary while trying to build the foundations for a future more receptive climate. He didn't want those compromises made twice, once by us and secondly by them.

Today the main basis for assuming that there is nothing much that can be done about a significant loss of parity and crisis stability is the judgment that Congressional and public opinion will not support the measures necessary to halt present trends. But is the Executive Branch taking the steps which might lay a foundation for a more favorable climate next year and the year after? There is, moreover, a prior question—is there a consensus within the Executive Branch as to what it would be desirable to do first to maintain crisis stability and then to assure sufficiency, even if not parity, in the absence of a SALT agreement which would serve to unstress our defense problem? And may this not go back, in turn, to lack of agreement on the current prospects for such a SALT agreement and the long term value of detente?

I might conclude by outlining, in reverse order, my views on each of these points.

As I see it, "detente" in the sense of warm formal relations with the Soviet Union, a special relationship to mitigate those crisis situations where their exacerbation would serve neither of our interests, and a wide range of negotiations between the two sides, is desirable and should be continued. But detente does not imply any change in Soviet long term aims or expectations, or any reliable continuing restraint on Soviet actions. Their interest in maintaining the atmosphere of detente can, however, impose a certain tactical restraint upon what they say and do from time to time. I further believe that they consider progress in detente to be a reflection of what they judge to have been an improvement in the correlation of forces in their favor. I therefore have difficulty in seeing them settle for a SALT TWO agreement which would place a real restraint on the further evolution in their favor of the strategic military component of the correlation of forces.

Such an assessment of detente supports the view which I have earlier stated that [it] is unlikely that we can negotiate a SALT TWO agreement which will significantly unstress our defense problem.

I believe that a zero base review of our strategic programs would establish that there is much that we could do to preserve the quality of deterrence and at not too great an increase in cost above the current level of some seven billions in 1974 dollars in Program I. The cost would certainly be far less than that which we sustained in the late fifties and early sixties to meet a lesser problem. We would have to take care, however, that a SALT TWO agreement did not ban those technological developments necessary to maintain crisis stability in the face of anticipated Soviet deployments.

I further believe that if, after the necessary analyses, a consensus were to emerge within the Executive Branch on pertinent judgments on these points, then over time, the necessary public and Congressional support could be mobilized to authorize the required programs.

In summary, it is my suggestion that the basic analysis be done along the lines of the [Dean] Acheson formula. Only then will it be possible to judge how important a given course of action is likely to be to the nation's future. If it is in truth important, I am confident the President and his close advisors can judge how best to present the considerations to the Congress and the public.

Source: Excerpt, Paul H. Nitze to Donald Rumsfeld, Assistant to President Gerald Ford, December 19, 1974, White House Central Files, Box 33, Gerald R. Ford Library.

6

CONSERVATIVE VALUES: RONALD REAGAN, "REMARKS AT THE ANNUAL CONVENTION OF THE NATIONAL ASSOCIATION OF THE EVANGELICALS" (MARCH 8, 1983)

In this speech to evangelical Christians in 1983, President Ronald Reagan articulated the conservative view that cultural values are essential to maintaining American democracy. Why does Reagan argue that a transcendent faith is essential to American democracy? What examples does he use to cite moral decay in America? Is religion essential to American democracy? Are the examples he uses to suggest moral decay accurate? How does he link cultural issues to his defense policy?

Reverend clergy all, Senator Hawkins, distinguished members of the Florida congressional delegation, and all of you:

I can't tell you how you have warmed my heart with your welcome. I'm delighted to be here today.

Those of you in the National Association of Evangelicals are known for your spiritual and humanitarian work. And I would be especially remiss if I didn't discharge right now one personal debt of gratitude. Thank you for your prayers. Nancy and I have felt their presence many times in many ways. And believe me, for us they've made all the difference.

The other day in the East Room of the White House at a meeting there, someone asked me whether I was aware of all the people out there who were praying for the President. And I had to say, "Yes, I am. I've felt it. I believe in intercessionary prayer." But I couldn't help but say to that questioner after he'd asked the question that—or at least say to them that if sometimes when he was praying he got a busy signal, it was just me in there ahead of him. [Laughter] I think I understand how Abraham Lincoln felt when he said, "I have been driven many times to my knees by the overwhelming conviction that I had nowhere else to go."

From the joy and the good feeling of this conference, I go to a political reception. [Laughter] Now, I don't know why, but that bit of scheduling reminds me of a story—[laughter]—which I'll share with you.

An evangelical minister and a politician arrived at Heaven's gate one day together. And St. Peter, after doing all the necessary formalities, took them in hand to show them where their quarters would be. And he took them to a small, single room with a bed, a chair, and a table and said this was for the clergyman. And the politician was a little worried about what might be in store for him. And he couldn't believe it then when St. Peter stopped in front of a beautiful mansion with lovely grounds, many servants, and told him that these would be his quarters.

And he couldn't help but ask, he said, "But wait, how—there's something wrong—how do I get this mansion while that good and holy man only gets a single room?" And St. Peter said, "You have to understand how things are up here. We've got thousands and thousands of clergy. You're the first politician who ever made it." [Laughter]

But I don't want to contribute to a stereotype. [Laughter] So, I tell you there are a great many God-fearing, dedicated, noble men and women in public life, present company included. And, yes, we need your help to keep us ever mindful of the ideas and the principles that brought us into the public arena in the first place. The basis of those ideals and principles is a commitment to freedom and personal liberty that, itself, is grounded in the much deeper realization that freedom prospers only where the blessings of God are avidly sought and humbly accepted.

The American experiment in democracy rests on this insight. Its discovery was the great triumph of our Founding Fathers, voiced by William Penn when he said: "If we will not be governed by God, we must be governed by tyrants." Explaining the inalienable rights of men, Jefferson said, "The God who gave us life, gave us liberty at the same time." And it was George Washington who said that "of all the dispositions and habits which lead to political prosperity, religion and morality are indispensable supports."

And finally, that shrewdest of all observers of American democracy, Alexis de Tocqueville, put it eloquently after he had gone on a search for the secret of America's greatness and genius—and he said: "Not until I went into the churches of America and heard her pulpits aflame with righteousness did I understand the greatness and the genius of America. . . . America is good. And if America ever ceases to be good, America will cease to be great."

Well, I'm pleased to be here today with you who are keeping America great by keeping her good. Only through your work and prayers and those of millions of others can we hope to survive this perilous century and keep alive this experiment in liberty, this last, best hope of man.

I want you to know that this administration is motivated by a political philosophy that sees the greatness of America in you, her people, and in your families, churches, neighborhoods, communities—the institutions that foster and nourish values like concern for others and respect for the rule of law under God.

Now, I don't have to tell you that this puts us in opposition to, or at least out of step with, a prevailing attitude of many who have turned to a modern-day secularism, discarding the tried and time-tested values upon which our very civilization is based. No matter how well intentioned, their value system is radically different from that of most Americans. And while they proclaim that they're freeing us from superstitions of the past, they've taken upon themselves the job of superintending us by government rule and regulation. Sometimes their voices are louder than ours, but they are not yet a majority.

An example of that vocal superiority is evident in a controversy now going on in Washington. And since I'm involved, I've been waiting to hear from the parents of young America. How far are they willing to go in giving to government their prerogatives as parents?

Let me state the case as briefly and simply as I can. An organization of citizens, sincerely motivated and deeply concerned about the increase in illegitimate births and abortions involving girls well below the age of consent, sometime ago established a nationwide network of clinics to offer help to these girls and, hopefully, alleviate this situation. Now, again, let me say, I do not fault their intent. However, in their well-intentioned effort, these clinics have decided to provide advice and birth control drugs and devices to underage girls without the knowledge of their parents.

For some years now, the Federal Government has helped with funds to subsidize these clinics. In providing for this, the Congress decreed that every effort would be made to maximize parental participation. Nevertheless, the drugs and devices are prescribed without getting parental consent or giving notification after they've done so. Girls termed "sexually active"—and that has replaced the word "promiscuous"—are given this help in order to prevent illegitimate birth or abortion.

Well, we have ordered clinics receiving Federal funds to notify the parents such help has been given. One of the Nation's leading newspapers has created the term "squeal rule" in editorializing against us for doing this, and we're being criticized for violating the privacy of young people. A judge has recently granted an injunction against an enforcement of our rule. I've watched TV panel shows discuss this issue, seen columnists pontificating on our error, but no one seems to mention morality as playing a part in the subject of sex.

Is all of Judeo-Christian tradition wrong? Are we to believe that something so sacred can be looked upon as a purely physical thing with no potential for emotional and psychological harm? And isn't it the parents' right to give counsel and advice to keep their children from making mistakes that may affect their entire lives?

Many of us in government would like to know what parents think about this intrusion in their family by government. We're going to fight in the courts. The right of parents and the rights of family take precedence over those of Washington-based bureaucrats and social engineers.

But the fight against parental notification is really only one example of many attempts to water down traditional values and even abrogate the original terms of American democracy. Freedom prospers when religion is vibrant and the rule of law under God is acknowledged. When our Founding Fathers passed the first amendment they sought to protect churches from government interference. They never intended to construct a wall of hostility between government and the concept of religious belief itself.

The evidence of this permeates our history and our government. The Declaration of Independence mentions the Supreme Being no less than four times. "In God We Trust" is engraved on our coinage. The Supreme Court opens its proceedings with a religious invocation. And the Members of Congress open their sessions with a prayer. I just happen to believe the schoolchildren of the United States are entitled to the same privileges as Supreme Court Justices and Congressmen.

Last year, I sent the Congress a constitutional amendment to restore prayer to public schools. Already this session, there's growing bipartisan support for the amendment, and I am calling on the Congress to act speedily to pass it and to let our children pray.

Perhaps some of you read recently about the Lubbock school case, where a judge actually ruled that it was unconstitutional for a school district to give equal treatment to religious and nonreligious student groups, even when the group meetings were being held during the students' own time. The first amendment never intended to require government to discriminate against religious speech.

Senators Denton and Hatfield have proposed legislation in the Congress on the whole question of prohibiting discrimination against religious forms of student speech. Such legislation could go far to restore freedom of religious speech for public school students. And I hope the Congress considers these bills quickly. And with your help, I think it's possible we could also get the constitutional amendment through the Congress this year.

More than a decade ago, a Supreme Court decision literally wiped off the books of 50 States statutes protecting the rights of unborn children. Abortion on demand now takes the lives of up to 1½ million unborn children a year. Human life legislation ending this tragedy will some day pass the Congress, and you and I must never rest until it does. Unless and until it can be proven that the unborn child is not a living entity, then its right to life, liberty, and the pursuit of happiness must be protected.

You may remember that when abortion on demand began, many, and, indeed, I'm sure many of you, warned that the practice would lead to a decline in respect for human life, that the philosophical premises used to justify abortion on demand would ultimately be used to justify other attacks on the sacredness of human life—infanticide or mercy killing. Tragically enough, those warnings proved all too true. Only last year a court permitted the death by starvation of a handicapped infant.

I have directed the Health and Human Services Department to make clear to every health care facility in the United States that the Rehabilitation Act of 1973 protects all handicapped persons against discrimination based on handicaps, including infants. And we have taken the further step of requiring that each and every recipient of Federal funds who provides health care services to infants must post and keep posted in a conspicuous place a notice stating that "discriminatory failure to feed and care for handicapped infants in this facility is prohibited by Federal law." It also lists a 24-hour, toll-free number so that nurses and others may report violations in time to save the infant's life.

In addition, recent legislation introduced in the Congress by Representative Henry Hyde of Illinois not only increases restrictions on publicly financed abortions, it also addresses this whole problem of infanticide. I urge the Congress to begin hearings and to adopt legislation that will protect the right of life to all children, including the disabled or handicapped.

Now, I'm sure that you must get discouraged at times, but you've done better than you know, perhaps. There's a great spiritual awakening in America, a renewal of the traditional values that have been the bedrock of America's goodness and greatness.

One recent survey by a Washington-based research council concluded that Americans were far more religious than the people of other nations; 95 percent of those surveyed expressed a belief in God and a huge majority believed the Ten Commandments had real meaning in their lives. And another study has found that an overwhelming majority of Americans disapprove of adultery, teenage sex, pornography, abortion, and hard drugs. And this same study showed a deep reverence for the importance of family ties and religious belief.

I think the items that we've discussed here today must be a key part of the Nation's political agenda. For the first time the Congress is openly and seriously debating and dealing with the prayer and abortion issues—and that's enormous progress right there. I repeat: America is in the midst of a spiritual awakening and a moral renewal. And with your Biblical keynote, I say today, "Yes, let justice roll on like a river, righteousness like a never-failing stream."

Now, obviously, much of this new political and social consensus I've talked about is based on a positive view of American history, one that takes pride in our country's accomplishments and record. But we must never forget that no government schemes are going to perfect man. We know that living in this world means dealing with what philosophers would call the phenomenology of evil or, as theologians would put it, the doctrine of sin.

There is sin and evil in the world, and we're enjoined by Scripture and the Lord Jesus to oppose it with all our might. Our nation, too, has a legacy of evil with which it must deal. The glory of this land has been its capacity for transcending the moral evils of our past. For example, the long struggle of minority citizens for equal rights, once a source of disunity and civil war, is now a point of pride for all Americans. We must never go back. There is no room for racism, anti-Semitism, or other forms of ethnic and racial hatred in this country.

I know that you've been horrified, as have I, by the resurgence of some hate groups preaching bigotry and prejudice. Use the mighty voice of your pulpits and the powerful standing of your churches to denounce and isolate these hate groups in our midst. The commandment given us is clear and simple: "Thou shalt love thy neighbor as thyself."

But whatever sad episodes exist in our past, any objective observer must hold a positive view of American history, a history that has been the story of hopes fulfilled and dreams made into reality. Especially in this century, America has kept alight the torch of freedom, but not just for ourselves but for millions of others around the world.

And this brings me to my final point today. During my first press conference as President, in answer to a direct question, I pointed out that, as good Marxist-Leninists, the Soviet leaders have openly and publicly declared that the only morality they recognize is that which will further their cause, which is world revolution. I think I should point out I was only quoting Lenin, their guiding spirit, who said in 1920 that they repudiate all morality that proceeds from supernatural ideas—that's their name for religion—or ideas that are outside class conceptions. Morality is entirely subordinate to the interests of class war. And everything is moral that is necessary for the annihilation of the old, exploiting social order and for uniting the proletariat.

Well, I think the refusal of many influential people to accept this elementary fact of Soviet doctrine illustrates an historical reluctance to see totalitarian powers for what they are. We saw this phenomenon in the 1930s. We see it too often today.

This doesn't mean we should isolate ourselves and refuse to seek an understanding with them. I intend to do everything I can to persuade them of our peaceful intent, to remind them that it was the West that refused to use its nuclear monopoly in the forties and fifties for territorial gain and which now proposes a 50-percent cut in strategic ballistic missiles and the elimination of an entire class of land-based, intermediate-range nuclear missiles.

At the same time, however, they must be made to understand we will never compromise our principles and standards. We will never give away our freedom. We will never abandon our belief in God. And we will never stop searching for a genuine peace. But we can assure none of these things America stands for through the so-called nuclear freeze solutions proposed by some.

The truth is that a freeze now would be a very dangerous fraud, for that is merely the illusion of peace. The reality is that we must find peace through strength.

I would agree to a freeze if only we could freeze the Soviets' global desires. A freeze at current levels of weapons would remove any incentive for the Soviets to negotiate seriously in Geneva and virtually end our chances to achieve the major arms reductions which we have proposed. Instead, they would achieve their objectives through the freeze.

A freeze would reward the Soviet Union for its enormous and unparalleled military buildup. It would prevent the essential and long overdue modernization of United States and allied defenses and would leave our aging forces increasingly vulnerable. And an honest freeze would require extensive prior negotiations on the systems and numbers to be limited and on the measures to ensure effective verification and compliance. And the kind of a freeze that has been suggested would be virtually impossible to verify. Such a major effort would divert us completely from our current negotiations on achieving substantial reductions.

A number of years ago, I heard a young father, a very prominent young man in the entertainment world, addressing a tremendous gathering in California. It was during the time of the Cold War, and Communism and our own way of life were very much on people's minds. And he was speaking to that subject. And suddenly, though, I heard him saying, "I love my little girls more than anything—" And I said to myself, "Oh, no, don't. You can't—don't say that." But I had underestimated him. He went on: "I would rather see my little girls die now, still believing in God, than have them grow up under Communism and one day die no longer believing in God."

There were thousands of young people in that audience. They came to their feet with shouts of joy. They had instantly recognized the profound truth in what he had said, with regard to the physical and the soul and what was truly important.

Yes, let us pray for the salvation of all of those who live in that totalitarian darkness—pray they will discover the joy of knowing God. But until they do, let us be aware that while they preach the supremacy of the state, declare its omnipotence over individual man, and predict its eventual domination of all peoples on the Earth, they are the focus of evil in the modern world.

It was C. S. Lewis who, in his unforgettable "Screwtape Letters," wrote: "The greatest evil is not done now in those sordid 'dens of crime' that Dickens loved to paint. It is not even done in concentration camps and labor camps. In those we see its final result. But it is conceived and ordered (moved, seconded, carried and minuted) in clear, carpeted, warmed, and well-lighted offices, by quiet men with white collars and cut fingernails and smooth-shaven cheeks who do not need to raise their voice."

Well, because these "quiet men" do not "raise their voices," because they sometimes speak in soothing tones of brotherhood and peace, because, like other dictators before them, they're always making "their final territorial demand," some would have us accept them at their word and accommodate ourselves to their aggressive impulses. But if history teaches anything, it teaches that simple-minded appeasement or wishful thinking about our adversaries is folly. It means the betrayal of our past, the squandering of our freedom.

So, I urge you to speak out against those who would place the United States in a position of military and moral inferiority. You know, I've always believed that old Screwtape reserved his best efforts for those of you in the church. So, in your discussions of the nuclear freeze proposals, I urge you to beware the temptation of pride—the temptation of blithely declaring yourselves above it and label both sides equally at fault, to ignore the facts of history and the aggressive impulses of an evil empire, to simply call the arms race a giant misunderstanding and thereby remove yourself from the struggle between right and wrong and good and evil.

I ask you to resist the attempts of those who would have you withhold your support for our efforts, this administration's efforts, to keep America strong and free, while we negotiate real and verifiable reductions in the world's nuclear arsenals and one day, with God's help, their total elimination.

While America's military strength is important, let me add here that I've always maintained that the struggle now going on for the world will never be decided by bombs or rockets, by armies or military might. The real crisis we face today is a spiritual one; at root, it is a test of moral will and faith.

Whittaker Chambers, the man whose own religious conversion made him a witness to one of the terrible traumas of our time, the Hiss-Chambers case, wrote that the crisis of the Western World exists to the degree in which the West is indifferent to God, the degree to which it collaborates in Communism's attempt to make man stand alone without God. And then he said, for Marxism-Leninism is actually the second oldest faith, first proclaimed in the Garden of Eden with the words of temptation, "Ye shall be as gods."

The Western World can answer this challenge, he wrote, "but only provided that its faith in God and the freedom He enjoins is as great as communism's faith in Man."

I believe we shall rise to the challenge. I believe that Communism is another sad, bizarre chapter in human history whose last pages even now are being written. I believe this because the source of our strength in the quest for human freedom is not material, but spiritual. And because it knows no limitation, it must terrify and ultimately triumph over those who would enslave their fellow man. For in the words of Isaiah: "He giveth power to the faint; and to them that have no might He increased strength. . . . But they that wait upon the Lord shall renew their strength; they shall mount up with wings as eagles; they shall run, and not be weary. . . ."

Yes, change your world. One of our Founding Fathers, Thomas Paine, said, "We have it within our power to begin the world over again." We can do it, doing together what no one church could do by itself.

God bless you, and thank you very much.

Note: The President spoke at 3:04 p.m. in the Citrus Crown Ballroom at the Sheraton Twin Towers Hotel.

Following his appearance before the convention, the President attended a Florida Republican fundraising reception at the hotel and then returned to Washington, D.C.

Source: Ronald Reagan, "Remarks at the Annual Convention of the National Association of the Evangelicals," Orlando, Florida, March 8, 1983.

7

RONALD REAGAN, "CREATORS OF THE FUTURE" (MARCH 1, 1985)

> In this speech before a conservative audience in 1985, President Ronald Reagan spoke about why conservatives had become the "creators of the future," and why he believed modern liberalism was exhausted. Why have conservatives become the creators of the future in Reagan's view? Is it an accurate statement to maintain that modern liberalism is without ideas? Is this view accurate today?

Thank you, Vice Chairman Linen, for those very kind words. I'm grateful to the American Conservative Union, Young Americans for Freedom, *National Review*, *Human Events*, for organizing this wonderful evening. When you work in the White House, you don't get to see your old friends as much as you'd like. And I always see the CPAC speech as my opportunity to "dance with the one that brung ya."

There's so much I want to talk about tonight. I've been thinking, in the weeks since the inauguration, that we are at an especially dramatic turning point in American history. And just putting it all together in my mind, I've been reviewing the elements that have led to this moment.

Ever since F.D.R. and the New Deal, the opposition party, and particularly those of a liberal persuasion, have dominated the political debate. Their ideas were new; they had momentum; they captured the imagination of the American people. The left held sway for a good long time. There was a right, but it was, by the forties and fifties, diffuse and scattered, without a unifying voice.

But in 1964 came a voice in the wilderness—Barry Goldwater; the great Barry Goldwater, the first major party candidate of our time who was a true-blue, undiluted conservative. He spoke from principle, and he offered vision. Freedom—he spoke of freedom: freedom from the Government's increasing demands on the family purse, freedom from the Government's increasing usurpation of individual rights and responsibilities, freedom from the leaders who told us the price of world peace is continued acquiescence to totalitarianism. He was ahead of his time. When he ran for President, he won 6 States and lost 44. But his candidacy worked as a precursor of things to come.

A new movement was stirring. And in the 1960s Young Americans for Freedom is born; *National Review* gains readership and prestige in the intellectual community; *Human Events* becomes a major voice on the cutting edge. In the seventies the antitax movement begins.

Actually, it was much more than an antitax movement, just as the Boston Tea Party was much more than antitax initiative. [Laughter] In the late seventies Proposition 13 and the Sagebrush Rebellion; in 1980, for the first time in 28 years, a Republican Senate is elected; so, may I say, is a conservative President. In 1984 that conservative administration is reelected in a 49-state sweep. And the day the votes came in, I thought of Walt Whitman: "I hear America singing." [Laughter]

This great turn from left to right was not just a case of the pendulum swinging—first, the left held sway and then the right, and here comes the left again. The truth is, conservative thought is no longer over here on the right; it's the mainstream now.

And the tide of history is moving irresistibly in our direction. Why? Because the other side is virtually bankrupt of ideas. It has nothing more to say, nothing to add to the debate. It has spent its intellectual capital, such as it was—[laughter]—and it has done its deeds.

Now, we're not in power now because they failed to gain electoral support over the past 50 years. They did win support. And the result was chaos, weakness, and drift. Ultimately, though, their failures yielded one great thing—us guys. [Laughter] We in this room are not simply profiting from their bankruptcy; we are where we are because we're winning the contest of ideas. In fact, in the past decade, all of a sudden, quietly, mysteriously, the Republican Party has become the party of ideas.

We became the party of the most brilliant and dynamic young minds. I remember them, just a few years ago, running around scrawling Laffer curves on table napkins—[laughter]—going to symposia and talking about how social programs did not eradicate poverty, but entrenched it; writing studies on why the latest weird and unnatural idea from the social engineers is weird and unnatural. [Laughter] You were there. They were your ideas, your symposia, your books, and usually somebody else's table napkins. [Laughter]

All of a sudden, Republicans were not defenders of the status quo but creators of the future. They were looking at tomorrow with all the single-mindedness of an inventor. In fact, they reminded me of the American inventors of the 19th and 20th centuries who filled the world with light and recorded sound.

The new conservatives made anew the connection between economic justice and economic growth. Growth in the economy would not only create jobs and paychecks, they said; it would enhance familial stability and encourage a healthy optimism about the future. Lower those tax rates, they said, and let the economy become the engine of our dreams. Pull back regulations, and encourage free and open competition. Let the men and women of the marketplace decide what they want.

But along with that, perhaps the greatest triumph of modern conservatism has been to stop allowing the left to put the average American on the moral defensive. By average American I mean the good, decent, rambunctious, and creative people who raise the families, go to church, and help out when the local library holds a fundraiser; people who have a stake in the community because they are the community.

These people had held true to certain beliefs and principles that for 20 years the intelligentsia were telling us were hopelessly out of date, utterly trite, and reactionary. You want prayer in the schools? How primitive, they said. You oppose abortion? How oppressive, how antimodern. The normal was portrayed as eccentric, and only the abnormal was worthy of emulation. The irreverent was celebrated, but only irreverence about certain things: irreverence toward, say, organized religion, yes; irreverence toward establishment liberalism, not too much of that. They celebrated their courage in taking on safe targets and patted each other on the back for slinging stones at a confused Goliath, who was too demoralized and really too good to fight back.

But now one simply senses it. The American people are no longer on the defensive. I believe the conservative movement deserves some credit for this. You spoke for the permanent against the merely prevalent, and ultimately you prevailed.

I believe we conservatives have captured the moment, captured the imagination of the American people. And what now? What are we to do with our success? Well, right now, with conservative thought accepted as mainstream thought and with the people of our country leading the fight to freedom, now we must move.

You remember your Shakespeare: "There is a tide in the affairs of men which, taken at the flood, leads on to fortune. Omitted, all the voyage of their life is bound in shallows and in miseries. On such a full sea are we now afloat. And we must take the current when it serves, or lose our ventures." I spoke in the—[applause]. It's typical, isn't it? I just quoted a great writer, but as an actor, I get the bow. [Laughter]

I spoke in the State of the Union of a second American revolution, and now is the time to launch that revolution and see that it takes hold. If we move decisively, these years will not be just a passing era of good feeling, not just a few good years, but a true golden age of freedom.

The moment is ours, and we must seize it. There's work to do. We must prolong and protect our growing prosperity so that it doesn't become just a passing phase, a natural adjustment between periods of recession. We must move further to provide incentive and make America the investment capital of the world.

We must institute a fair tax system and turn the current one on its ear. I believe there is natural support in our country for a simplified tax system, with still lower tax rates but a broader base, with everyone paying their fair share and no more. We must eliminate unproductive tax shelters. Again, there is natural support among Americans, because Americans are a fairminded people.

We must institute enterprise zones and a lower youth minimum wage so we can revitalize distressed areas and teenagers can get jobs. We're going to take our revolution to the people, all of the people. We're going to go to black Americans and members of all minority groups, and we're going to make our case.

Part of being a revolutionary is knowing that you don't have to acquiesce to the tired, old ideas of the past. One such idea is that the opposition party has black America and minority America locked up, that they own black America. Well, let me tell you, they own nothing but the past. The old alignments are no longer legitimate, if they ever were.

We're going to reach out, and we need your help. Conservatives were brought up to hate deficits, and justifiably so. We've long thought there are two things in Washington that are unbalanced—the budget and the liberals. [Laughter]

But we cannot reduce the deficit by raising taxes. And just so that every "i" is dotted and every "t" is crossed, let me repeat tonight for the benefit of those who never seem to get the message: We will not reduce the deficit by raising taxes. We need more taxes like John McLaughlin

[Washington executive editor, *National Review* magazine] needs assertiveness training. [Laughter]

Now, whether government borrows or increases taxes, it will be taking the same amount of money from the private economy, and either way, that's too much. We must bring down government spending. We need a constitutional amendment requiring a balanced budget.

It's something that 49 States already require—no reason the Federal Government should be any different.

We need the line-item veto, which 43 Governors have—no reason that the President shouldn't. And we have to cut waste. The Grace commission has identified billions of dollars that are wasted and that we can save.

But the domestic side isn't the only area where we need your help. All of us in this room grew up, or came to adulthood, in a time when the doctrine of Marx and Lenin was coming to divide the world. Ultimately, it came to dominate remorselessly whole parts of it. The Soviet attempt to give legitimacy to its tyranny is expressed in the infamous Brezhnev doctrine, which contends that once a country has fallen into Communist darkness, it can never again be allowed to see the light of freedom.

Well, it occurs to me that history has already begun to repeal that doctrine. It started one day in Grenada. We only did our duty, as a responsible neighbor and a lover of peace, the day we went in and returned the government to the people and rescued our own students. We restored that island to liberty. Yes, it's only a small island, but that's what the world is made of—small islands yearning for freedom.

There's much more to do. Throughout the world the Soviet Union and its agents, client states, and satellites are on the defensive—on the moral defensive, the intellectual defensive, and the political and economic defensive. Freedom movements arise and assert themselves. They're doing so on almost every continent populated by man—in the hills of Afghanistan, in Angola, in Kampuchea, in Central America. In making mention of freedom fighters, all of us are privileged to have in our midst tonight one of the brave commanders who lead the Afghan freedom fighters—Abdul Haq. Abdul Haq, we are with you.

They are our brothers, these freedom fighters, and we owe them our help. I've spoken recently of the freedom fighters of Nicaragua. You know the truth about them. You know who they're fighting and why. They are the moral equal of our Founding Fathers and the brave men and women of the French Resistance. We cannot turn away from them, for the struggle here is not right versus left; it is right versus wrong.

Now, I am against sending troops to Central America. They are simply not needed. Given a chance and the resources, the people of the area can fight their own fight. They have the men and women. They're capable of doing it. They have the people of their country behind them. All they need is our support. All they need is proof that we care as much about the fight for freedom 700 miles from our shores as the Soviets care about the fight against freedom 5,000 miles from theirs. And they need to know that the U.S. supports them with more than just pretty words and good wishes. We need your help on this, and I mean each of you—involved, active, strong, and vocal. And we need more.

All of you know that we're researching nonnuclear technologies that may enable us to prevent nuclear ballistic missiles from reaching U.S. soil or that of our allies. I happen to believe—logic forces me to believe—that this new defense system, the Strategic Defense Initiative, is the most hopeful possibility of our time. Its primary virtue is clear. If anyone ever attacked us, Strategic Defense would be there to protect us. It could conceivably save millions of lives.

SDI has been criticized on the grounds that it might upset any chance of an arms control agreement with the Soviets. But SDI is arms control. If SDI is, say, 80 percent effective, then it will make any Soviet attack folly. Even partial success in SDI would strengthen deterrence and keep the peace. And if our SDI research is successful, the prospects for real reduction in U.S. and Soviet offensive nuclear forces will be greatly enhanced.

It is said that SDI would deal a blow to the so-called East-West balance of power. Well, let's think about that. The Soviets already are investing roughly as much on strategic defenses as they are on their offensive nuclear forces. This could quickly tip the East-West balance if we had no defense of our own. Would a situation of comparable defenses threaten us? No, for we're not planning on being the first to use force.

As we strive for our goal of eventual elimination of nuclear weapons, each side would retain a certain amount of defensive—or of, I should say, destructive power—a certain number of missiles. But it would not be in our interest, or theirs, to build more and more of them.

Now, one would think our critics on the left would quickly embrace, or at least be openminded about a system that promises to reduce the size of nuclear missile forces on both sides and to greatly enhance the prospects for real arms reductions. And yet we hear SDI belittled by some with nicknames, or demagogued with charges that it will bring war to the heavens.

They complain that it won't work, which is odd from people who profess to believe in the perfectability of man-machines after all. [Laughter]

And man-machines are so much easier to manipulate. They say it won't be 100 percent effective, which is odd, since they don't ask for 100 percent effectiveness in their social experiments. [Laughter] They say SDI is only in the research stage and won't be realized in time to change things. To which, as I said last month, the only reply is: Then let's get started.

Now, my point here is not to question the motives of others. But it's difficult to understand how critics can object to exploring the possibility of moving away from exclusive reliance upon nuclear weapons. The truth is, I believe that they find it difficult to embrace any idea that breaks with the past, that breaks with consensus thinking and the common establishment wisdom. In short, they find it difficult and frightening to alter the status quo.

And what are we to do when these so-called opinion leaders of an outworn philosophy are out there on television and in the newspapers with their steady drumbeat of doubt and distaste? Well, when all you have to do to win is rely on the good judgment of the American people, then you're in good shape, because the American people have good judgment. I know it isn't becoming of me, but I like to think that maybe 49 of our 50 States displayed that judgment just a few months ago. [Laughter]

What we have to do, all of us in this room, is get out there and talk about SDI. Explain it, debate it, tell the American people the facts. It may well be the most important work we do in the next few years. And if we try, we'll succeed. So, we have great work ahead of us, big work. But if we do it together and with complete commitment, we can change our country and history forever.

Once during the campaign, I said, "This is a wonderful time to be alive." And I meant that. I meant that we're lucky not to live in pale and timid times. We've been blessed with the opportunity to stand for something—for liberty and freedom and fairness. And these are things worth fighting for, worth devoting our lives to. And we have good reason to be hopeful and optimistic.

We've made much progress already. So, let us go forth with good cheer and stout hearts—happy warriors out to seize back a country and a world to freedom.

Thank you, and God bless you.

Source: Ronald Reagan, "Creators of the Future," speech before the Conservative Political Action Conference, Washington, DC, March 1, 1985.

8

CONSERVATIVES ON RELIGIOUS FREEDOM: MITT ROMNEY, "RELIGIOUS LIBERTY" (2008)

During the 2008 primaries, Republican presidential candidate Mitt Romney spoke at the George H. W. Bush Presidential Library in College Station, Texas. Romney had come under criticism for his Mormon faith. His views on faith spoke of a tradition of religious liberty and tolerance in America. In this document, how does he define religious liberty and religious freedom? What role does religion play in American life in Romney's view? Are his views conservative? The speech begins with Romney addressing former President George H. W. Bush, who introduced the former governor.

Romney: Thank you, Mr. President, for your kind introduction. America faces a new generation of challenges. Radical violent Islam seeks to destroy us. An emerging China endeavors to surpass our economic leadership. And we are troubled at home by government overspending, overuse of foreign oil, and the breakdown of the family.

Over the last year, we have embarked on a national debate on how best to preserve American leadership. Today, I wish to address a topic which I believe is fundamental to America's greatness: our religious liberty. I will also offer perspectives on how my own faith would inform my presidency, if I were elected.

There are some who may feel that religion is not a matter to be seriously considered in the context of the weighty threats that face us. If so, they are at odds with the nation's founders, for they, when our nation faced its greatest peril, sought the blessings of the Creator. And further, they discovered the essential connection between the survival of a free land and the protection of religious freedom. In John Adams' words: "We have no government armed with power capable of contending with human passions unbridled by morality and religion. . . . Our Constitution was made for a moral and religious people."

Freedom requires religion just as religion requires freedom. Freedom opens the windows of the soul so that man can discover his most profound beliefs and commune with God. Freedom and religion endure together, or perish alone.

Given our grand tradition of religious tolerance and liberty, some wonder whether there are any questions regarding an aspiring candidate's religion that are appropriate. I believe there are. And I will answer them today.

Almost 50 years ago another candidate from Massachusetts explained that he was an American running for president, not a Catholic running for president. Like him, I am an American running for president. I do not define my candidacy by my religion. A person should not be elected because of his faith nor should he be rejected because of his faith.

Let me assure you that no authorities of my church, or of any other church for that matter, will ever exert influence on presidential decisions. Their authority is theirs, within the province of church affairs, and it ends where the affairs of the nation begin.

As governor, I tried to do the right as best I knew it, serving the law and answering to the Constitution. I did not confuse the particular teachings of my church with the obligations of the office and of the Constitution—and of course, I would not do so as president. I will put no doctrine of any church above the plain duties of the office and the sovereign authority of the law.

As a young man, Lincoln described what he called America's "political religion"—the commitment to defend the rule of law and the Constitution. When I place my hand on the Bible and take the oath of office, that oath becomes my highest promise to God. If I am fortunate to become your president, I will serve no one religion, no one group, no one cause, and no one interest. A president must serve only the common cause of the people of the United States.

There are some for whom these commitments are not enough. They would prefer it if I would simply distance myself from my religion, say that it is more a tradition than my personal conviction, or disavow one or another of its precepts. That I will not do. I believe in my Mormon faith and I endeavor to live by it. My faith is the faith of my fathers—I will be true to them and to my beliefs.

Some believe that such a confession of my faith will sink my candidacy. If they are right, so be it. But I think they underestimate the American people. Americans do not respect believers of convenience.

Americans tire of those who would jettison their beliefs, even to gain the world.

There is one fundamental question about which I often am asked. What do I believe about Jesus Christ? I believe that Jesus Christ is the Son of God and the Savior of mankind. My church's beliefs about Christ may not all be the same as those of other faiths. Each religion has its own unique doctrines and history. These are not bases for criticism but rather a test of our tolerance. Religious tolerance would be a shallow principle indeed if it were reserved only for faiths with which we agree.

There are some who would have a presidential candidate describe and explain his church's distinctive doctrines. To do so would enable the very religious test the founders prohibited in the Constitution. No candidate should become the spokesman for his faith. For if he becomes president he will need the prayers of the people of all faiths.

I believe that every faith I have encountered draws its adherents closer to God. And in every faith I have come to know, there are features I wish were in my own: I love the profound ceremony of the Catholic Mass, the approachability of God in the prayers of the Evangelicals, the tenderness of spirit among the Pentecostals, the confident independence of the Lutherans, the ancient traditions of the Jews, unchanged through the ages, and the commitment to frequent prayer of the Muslims. As I travel across the country and see our towns and cities, I am always moved by the many houses of worship with their steeples, all pointing to heaven, reminding us of the source of life's blessings.

It is important to recognize that while differences in theology exist between the churches in America, we share a common creed of moral convictions. And where the affairs of our nation are concerned, it's usually a sound rule to focus on the latter—on the great moral principles that urge us all on a common course. Whether it was the cause of abolition, or civil rights, or the right to life itself, no movement of conscience can succeed in America that cannot speak to the convictions of religious people.

We separate church and state affairs in this country, and for good reason. No religion should dictate to the state nor should the state interfere with the free practice of religion. But in recent years, the notion of the separation of church and state has been taken by some well beyond its original meaning. They seek to remove from the public domain any acknowledgment of God. Religion is seen as merely a private affair with no place in public life. It is as if they are intent on establishing a new religion in America—the religion of secularism. They are wrong.

The founders proscribed the establishment of a state religion, but they did not countenance the elimination of religion from the public square. We are a nation "Under God" and in God, we do indeed trust.

We should acknowledge the Creator as did the Founders—in ceremony and word. He should remain on our currency, in our pledge, in the teaching of our history, and during the holiday season, nativity scenes and menorahs should be welcome in our public places. Our greatness would not long endure without judges who respect the foundation of faith upon which our constitution rests. I will take care to separate the affairs of government from any religion, but I will not separate us from "the God who gave us liberty."

Nor would I separate us from our religious heritage. Perhaps the most important question to ask a person of faith who seeks a political office, is this: does he share these American values: the equality of human kind, the obligation to serve one another, and a steadfast commitment to liberty?

They are not unique to any one denomination. They belong to the great moral inheritance we hold in common. They are the firm ground on which Americans of different faiths meet and stand as a nation, united.

We believe that every single human being is a child of God—we are all part of the human family. The conviction of the inherent and inalienable worth of every life is still the most revolutionary political proposition ever advanced. John Adams put it that we are "thrown into the world all equal and alike."

The consequence of our common humanity is our responsibility to one another, to our fellow Americans foremost, but also to every child of God. It is an obligation which is fulfilled by Americans every day, here and across the globe, without regard to creed or race or nationality.

Americans acknowledge that liberty is a gift of God, not an indulgence of government. No people in the history of the world have sacrificed as much for liberty. The lives of hundreds of thousands of America's sons and daughters were laid down during the last century to preserve freedom, for us and for freedom loving people throughout the world. America took nothing from that Century's terrible wars—no land from Germany or Japan or Korea; no treasure; no oath of fealty. America's resolve in the defense of liberty has been tested time and again. It has not been found wanting, nor must it ever be. America must never falter in holding high the banner of freedom.

These American values, this great moral heritage, is shared and lived in my religion as it is in yours. I was taught in my home to honor God and love my neighbor. I saw my father march with Martin Luther King. I saw my parents provide compassionate care to others, in personal ways to people nearby, and in just as consequential ways in leading national volunteer movements. I am moved by the Lord's words: "For I was an hungered, and ye gave me meat: I was thirsty, and ye gave me drink: I was a stranger, and ye took me in: naked, and ye clothed me. . . ."

My faith is grounded on these truths. You can witness them in Ann and my marriage and in our family. We are a long way from perfect and we have surely stumbled along the way, but our aspirations, our values, are the self-same as those from the other faiths that stand upon this common foundation. And these convictions will indeed inform my presidency.

Today's generations of Americans have always known religious liberty. Perhaps we forget the long and arduous path our nation's forbearers took to achieve it. They came here from England to seek freedom of religion. But upon finding it for themselves, they at first denied it to others. Because of their diverse beliefs, Ann Hutchinson was exiled from Massachusetts Bay, a banished Roger Williams founded Rhode Island, and two centuries later, Brigham Young set out for the West. Americans were unable to accommodate their commitment to their own faith with an appreciation for the convictions of others to different faiths. In this, they were very much like those of the European nations they had left.

It was in Philadelphia that our founding fathers defined a revolutionary vision of liberty, grounded on self-evident truths about the equality of all, and the inalienable rights with which each is endowed by his Creator.

We cherish these sacred rights, and secure them in our Constitutional order. Foremost do we protect religious liberty, not as a matter of policy but as a matter of right. There will be no established church, and we are guaranteed the free exercise of our religion.

I'm not sure that we fully appreciate the profound implications of our tradition of religious liberty. I have visited many of the magnificent cathedrals in Europe. They are so inspired, so grand, so empty. Raised up over generations, long ago, so many of the cathedrals now stand as the postcard backdrop to societies just too busy or too "enlightened" to venture inside and kneel in prayer. The establishment of state religions in Europe did no favor to Europe's churches. And though you will find many people of strong faith there, the churches themselves seem to be withering away.

Infinitely worse is the other extreme, the creed of conversion by conquest: violent jihad, murder as martyrdom . . . killing Christians, Jews, and

Muslims with equal indifference. These radical Islamists do their preaching not by reason or example, but in the coercion of minds and the shedding of blood. We face no greater danger today than theocratic tyranny, and the boundless suffering these states and groups could inflict if given the chance.

The diversity of our cultural expression, and the vibrancy of our religious dialogue, has kept America in the forefront of civilized nations even as others regard religious freedom as something to be destroyed.

In such a world, we can be deeply thankful that we live in a land where reason and religion are friends and allies in the cause of liberty, joined against the evils and dangers of the day. And you can be certain of this: Any believer in religious freedom, any person who has knelt in prayer to the Almighty, has a friend and ally in me. And so it is for hundreds of millions of our countrymen: We do not insist on a single strain of religion—rather, we welcome our nation's symphony of faith.

Recall the early days of the First Continental Congress in Philadelphia, during the fall of 1774. With Boston occupied by British troops, there were rumors of imminent hostilities and fears of an impending war. In this time of peril, someone suggested that they pray. But there were objections. They were too divided in religious sentiments, what with Episcopalians and Quakers, Anabaptists and Congregationalists, Presbyterians and Catholics.

Then Sam Adams rose, and said he would hear a prayer from anyone of piety and good character, as long as they were a patriot. And so together they prayed, and together they fought, and together, by the grace of God, they founded this great nation.

In that spirit, let us give thanks to the divine author of liberty. And together, let us pray that this land may always be blessed with freedom's holy light.

God bless this great land, the United States of America.

Source: Republican presidential candidate Mitt Romney's speech at the George H. W. Bush Presidential Library in College Station, Texas, 2008.

GUARDIANS OF PRIVILEGE

Nancy MacLean

Ronald Reagan chose an odd site for the opening speech of his 1980 presidential campaign. Fresh from receiving the Republican nomination, he headed not for California, where he had served as governor, nor a Republican stronghold in the Midwest, where he was born, nor even a major population center like Atlanta. Instead, he chose the Neshoba County Fair in Philadelphia, Mississippi, where three student civil rights workers had been murdered in 1964. Why would he take his message to rural Mississippi? Reagan made his purpose clear: In today's marketing language, he was branding his campaign. "I believe in states' rights," he announced to the crowd of fifteen thousand fairgoers. His presidency would "restore to states and local governments the power that belongs to them."

States' rights was the rallying cry of the southern whites who fought the civil rights movement and defended the state-enforced racial hierarchy known as Jim Crow. Mississippi Republican officials had selected the fair as a way for Reagan to bring his campaign message to such "George Wallace–inclined voters," referring to the Alabama governor who had once stood in a schoolhouse door and declared, "I say segregation now, segregation tomorrow, and segregation forever!" Reagan's Mississippi campaign was run by then U.S. representative Trent Lott, who at one rally praised Strom Thurmond, the States' Rights Democratic Party candidate of 1948, who ran a hard-line segregationist third-party campaign in protest when President Harry Truman ordered desegregation of the armed forces and action on civil rights. "If we had elected this man thirty years ago," Lott told the 1980 audience of Reagan supporters, gesturing to Thurmond's candidacy, "we wouldn't be in the mess we are today."

How are we to make sense of this? Reagan is remembered today as an advocate of free enterprise, anti-Communism, limited government, and traditional morality. Why was he currying favor with white voters who mourned the passing of segregation? For that matter, why was a candidate who promised a stronger America appealing to some of the most divisive forces in the country—and doing so with slogans used, within living memory, to justify the forcible subordination of those they considered their racial inferiors? To explain this seeming contradiction, we need to understand Ronald Reagan's relationship with the conservative movement and examine how that movement built its popular following.

As a standard bearer of conservatism, Reagan was following a strategy developed over more than a quarter century. Since the mid-1950s, conservative intellectuals and political leaders had reached out to southern segregationists to expand their ranks. After 1964, when Barry Goldwater ran for president, they set out in earnest to build the right wing of the Republican Party with southern conservatives. By Reagan's second term in the White House, Trent Lott, then the Republican House Minority Whip, told a white southern audience that "the 1984 Republican platform, all the ideas we supported there—from tax policy, to foreign policy; from individual rights to neighborhood security—are things that Jefferson Davis and his people believed in." Davis, of course, was the president of the Confederate States of America, which waged war against the federal government of the United States from 1861 to 1865.

How could the party of Abraham Lincoln, which saved the Union and abolished slavery, promote itself in the late twentieth century as the party of neo-Confederacy? It seems nonsensical—until one learns the deeper history of the conservative movement. That movement came together in the wake of World War II, but built on foundations laid in the resistance to Reconstruction and the New Deal. Over more than six decades, its thinkers and strategists chose to act as guardians of privilege in national life. Each time groups of Americans who had been denied full citizenship rights and social dignity organized to achieve fair treatment, conservatives assembled to block their path and secure the advantages of those already favored. Indeed, they actively enlisted prejudice to do so. The pattern holds true from the European immigrant workers who built the industrial unions of the 1930s and helped win a New Deal for all Americans, through the African American civil rights movement of the postwar years and the feminist movement that gained momentum in its wake, to gay men and lesbians seeking to end discrimination on the basis of sexual orientation today. The prime means for those with limited wealth and lesser power to better their situation has been the democratic capacity to organize through trade union struggle and other social movements that enlist the federal government's help to ensure fair treatment. The political Right has steadfastly opposed all such efforts. Calling for property rights, small government, and its version of traditional morality in order to safeguard privilege, it has fought those who sought justice.

Conservative leaders felt a deep and understandable sense of legitimacy in their quest to safeguard established advantages, however. That confidence came from the nation's dual origins in slavery and freedom. As the first modern republic, which inspired human rights activists around the world with its clarion call that "all men are created equal," the United States was founded in part by slaveholders. They built protections for their right to treat other people as property into the Constitution (article I, section 2 counted a slave as three-fifths of a person for purposes of representation and taxation). From the drafting of the nation's founding documents forward, the tension between the quest for equality and representative government, on one side, and the determination to preserve powers of domination and privilege, on the other, has animated the main battles of American history. Whereas the abolition movement, the Populist movement, the labor movement, the civil rights movement, the women's movement, and the gay rights movement have looked to the expansive promise of the Declaration of Independence, conservatives have looked to the Constitution's protections for property rights and its related restrictions on popular democracy. No one promoted those restrictive traditions more strenuously than antebellum slave-owning politicians such as John C. Calhoun and their admirers among later southern white conservatives, so it is not surprising that northern and western conservatives looked south for aid from the very outset of their movement. Conservatism meant various things to various people as it evolved over the years, but without the appeal to white prejudice in the South it would never have acquired the power it did in recent decades.

To understand these dynamics, it helps to focus on the movement's thinkers and strategists, rather than on individual voters with conservative sensibilities. This is very important to making sense of what happened and why. Ordinary Americans responded to the conservative appeals and sometimes organized themselves on particular issues of concern to them, such as taxes and abortion. But they were not in the driver's seat of this movement. Most had little sense of the conservative leaders' overall project, let alone their strategy for achieving it, and many would in time find some of their own interests hurt by it. The rise of the Right is above all the story of organizing by conservative intellectuals and politicians who stirred anxiety about where the country was headed in order to build the power to turn national policy away from the inclusive social citizenship inaugurated in the New Deal and expanded thereafter. Deep economic, social, and cultural changes opened up many ordinary Americans to appeals for new directions by the 1960s and 1970s, but the country never would have turned right as it did without the arguments and organizing of the conservative movement's movers and shakers.

They built the postwar Right in three phases. In the first, from 1955 to 1963, conservative intellectuals developed the ideas, institutions, and alliances that laid the groundwork for later successes. In the second phase, from 1964 to 1980, starting with the fight against the Civil Rights Act and the presidential candidacy of Barry Goldwater, they gathered a mass following by tapping into popular white fears and prejudices at a time of profound change and challenge, including alterations in race relations and in family life, gender roles, and sexuality. That grassroots outreach enabled the cause to expand far beyond the elite founding cohort and begin winning elections. In the third period, from 1980 to the present, conservatives used the power thus acquired to attempt a U-turn in national policy. Hoping to roll back the more egalitarian, opportunity-enhancing public policies enacted during the Great Depression and expanded in the Great Society programs of the 1960s, they managed to restore levels of corporate power and social inequality not seen since the 1920s.

Yet, while conservatives have succeeded in cutting budgets and deforming enforcement of many elements of the Great Society in particular, they have failed in their mission to reverse the trajectory of government, precisely because core New Deal and Great Society reforms such as Social Security, Medicare and Medicaid, civil rights, and environmental protection remain so popular with voters. Even on issues where they have amassed a stronger (if still minority) following, such as restoring school prayer and recriminalizing abortion, conservatives have proven unable to win the reversals to which they pledged themselves. Acrimony they have produced in abundance, but across-the-board success appears unlikely while majority rule prevails. To explain this outcome, a long look at the formative years is helpful, because once one understands that era, everything conservatives did with their expanding resources thereafter makes more sense.

LAYING THE GROUNDWORK, 1955–1963

Historians and conservative organizers alike identify 1955 as the official start of modern American conservatism as a movement, no longer just a way of thinking or voting. That was when William F. Buckley Jr. and his collaborators founded the *National Review*, a magazine that became the cause's organizing center. The magazine's founding was not the only omen of the movement ahead. In the span of a few years, core tracts of the new cause appeared in print, among them Richard Weaver's *Ideas Have Consequences*, Russell Kirk's *The Conservative Mind*, and Willmoore Kendall's *The Conservative Affirmation*. Before this, recalled one insider, "there did not exist anything in the nature of a broadly principled, coherent conservative movement."

But the magazine launch was unique. It signaled a determination to draw like thinkers into a network to promote change: a collective, self-conscious movement to alter the country. In its inaugural issue, *National Review* proclaimed it would "stand athwart history, yelling Stop." The editors promised to challenge "the Liberal orthodoxy." Theirs would be a forum for "radical conservatives," those "who have not made their peace with the New Deal," which, the editors charged, "the well-fed Right"—presided over by President Dwight Eisenhower himself—had. Tellingly, the magazine's statement of its core "convictions" recast the wording of the Declaration of Independence. Where the Declaration had declared the "unalienable Rights" of "Life, Liberty, and *the pursuit of Happiness*," the *National Review* proclaimed that government must "protect its citizens' lives, liberty, and *property*." It insisted that "all other activities tend to diminish freedom and hamper progress" and so "the growth of government—the dominant feature of this century—must be fought relentlessly." "Satanic" Communism must be defeated, first and foremost. But so, too, should the "Social-Democrat" in "both parties." Indeed, the *National Review* signaled irrevocable hostility toward the direction the United States had taken after Franklin Delano Roosevelt's election. It decried "politically oriented [labor] unionism" and the welfare state and vowed to "tell the violated businessman's side of the story." And it pledged to fight any "surrender of U.S. sovereignty to a world organization" such as the United Nations. The magazine placed its faith in "the market economy" and "the organic moral order" in the conviction that "freedom goes hand in hand with a state of political decentralization."

In conservatives' view, the New Deal violated the aims of the nation's founders. "Freedom and equality are opposites," *National Review* senior editor Frank Meyer declared. "The tradition of Western civilization and the American republic," Meyer claimed, had "been subjected to a revolutionary attack in the years since 1932" when Roosevelt was elected. What appalled Meyer and the budding modern conservative movement was not so much the early New Deal, which tackled the economic crisis by allowing employers to form cartels and by paying subsidies to farm owners to reduce output. What they most objected to was the so-called Second New Deal. It empowered working-class Americans with measures such as federally enforced fair labor standards in wages, hours, and working conditions; legal backing for workers to organize trade unions; and tax-funded public works programs for the unemployed. Conservatives scorned all this. Detesting what Meyer called "the characteristic leveling egalitarianism of the time," they maintained that social hierarchy was mandated by nature and in the best interest of all.

Conservatives sought to undermine the consensus among Americans at midcentury that in a modern capitalist society true freedom and opportunity for all required greater economic equality and security. It was a conclusion most of the nation's citizens and leaders reached as they confronted the cataclysmic trauma of the Great Depression. By the spring of 1933, thirteen million Americans had lost their jobs; one hundred thousand businesses had failed in four years. With one in four out of work, so many men were reduced to selling apples that the Census began listing apple-seller as an occupation. Unable to pay their rent or mortgages, people lost their homes. Parents couldn't buy food or milk. Nine out of every ten schoolchildren in the coal counties of West Virginia suffered malnutrition; in New York City, one in five did. Desperate for income, between one and two million Americans became permanent migrants—hoboes, they were called—riding the rails in search of temporary jobs. The have-nots suffered most, but middle-class, white-collar families also learned that decades of hard work and thrift proved no protection from catastrophe in a laissez-faire system. When the banks failed, nine million households lost their life savings. African Americans, already struggling, hit bottom. During the 1930s, studies found, the income of eight of every ten black households hovered between minimal subsistence and utter disaster. Humiliated by their inability to provide for their wives and children—to act as breadwinners in the way gender norms mandated—many men of all backgrounds deserted their families. Some took their own lives. One told an investigator: "I would rather turn on the gas, and put an end to the whole family than let my wife support me." "All this—it breaks you down," said a businessman who lost everything. "You get so you feel so whipped."

Citizens began to look to the federal government for help because everything else they relied on had failed. Before giving up on the laissez-faire, small government model that prevailed in the 1920s, however, they tried every avenue of relief its advocates urged. Extended families helped where they could, but that usually wasn't much because so many needed help. Some large employers in the 1920s had developed what was called welfare capitalism, providing various kinds of insurance, pensions, and services to keep their employees loyal by helping them through tough times. But once the Depression decimated their profit margins, businesses stopped providing all but the bare minimum to those lucky enough to stay on the payroll. As those who needed help appealed to private charities, religious groups, and local government, the demand overwhelmed these institutions. Total public and private spending for relief in 1932 amounted to less than $27 a year for each of the twelve million jobless; only one in four of the unemployed was getting anything at all. Depleted, private charities closed their doors, and city and state governments exhausted their resources.

As all traditional remedies proved woefully inadequate, citizens and city and state officials began looking to Washington, DC, for salvation. Doing nothing, more and more feared, would not only hurt people, it would fuel extremism. In Italy and Germany, fascists had taken power and used militarism to revive their economies; in the Soviet Union, Communists maintained control through a centralized police state. In America, both Right and Left were organizing and winning recruits for radical change. Most voters rejected their offerings, yet still wanted more relief than the Republican president, Herbert Hoover, was willing to provide. Turning him out of office in 1932, they voted for the candidate who promised "a new deal for the American people." Carrying all but six states in 1932, Franklin D. Roosevelt won a mandate for change. Thanks to wide-ranging grassroots organizing for remedies ranging from trade union representation to public works jobs and old-age retirement pensions, the era that followed proved one of stunning innovation in the use of democracy to address social problems.

The fact that the resulting New Deal welfare state accepted some responsibility for popular well-being and curbed the once-absolute freedoms of employers seemed an abrogation of national traditions to the nascent conservative movement of the 1950s. As the popular ex-Communist conservative hero Whittaker Chambers put it, in allowing "the power of politics" to eclipse "the power of business," the New Deal had created a system akin to that of the Soviet Union. The Rooseveltian model of government was "that great socialist revolution, which, in the name of liberalism . . . has been inching its ice cap over the nation for two decades." In this view, liberalism not only froze economic initiative but also bordered on treason. The federal government had no business doing any more than defending the nation from foreign threats, punishing criminal wrongdoing, and preserving public order. The only point of dispute among conservatives was whether the state should also enforce private morality, something the social traditionalists advocated and the economic libertarians opposed.

Conservatives were right that the New Deal inaugurated an epochal change in the relationship of citizens to the government. In cultural terms, it marked national acceptance of a value system urged by farmers in the Populist movement, settlement house reformers in the Progressive era, and labor organizers in the Depression: that economics should not be divorced from ethics. Those who wanted government to do more for citizens accepted the market as an efficient system for the production of goods and services, but they sought a "moral capitalism," as one historian put it, in place of a business free-for-all. Recognizing that economies are human creations, not forces of nature, they maintained that markets ought not to dehumanize those who enable their functioning. Though not to the degree that some European nations did, the New Deal enshrined these principles of social solidarity and mutual obligation. Its premise was that when risks are shared and citizens are protected from catastrophes of others' making, everyone is more secure and able to achieve their full potential. Conversely, when economic inequality reached the level it had in the 1920s, when the income of the wealthiest 1 percent of the population was as great as the combined incomes of the bottom 42 percent and when almost half of American families took in less than was needed to live in "minimum health and decency," that endangered not only their well-being but the very functioning of the economy. Such skewed distribution meant that millions could not buy the goods the economy was generating. Their underconsumption contributed to the Depression and imperiled recovery. Hard experience thus taught most Americans that for capitalism to flourish, government must defend the common good.

Many contemporaries spoke of what they were developing as industrial democracy, of bringing some self-government to the nation's corporate workplaces, which before had run more or less as autocracies. Scholars have since called it social citizenship. By enhancing the economic security of Americans, government intervention boosted their courage to challenge abuses of power at work and strengthen democracy in public life. In practical terms, the New Deal expanded the government's presence in everyday life and so connected citizens as never before to Washington. (Ordinary Americans invited a deeper relationship: fifteen million, for example, wrote personal letters to Franklin and Eleanor Roosevelt during his time in office. Where Herbert Hoover received an average of one hundred letters a day, FDR got four hundred fifty thousand in the first week of his presidency, and generally about eight thousand a day thereafter.) The government financed its new activities to promote popular well-being through progressive taxation, which operated on a secular version of the biblical maxim that of those to whom much is given, much is expected. That, too, offended many wealthy people, who were required to pay taxes at higher rates than their struggling fellow citizens. Corporate executives first began using the phrase "free enterprise" in these years to signal their opposition to all this.

Together, the cultural change and the public policies of the New Deal altered the balance of power between the richest Americans and the rest. The most immediate beneficiaries were the nation's working people, above all the children of southern and eastern European immigrants who worked in factories making cars, rubber, steel, and more. They built the Congress of Industrial Organizations, or CIO, America's first enduring federation of industrial unions. Energetically entering electoral politics, the CIO pushed for the kinds of measures that in Europe gained the name social democracy, measures that enabled the mass expansion of the middle class over the ensuing three decades. Those organizations and the new government regulatory capacity also laid the groundwork for the postwar civil rights movement and feminism. Without that widespread belief in government as a force for social justice and without the institutional capacity for its intervention to stop wrongdoing and solve social problems, those movements would have been unimaginable.

The Second World War deepened the change when the government oversaw the economy to a novel degree to win the war against imperial Japan, fascist Italy, and Nazi Germany. This development offered new leverage for subordinated groups to demand fair treatment, as in the 1941 March on Washington Movement, a black-led effort to desegregate defense industries and the armed forces and ensure equal opportunity. Prompted by the horrors of Nazi anti-Semitism, Jewish Americans similarly rallied to end discrimination. Like trade unionists and African Americans, they took confidence from the Roosevelt administration's January 1941 proclamation of the Four Freedoms required for a secure world order: freedom of speech, freedom of worship, freedom from want, and freedom from fear. The United States was thus now committed to economic security, democratic rights and dignity, and multilateral cooperation to protect against armed aggression.

Where nearly all Americans appreciated that departure from tradition, conservatives steadfastly opposed it. They girded themselves for what most expected to be an epochal battle that would likely require decades before its success. What especially bothered the nascent Right was how the Republican Party mainstream had come to accept the new order by the mid-1950s. As president, the hugely popular General Dwight D. Eisenhower treated the New Deal as settled tradition to be conserved, if contained. He sought to avoid a frontal battle with the USSR in the knowledge that it would be cataclysmic. In Buckley's view, this was "measured socialism." Eisenhower also accepted the Supreme Court's *Brown v. Board of Education* decision requiring school desegregation, and he enforced it when segregationists defied the court in Little Rock, Arkansas, in 1957. Scorning the right wing as an anachronism, Eisenhower had written his brother in 1954, "Should any political party attempt to abolish social security, unemployment insurance, and eliminate labor laws and farm programs, you would not hear of that party again in our political history. There is a tiny splinter group, of course, that believes you can do these things. . . . Their number is negligible and they are stupid." Reciprocating the contempt, the founding issue of *National Review* derided Republican centrists as "the well-fed Right" and accused them of "amorality."

Conservatives like to portray their movement in this founding decade as a "movement of ideas." That is the oft-told story. But it distracts attention from how theirs was also a movement of action. In their writings and speeches, conservatives exalted "liberty" and "tradition"; in practice, they aligned with the forces of privilege and prejudice. One telling illustration is the figures they held up for praise in American history. John C. Calhoun, the antebellum South Carolinian planter and politician known for proclaiming on the Senate floor that slavery was "a positive good," claimed a special place in the conservative pantheon. Calhoun had devised an interpretation of the Constitution that could constrain democracy so as to protect property and privilege. His theory of nullification asserted that states had the right to nullify (that is, invalidate and defy) any federal law they deemed unconstitutional. His purpose was to defend slaveholders from reformers in Congress, but 1950s conservatives found his states' rights ideas helpful to buttress corporate and white power. In a tribute to him, *National Review* contributor Donald Davidson thus insisted that slavery was but "a minor issue" in the conflict between North and South: "the difficulty was with egalitarianism itself." Calhoun had understood early on that his region could hold back reform movements of all kinds in the United States because it acted as "the great conservative power." "In this tendency to conflict in the North, between labor and capital," Calhoun had written, "the South has been and ever will be found on the conservative side." Agreeing, later conservatives looked to Dixie for support.

They championed what Martin Luther King Jr. later called "the tragic coalition in Congress": the alliance that after 1937 united segregationist white southern Democrats with northern business-minded Republicans to fight egalitarian measures at home and rachet up the Cold War abroad. *Na-*

tional Review cofounder Willmoore Kendall identified Senator Harry Byrd of Virginia, Senator Patrick McCarran of Nevada, and Senator Joseph Mc-Carthy of Wisconsin as "the Rightists' most far-seeing commanders" in Congress. Each man fought the New Deal and promoted repression of human rights and civil liberties in the name of anti-Communism. Harry Byrd opposed virtually all of the New Deal, *Brown v. Board of Education*, and, one contemporary quipped, "the twentieth century." Patrick McCarran sponsored legislation that enabled the firing and deportation of people with left-wing views and affiliations. Joseph McCarthy's preposterous allegations of Communism in high places led his fellow senators to censure him for bringing the Senate "into dishonor and disrepute." William F. Buckley and his brother-in-law Brent Bozell brooked no criticism, however. They portrayed him as a hero of the war on subversion in their book *McCarthy and His Enemies: The Record and Its Meaning.*

Yet in these years conservative commitments never translated neatly into electoral politics because of the crazy-quilt nature of American party coalitions. While business interests and centrists like Dwight Eisenhower dominated the Republican Party, it also contained a vocal liberal wing based in the Northeast that included African Americans and other advocates of civil rights enforcement. Some self-identified feminists also appreciated the Republican Party's support for an Equal Rights Amendment, a measure Democrats feared would undermine protective legislation for working women. The Democratic Party, for its part, was the party of the New Deal, but also of segregationists and disfranchisers such as Harry Byrd. Dating back to the 1860s, large landowners in the South had used their power in the party to keep black sharecroppers and domestic workers uneducated, intimidated, and largely unaided by the New Deal. Roosevelt tried to purge the party of such reactionaries in the late 1930s, when he condemned the region's "feudal system" for propping up "selfish minorities." However, his clumsy attempt to add justices to the Supreme Court to end its obstruction of reform redounded to the advantage of the conservative southerners.

Their 1937 "Conservative Manifesto" protest against Roosevelt was an omen of the right-wing movement to come. "So long as the New Deal did not disturb southern agricultural, industrial, or racial patterns," noted one historian, the rural southern conservatives in Congress "would support it, sometimes with enthusiasm." But "as the administration drew closer to the CIO, Negroes, and other 'forgotten men,' conservative Democrats gradually discovered their philosophical kinship with conservative Republicans." The document the southern conservative Democrats and northern business Republicans produced was short, but anticipated much of the postwar conservatives' platform. Writing in the midst of the sit-down strikes that unionized General Motors, the signers expressed their desire to curb both industrial unions and President Roosevelt. The manifesto urged cutting taxes, restoring powers to "private enterprise," and balancing the budget by cutting back social welfare and public works. Lastly, the authors emphasized, in deference to the low-wage southern employers who were their prime constituency, "we favor the vigorous maintenance of States' rights, home rule and local self government."

After the war, such sentiments drove the passage of the Taft-Hartley Act of 1947, another landmark of the cross-regional, anti–New Deal alliance on which the conservative movement built. Capitalizing on the fear of Communism spreading with the Cold War, the act weakened New Deal forces in lasting ways. It tied the hands of labor political activists and effectively kept industrial unions from organizing the South. Taft-Hartley outlawed or limited many of the tools that had leveled the playing field between labor and capital, such as closed shops, the right to strike, and the ability of white-collar workers to form unions. Allowing states to pass their own antiunion laws, it also produced a purge of left-wing union leaders—those who worked hardest to make the labor movement a power for wider social justice along with better wages and hours.

All of this provides vital context for understanding the conservative movement that assembled in the 1950s. The Right's thinkers trumpeted "liberty," but they aligned with the opponents of workers' rights and the defenders of segregation. Indeed, although *National Review* was founded in the same year as the Montgomery bus boycott led by the Reverend Martin Luther King Jr., only one leading conservative (Garry Wills) responded positively to African Americans' quest for fair treatment—and he quit the movement within a few years. With stunning uniformity, right-wing intellectuals in the 1950s and 1960s refused to recognize the unfreedom of the nation's largest minority as a problem in need of correction, even as other white Americans began to.

How could a movement for freedom and against big government fail to object to the state-sponsored repression of a large section of the citizenry? Because conservatives defined the liberty they cherished in precise and narrow ways: above all, as autonomy for property owners. On both sides of the Mason-Dixon Line, they understood liberty as the nation's slave-owning founders had. They viewed it as essential to the preservation of republican institutions, yet something only certain men were fit to exercise. That was why conservatives consistently backed employers in conflicts with labor, urged McCarthyite attacks on civil liberties, and sought to limit the rights of poorer Americans.

Moreover, the same U.S. history that upset African Americans emboldened conservatives to think that their interpretation of the founders' intentions was correct. The nation's dual origins in slavery and freedom imbued modern conservatives with a deep sense of cultural authenticity in their fight against democratic inclusion. They saw no problem in professing liberty while opposing the black freedom movement because they revered a tradition that silenced and subordinated blacks. "Integration," said a writer for *Modern Age*, another leading conservative journal, "is patently a radical departure from the explicit provisions of the contract between the states that established the federal union." "The Liberal propaganda machine," wrote Willmoore Kendall, Buckley's teacher at Yale and colleague at *National Review*, "never gives up on the desegregation issue in the South . . . the indispensable next step . . . in the leveling program to which . . . the Liberals are pledged."

Steeped in such beliefs, conservative movement builders actively influenced the outcome of the struggle for racial justice. Just when civil rights proponents were bringing a majority of Americans to see the need for reform, conservative leaders galvanized the will of those fighting to preserve white advantage over blacks by portraying their cause as an honorable pursuit. As the leading conservative historian, George Nash, acknowledges, "*National Review* was one of the very few journals receptive to the viewpoint of conservative white Southerners in the tempestuous decade after which it was founded."

Most scholars view the Supreme Court's *Brown v. Board of Education* decision outlawing racial segregation in public schools as a pivotal step toward full citizenship for all Americans. How did conservatives react? So often at odds on other questions, libertarians, cultural traditionalists, and anti-Communist hawks all agreed that *Brown* was an outrage. The leader praised for "fusion" of the rival factions, Frank Meyer, vividly expressed their consensus when he denounced the decision as a "rape of the Constitution." The fledgling conservative movement chose as one of its top spokespersons the Virginia newspaperman who was leading "massive resistance" to school desegregation, James Jackson Kilpatrick. As editor of the *Richmond News Leader*, Kilpatrick had attacked the Supreme Court and urged white southerners to fight implementation of its decision. Resurrecting John C. Calhoun's proslavery states' rights theory for use against integration, Kilpatrick exulted in how it was "catching fire across the lower South, because it's right." The head of the white Citizens' Councils of

Mississippi, an arch-segregationist organizer, praised Kilpatrick as "one of the South's most talented leaders." The *National Review* chose him as its featured voice on the civil rights movement, as Buckley and Kilpatrick united readers north and south behind a conservative vision that included upholding white supremacy against challenges from civil rights activists and their allies in government.

Some leading conservative intellectuals were unabashed in their denial that blacks deserved to be treated as full members of the polity. "The White community in the South," Buckley editorialized in 1957, "is entitled to take such measures as are necessary to prevail, politically and culturally, in the areas in which it does not predominate numerically." Why did he endorse the refusal of basic civil rights to blacks, such as the ability to vote and serve on juries, and wave away with derision "political abstractions" about "the rights of American citizens, born Equal" raised in objection to such racial tyranny? Whites were "the advanced race," insisted Buckley, so their "claims of civilization supersede those of universal suffrage." Willmoore Kendall similarly condemned liberals for their belief in "one-man one-equal-vote."

Across regional lines, conservative movement builders took for granted that segregating blacks from whites was natural. In the view of the most vocal, it was simply the "realistic" way for a society to handle two fundamentally different populations living side by side, one of which they believed to be inferior. Russell Kirk urged readers to consider "the immense problem which must exist when two races occupy the same territory." Donald Davidson, a *National Review* writer and Vanderbilt professor who led a Tennessee pro-segregation organization, argued that realism dictated that "the alien element" must "be strictly controlled" in order to ensure "democracy for white people." Buckley himself approached the white Citizens' Councils then working to crush the civil rights struggle as a fertile pool of potential *National Review* subscribers. Conservative political leaders including Barry Goldwater and the Texas Republican John Tower were guests on the *Citizens' Council Forum* talk show, where they joined its segregationist regulars.

Indeed, as the rest of the country was coming to look askance at the South's system of white racial privilege, conservatives held out the slave South and the Jim Crow South as models of their values in action. Richard Weaver, a leading conservative intellectual, effused over the region's devotion to what he called the "principle of exclusion" and an "aristocratic" social order and denounced what he described as the "heavy assault" on it "by Liberalism." Anthony Harrigan, another *National Review* writer, praised the South for its "essential conservatism" and "built-in power brake." To the

Michigan-based Russell Kirk, the South was "the citadel of tradition," the front line of defense for "civilization." "The South," he instructed his readers, "need feel no shame for its defense of beliefs that were not concocted yesterday."

Conservatives especially looked to the South for legitimacy for an interpretation of the Constitution they came to refer to as "original intent." As Felix Morley, one of the founders of the conservative journal *Human Events*, noted of elite white southerners' contribution, "to justify their part in the 'War Between the States' Southerners have had to study our constitutional history, and they are generally more familiar with it than are many in other sections of the country." It is largely forgotten today that the pioneers of so-called original intent jurisprudence were defenders of slavery in the antebellum era and its apologists thereafter. They used their "federalist" readings of the Constitution to limit what government could do for citizens. (As the historian Garry Wills has shown, this interpretation actually came from the anti-federalists who opposed ratification of the Constitution, not the document's advocates.) The Right enlisted its version of original intent to attack the New Deal state. As Frank Meyer later approvingly quoted Richard Weaver: "It took the study of John Calhoun to wake me up to a realization that a constitution is and should be primarily a negative document," that is, a restraint rather than an enabling framework. Conservative leaders wanted to turn the Supreme Court back to its habits in the Gilded Age and the 1920s, when it favored corporations and repelled Democratic attempts to aid workers seeking fair treatment as violations of the Constitution. Conservatives viewed the trend after 1937, when the Court accepted the New Deal, as the road to perdition.

Conservatives also expressed contempt for democratic modifications of the Constitution, particularly the Fourteenth Amendment. Enacted during Reconstruction to guarantee equal protection and due process to all citizens, the Fourteenth Amendment undergirded many subsequent reforms while the Fifteenth guaranteed voting rights to African American men. Explaining his support for white southerners' denial of civil rights to blacks, Buckley announced: "the Fourteenth and Fifteenth Amendments to the Constitution are regarded by much of the South as inorganic accretions to the original document, grafted upon it by victors-at-war by force." Such attacks on the legitimacy of the Fourteenth Amendment became a centerpiece of conservatives' advocacy of "authentic federalism." Today, most are more discreet, but as late as 1978, Henry Regnery, the leading conservative publisher in America, insisted that the Fourteenth Amendment had never "properly" become "part of the Constitution."

Even in these early years, an interesting pattern stands out: the southern white supremacists with whom *National Review* allied rarely referred to themselves as such. They simply called themselves "conservatives." Thus, when Regnery, a lifelong Midwesterner, invited James Kilpatrick to write *The Sovereign States*, a segregationist treatise, he described their shared convictions without regional modifiers as "the conservative point of view" on "constitutional problems as a result of the Supreme Court decision." Similarly, the Citizens' Council leader William J. Simmons portrayed his organization as "much more than a white supremacist group." It was, he said, "fundamentally the first stirrings of a conservative revolt in the country."

Conservatives usually wrapped commitment to white privilege in patriotism rather than regionalism. Many argued that the civil rights movement was a Communist front. Their hatred of Communism was sincere, as Donald Critchlow shows in his essay. But it was also eminently useful to block equal rights for blacks. When fair employment legislation was proposed for New York State in 1945, for example, the popular conservative columnist Westbrook Pegler insisted that "all such proposals . . . are the work of Communists and their kind." Within a few years, such thinking spread from the Right to the mainstream. "Of course," said the chair of a loyalty review panel in the postal service, "the fact that a person believes in racial equality doesn't *prove* that he's a Communist, but it certainly makes you look twice, doesn't it?" Most historians now concur that, as one summarized the pattern, "anticommunism proved invaluable to white supremacists during the 1940s and 1950s." Anti-Communism, moreover, enabled the blunting of global human rights when the conservative coalition in Congress stopped the United States from signing the U.N. Genocide Convention in 1948, which they feared would allow federal prosecution of lynching and action against Jim Crow.

Southern segregationists actively fostered the Red Scare to immunize white supremacy from democratic challenge. "The more national criticism of the region's racial institutions grew," historian Jeff Woods has demonstrated, "the more southern segregationists looked to anti-Communism to protect the traditional social order." Senator James Eastland of Mississippi, a leading segregationist in Congress, thus famously called the U.S. Supreme Court "pro-Communist" in the wake of *Brown*. Where the Texas-based Martin Dies established the House Un-American Activities Committee to fight the CIO in 1937, after the war Eastland set up the Internal Security Subcommittee. A plethora of state and local anti-Red initiatives followed in the South, of which Mississippi's State Sovereignty Commission was the most notorious. Woods concludes that "the southern red scare was in many ways a byproduct of the region's massive resistance to integration." Its target was less the Communist Party, which had few members in the South, than the anti-Communist NAACP, which had tens of thousands.

This is not to say that all conservatives bore a personal animus against African Americans. Certainly many did in these years; no doubt many did not. But what they may or may not have felt as individuals is beside the point, which is the side to which their shared convictions led them. Shoring up privilege of all kinds—not only race, but also class, national, gender, and religious privilege—by opposing those who fought to end it was hardwired into their cause by the logic of their core commitments, regardless of what was in their hearts. Conservatives disapproved all the democracy- and opportunity-promoting developments that had enabled the mounting challenge to racial hierarchy. The New Deal state; progressive labor unions; social gospel Christianity and prophetic Judaism; the right to organize mass direct-action protest; the popular movements for self-determination against colonialism in Africa, Asia, and Latin America—there was hardly a development that invigorated the civil rights movement that was not opposed by conservative spokespersons. Thus, even if not personally racist, they always lined up against the antiracist struggle.

Their project of rolling back the New Deal and returning America to the business domination of the Gilded Age and the 1920s drew them willy-nilly toward defense of white supremacy. American conservatives faced a particular challenge in a nation built on both racial slavery and popular self-government, because all philosophies whose advocates aspire to power have to explain the world as it exists, not simply depict the way they would like it to be. If capitalism was the perfect, self-regulating system and America's history was the blameless beacon they maintained, then how to explain persistent inequality such as that which the civil rights movement sought to correct?

After all, the civil rights movement aimed not just to wipe Jim Crow laws off the books but, as Martin Luther King Jr. put it in *Why We Can't Wait*, to win "concrete and prompt improvement" in the lives of African Americans. This drive to end their "financial servitude" inevitably led civil rights advocates toward alliances with the progressive wings of the Democratic Party and the labor movement—both forces hated by conservatives. King preached that the causes of "economic justice and the brotherhood of man" were indivisible. That was why he called in 1963 for "a broad-based and gigantic Bill of Rights for [All] the Disadvantaged," whites as well as blacks, in a domestic economic and social reconstruction effort analogous to the Marshall Plan that rebuilt Germany following World War II. As King explained during a strike by Memphis sanitation workers: "The fight of the Negro and of the underpaid worker is one situation in the United States. They go hand in hand. One won't advance without the other advancing." Nor could either advance without the aid of the federal government: there was no other force powerful enough to correct the injustices of centuries and equalize life chances.

To conservative eyes, however, such a social democratic approach looked like the slippery slope to the United States creating a Communist government. One activist in Young Americans for Freedom, the youth group launched by Buckley in 1960 to train conservative leaders, later put the clash this way: "Most blacks looked to the federal government to solve their problems. Most conservatives saw government as the problem." Unable to tolerate that challenge to their core beliefs, they had to come up with counterexplanations for the problems African Americans faced so as to refute the civil rights accounts that were winning many other whites to reform.

Consistently, conservatives found the causes of inequality not in American history and present-day practices, but in the victims themselves or their culture. Richard Weaver sneered at "the dogma that the Negro had the white man's nature and capacities." Claiming that blacks either lacked ability or failed to exert themselves, conservatives discounted the obstacles African Americans faced. The libertarian economist Henry Hazlitt thus insisted that "the market is color-blind" in 1964 in the face of study after study documenting pervasive bias against blacks. The finding that free enterprise operated unfairly defied such a core conservative axiom that believers had to find ways to rationalize inequality. "Most poor people in America today are poor because they want to be," summed up a *National Review* writer. "They cannot or will not compete." Instead, he claimed, "they make themselves the way they are by being lazy, uneducated, sick, undependable."

Like the conservatives of the late nineteenth century who embraced social Darwinism to justify the wealth and power of "robber barons," those of the postwar era excused the most glaring unfairness of their day by asserting that those who had the most were better by nature or tried harder. Attributing others' suffering to biology, some espoused racism by the most restrictive definition. Others pointed to culture, an approach that became ever more popular as biologically based racism lost legitimacy after the Holocaust. A campus leader of Young Americans for Freedom outlined the emerging emphasis on culture. "Part of the reason why so many Negroes have failed to achieve social and economic equality can be found in the discrepancy between their values and those of the industrial society around them." They "cling," he claimed, to "the stagnation of the tribe."

Whether the case was made via biology or culture, the practical import was the same. Conservatives lined up against the civil rights movement's quest for social justice. A scholarly study of contemporary public opinion regarding race thus concluded that the reason "why characterizations of blacks as irresponsible and lazy are so consequential" is "because *they supply the principle channel through which the influence of prejudice on whites' opinions about social welfare policy flows*" (emphasis in original). "The more conservative they perceive themselves to be," the authors summarized of the survey respondents, "the more negative are their images of blacks." Thus, all conservatives did not need to be racist for racism to advance their cause.

The Birmingham, Alabama, civil rights campaign of 1963 shows how hostility to civil rights and to liberal government were mutually reinforcing. In what Martin Luther King Jr. called "the toughest fight of our civil rights careers" conservatives backed Eugene "Bull" Connor, whose police force turned attack dogs against the nonviolent protestors. The same images of police cruelty that led President John F. Kennedy to declare civil rights an urgent "moral issue" led conservatives to opposite conclusions. "It is possible to pinpoint the time and place when the Negro movement became a revolution," opined the libertarian economist Murray Rothbard: "The time" was "May, 1963, the place, Birmingham, Alabama." Robert Bork, a conservative legal scholar, took the side of those he called the white "citizens" against the black "mob coercing and disturbing other private individuals in the exercise of their freedom." As fire hoses blasted children down city streets, Bork declared that for anyone to tell whites "that even as individuals they may not act on their racial preferences" was "unsurpassed ugliness."

Conservatives equated reform with appeasement. Rothbard wanted the struggle King led "crippled and defeated." Frank Meyer raged against the "sentimentality" of Kennedy's response to the "revolutionary situation" in Birmingham. Meyer praised the local police for having "successfully and humanely suppressed mob action." Buckley told his readers: "Repression is an unpleasant instrument, but it is absolutely necessary for civilizations that believe in order and human rights. I wish to God Hitler and Lenin had been repressed. And word should be got through to the non-violent avenger Dr. King, that in the unlikely event that he succeeds in mobilizing his legions, they will be most efficiently, indeed most zestfully, repressed." Conservative leaders simply could not abide a movement that made a convincing case for why the federal government must act in the interests of social justice.

Indeed, they mobilized to try to defeat the most important measure for racial equity since emancipation and Reconstruction: the Civil Rights Act of 1964. Support for it mounted as other Americans witnessed and finally understood the cruelty African Americans confronted. Yet not one prominent conservative movement leader approved of the Civil Rights Act, even when Senator Everett Dirksen at the eleventh hour brought his Republican colleagues in the Senate to vote for it. Quite to the contrary, the *National Review* publicized southern segregationists' arguments against it. James Kilpatrick wrote that the Civil Rights Act "would undermine the most precious rights of property." If "the citizen's right to discriminate" should "be destroyed, the whole basis of individual liberty is destroyed." "This precious right to discriminate," he insisted, "underlies our entire political and economic system." Echoing diehard segregationists, conservatives fulminated that legislation to outlaw unfair treatment would undermine liberty and the Constitution.

The conservatives lost the debate on the Civil Rights Act of 1964. The energetic coalition building and lobbying of civil rights activists and the political acumen of Lyndon Baines Johnson secured Senate passage of the Act by a vote of seventy-three to twenty-seven in July of 1964. Assuming the presidency after JFK was assassinated in Dallas in 1963, Johnson urged passage of the bill as a fitting memorial to Kennedy and "shoved in all my stack," as he later put it, to ensure passage.

By the end, white supremacist southern Democrats were nearly alone in the congressional opposition. One exception was the Republican U.S. senator from Arizona, Barry Goldwater. His fight against civil rights legislation, coming after his longtime backing of employers against unions, made him a hero to recalcitrant whites in the South who were eyeing the conservative movement with growing appreciation. Indeed, as far back as 1960 nearly all the Goldwater for President committees were formed in Dixie.

Thus, in the formative years of the conservative movement, its leaders' professed devotion to freedom sounded noble in theory, but in reality they sided with the most repressive men of power in American life. They backed businessmen who fought the application of democratic principles to their workplaces and defended autocratic fiefdoms under the banner of property rights. And they allied with southern segregationists who used those same principles to shore up a dictatorial system of white supremacy under the mantle of states' rights.

Organizers of the conservative movement reviled Franklin Delano Roosevelt and Lyndon Baines Johnson, the two twentieth-century presidents who did the most to promote economic security and social justice for all Americans. LBJ, shown here as a twenty-eight-year-old congressman-elect meeting his idol, FDR, envisioned his own Great Society programs as an extension of the New Deal. (Courtesy of the Associated Press)

AMASSING A GRASSROOTS FOLLOWING, 1964–1980

The events of 1964, above all the Senate civil rights debate and the election season that followed, galvanized the conservative movement. These events changed it from the project of relatively isolated intellectuals allied with diehard segregationists into a mass cause with a popular base strong enough, in time, to win elections that changed the country. For several years prior to 1964, in fact, a grassroots political right had been growing among middle- and upper-class whites, notably in new Sun Belt suburbs such as Orange County, California. Its participants avidly consumed the books and articles of the intellectual conservatives. They, too, believed that the centrist Republican president, Dwight D. Eisenhower, and his Democratic successor, John F. Kennedy, enabled the spread of Communism abroad and socialism at home. When grassroots conservatives first organized in the early 1960s they focused on local issues but the Civil Rights Act controversy drew their attention to national power.

With the 1964 election looming, conservatives at all levels turned to electoral activism. Defeating their moderate rivals for control of the Republican Party, they made Barry Goldwater its presidential candidate in 1964. In the limelight for his outspoken opposition to the Civil Rights Act, Goldwater was also a militant anti-Communist and a longtime enemy of the CIO. A pioneer of antiunion right-to-work laws, he had in the late 1950s called industry-wide bargaining by unions "an evil to be eliminated." He depicted the social justice–minded auto workers' leader Walter Reuther as "a more dangerous menace than the Sputnik or anything Soviet Russia might do in America." The federal minimum wage, he said, constituted "tampering with the natural laws of our free enterprise system." Denying the validity of *Brown v. Board of Education*, Goldwater said, "I am firmly convinced—not only that integrated schools are not required—but that the Constitution does not permit any interference whatsoever by the federal government in the field of education." His backers found the prevailing acceptance of the New Deal, civil rights, graduated income taxes, and multilateralism in foreign policy all to be anathema.

The Right aimed well in veering to the South to change the country because nowhere was Goldwater received as enthusiastically as in Dixie, where he derided the Texan Lyndon Johnson as a "counterfeit Confederate." At the San Francisco GOP convention where the conservative Republicans took over, one newspaper headline summarized, "Negro Delegates to GOP Convention Suffer Week of Humiliation." By a vote of more than two to one, the convention renounced the civil rights stands the party had endorsed in 1960. A New Jersey delegate reported that black delegates "had been shoved, pushed, spat on, and cursed with a liberal sprinkling of racial epithets." Jackie Robinson, the baseball Hall of Fame player who had integrated the major leagues and was a longtime Republican, emerged from the encounter saying, "I now believe I know how it felt to be a Jew in Hitler's Germany." After the convention, wrote one scholar, the southern state Republican parties began "systematically purging blacks," long their most loyal supporters. In South Carolina, Strom Thurmond, who had organized the "Southern Manifesto" of segregationist congressmen in opposition to *Brown v. Board of Education*, converted to the GOP in 1964. His radio ads announced, "A vote for Barry Goldwater is a vote to end judicial tyranny." The Republican Right's campaign so inflamed the region that President Johnson had to avoid visiting it to avert assassination attempts.

For all that Goldwater as a western libertarian differed from southern segregationists like Kilpatrick and Thurmond, Martin Luther King concluded that Goldwater was "the most dangerous man in America." Goldwater had attacked the Civil Rights Act as "special appeals for special

The 1964 Republican convention occurred toward the end of Freedom Summer, a student-led civil rights push in Mississippi. In just ten weeks, four civil rights workers were murdered, eighty volunteers were beaten, and thirty-seven churches were bombed or burned. Through it all, Barry Goldwater continued his opposition to the Civil Rights Act, which activists like these protesters at the convention viewed as the only way to end racial terrorism by the Ku Klux Klan. (Courtesy of Corbis)

welfare." "Our right of property," Goldwater insisted, "is probably our most sacred right" and now it would be subject to "a federal police force of mammoth proportions." King warned that Goldwater "talked soft and nice," using color-blind language, "but he gave comfort to the most vicious racists and most extreme rightists in America." Johnson thrashed Goldwater at the polls, winning a stunning victory. He garnered three of every five popular votes and more than nine times as many electoral college votes. Yet Johnson knew that the nation's electoral map would never be the same. The night he steered the Civil Rights Act to passage, he told an aide, "I think we just delivered the South to the Republican Party for my lifetime and yours."

He was right. In an omen of the regional party realignment on the horizon, the only states Goldwater won besides his own Arizona were in the Deep South. A majority of whites there found his opposition to the Civil Rights Act so appealing that they shifted the axis of the Republican Party south. The Goldwater-Johnson contest, said Trent Lott, the Mississippi-based later Republican Senate majority leader, was "the first time that we really started thinking, 'Gee, maybe we are Republicans.'" In his once solidly Democratic state of Mississippi, 87 percent of voters, still overwhelmingly white, took the same leap—in every one of the state's eighty-two counties. In fact, only one since 1964 has a Democratic presidential candidate carried the South. As a Goldwater biographer wrote of 1964: "A power shift had occurred that signaled the rise of a western-southern coalition and the decline of the East in Republican Party politics. The new conservative elite rejected Modern Republicanism's acceptance of New Deal social programs, the activist role of the federal government, and the importance of the black vote." Goldwater's campaign thus began the transformation of his party into the electoral arm of the conservative movement.

The Goldwater campaign energized that movement like nothing before. It taught conservatives how to organize, as it inspired potential members to get off their couches. It may have lost at the polls, but it attracted twenty-seven million voters and more volunteers (3.9 million) than any previous candidacy. Goldwater staked out a strong right-wing stance and stuck with it doggedly, to the delight of his backers, on every issue from civil rights to Vietnam, where he urged the use of atomic weapons. He disdained Social Security as encroaching socialism. He attacked the very idea of a War on Poverty as "the Santa Claus of the free lunch, the government hand-out." He expressed the established conservative explanation for poverty with gusto: "We are told that many people lack skills and cannot find jobs because they do not have an education. That's like saying that people have big feet because they wear big shoes. The fact is that most people who have no skill, have no education for the same reason—low intelligence or low ambition." Such talk lifted the morale of several million grassroots white voters tired of feeling defensive about privileges they believed to be rightfully theirs. Goldwater revived their fighting spirit.

The campaign illustrated, too, where conservatives' antipathy to government took them in the practical terms of the day. The mainstream Right had always been a coalition of varied ideological tendencies: militant anti-Communists alongside libertarians and traditionalists who eyed one another with some wariness. Although libertarians rarely backed white supremacy the way traditionalists such as Richard Weaver or Russell Kirk did, their conservative convictions led them to ally with the powers that enforced it. Milton Friedman, for example, the libertarian economist newly famous for his 1962 book *Capitalism and Freedom*, advised Barry Goldwater on economic policy in the campaign. Friedman, like Goldwater, personally disavowed racism. Yet the year after *Brown v. Board of Education* mandated public school desegregation, Friedman unveiled a school voucher program to enable parents to use tax monies to send their children to private schools. No one appreciated his idea more than southern white supremacists, who were deserting public schools in droves for private white academies and newly founded Christian schools. Mississippi led the way: ten years after the court's decision, only .02 percent of its black children attended school with white children. Neither Friedman nor other libertarians spoke out against this; they viewed it as an exercise of "choice" on the white parents' part. Nor did Friedman renounce the candidate who said Republicans should "hunt where the ducks are," which was to say, scour the South for white voters furious at Lyndon Johnson for embracing racial justice.

But the recalcitrant southerners weren't merely waiting to be bagged by northern and western hunters; they were actively shaping the larger conservative cause. They helped write the arch-conservative 1964 Republican platform, for example. Thereafter, they worked to bring the national movement and the party around to their way of seeing. Those who joined up from the Goldwater campaign made conservatism less an intellectual affair and more a popular movement of men and women who were often activists in local and state politics. With the infusion of their energies, the rhetoric of the movement turned away from the elitism that was once its proud signature and toward a new kind of populism, a shift sometimes characterized as country club to Main Street.

Yet the new approach was racially coded from the outset. Still appealing to prejudice and fear, it made "middle class," "law and order," and "family values" synonymous with white, and it made "welfare," "crime," and "family breakdown" synonymous with black. In 1969 Kevin Phillips summarized what he saw as the lessons of recent years for the building of, as his book title put it, *The Emerging Republican Majority*. He prescribed a "populist conservatism" to turn white working-class uneasiness over "the Negro socioeconomic revolution," as he called it, into defection from the Democrats. Racial conflict, he showed, had split open the New Deal coalition. It created openings for the Republicans not only in the South, but also in the North among white ethnics such as Irish, Polish, and Italian Americans. Phillips used poll numbers to demonstrate how the GOP could lose African Americans and still win elections if it reframed its message. "The new popular majority is white and conservative," he counseled, but it must be a "New Right" to succeed, one that renounced class elitism to fight liberalism in the name of the people. "The fulcrum of ideological gain is not adherence to classic conservatism," he elaborated, "but rather hostility toward the emerging liberal elite of amorality activists and social-change merchants." Heeding Phillips, *National Review* publisher William Rusher reached out to Alabama politician George Wallace as "the leading spokesman of social conservatism." Rusher wanted to win Wallace's following for a new conservative "majority party." It would unite white "middle Americans and hyphenated ethnics" against "establishment WASPs plus their minority group allies." "The whole secret of politics," as Kevin Phillips explained their approach, is "knowing who hates who."

Adopting a folksy style, the conservative movement appeared to surrender its earlier disdain for working-class people. Where once it purported that only a small group was fit to rule, now it embraced a rebel vocabulary. "We are no longer working to preserve the status quo," said the political marketing innovator Richard Viguerie, "we are radicals working to overthrow the power structure of this country." Viguerie volunteered to organize Wallace's direct mail campaigns, raising some $7 million from 1973 to 1976. But unlike the original Populists of the 1890s, who fought wealthy and powerful interests that held down the real producers, conservative populists did not take aim at corporations or the rich. "Populist dissent today," boasted one conservative, "is directed against liberal politics," those "committed to equality."

Conservatives made the phrase "liberal elite" one of the staples of their rhetoric. They hated liberals for allying with the poor, the excluded, and the unjustly treated. The premier example was Earl Warren, the chief justice of the U.S. Supreme Court over the years 1953–1969. The Warren Court, summarized one legal historian, was the first to stand for "equality of treatment as a necessary precondition of democracy." Warren's court opened the full promise of democracy to underdogs long denied a fair hearing, from black students deprived of equal education to Jewish youth forced to participate in Christian prayer and Bible reading at school, to criminal suspects abused by police, to city dwellers whose political representation was held down by voting systems stacked to favor agricultural interests. For these decisions, conservatives despised Earl Warren. As one conservative chronicler of the movement put it, gently, "dismay at the Warren Court was integral to American conservatism."

Seen in their historical context, the populist pitches made by the Right showed psychological savvy. Americans are by and large fair-minded people who do not like bullies. Most voters would recoil from a candidate who frontally attacked the poor or non-Christians or black children or residents of cities. However, portraying the source of trouble not as the vulnerable themselves, but as a "liberal elite" who cynically use the vulnerable to gain power for itself has a very different effect. It seeks the same ends, but by a less repellent route. It could even make listeners feel courageous for opposing egalitarian policies. Being democratically minded, most Americans (even wealthy Americans) instinctively distrust "elites," a term that conjures up a vision of ill-gained advantage, of surly snobs who would lord their power over others as the British Crown once did. To call people elite in the United States is thus to put them under automatic suspicion. Some middle-class liberals and radicals did condescend to working-class whites in this era, and government agencies sometimes did tie people up in stupid red tape, which gave the allegations plausibility. But conservatives' purpose in attacking "liberal elites" was to block measures for equal rights and economic justice.

The commitment to safeguard privilege could be seen in the cruel responses of some conservatives to the assassination of Martin Luther King in April 1968, as the rest of the nation, white and black, reeled in shock at the murder of the apostle of nonviolence. "The entire communications media," complained the *New Guard*, the magazine of the Buckley-sponsored Young Americans for Freedom, "paid unqualified tribute to Dr. King." "King was a collectivist" who failed to respect the rights of property, it charged. What King advocated was "what the looters did" in the riots that followed his death, "except that he advocated the government do it" with "stupid legislation" for "handouts." The man was "a lawbreaker" who did not deserve "the prevailing tone of praise." That summarized, if crudely, the conservative movement's contemporary assessment of America's foremost civil rights leader.

Yet its approach was about to change. Like most effective social movements, this one was capable of learning from experience, and its best strategists were smart men. Some of them began to see that arguing their case in such ugly ways was alienating potential supporters, backers they needed if they were ever to build an electoral majority for change. To continue selling their program in terms of property rights, anti-Communism, and racial aggression after the moral awakening the nation had been through in the 1960s was to embrace permanent marginality.

Veteran conservatives discovered better ways of conceiving and packaging their cause from a group of new recruits in the second half of the 1960s: intellectuals who came to be known as neoconservatives. Many were Jewish and once liberal. They disdained racism of the raw variety then seen on the Right, and they understood better how to address the millions of uneasy ethnic Americans wavering between liberalism and conservatism. The most distinguished neoconservatives were professors such as the philosopher Sidney Hook and the sociologist Nathan Glazer, who gave the cause gravitas. But the movers and shakers were Irving Kristol, a senior editor at Basic Books, and Norman Podhoretz, editor of *Commentary* magazine. Already actively anti-Communist in the 1950s, they moved to the right in the 1960s out of fear for the future of Israel and anger over the era's radical upheavals. The radical campus protests and black liberation struggles at home and the anticolonial movements of the so-called Third World often sympathized with the USSR and Communist China and criticized Israel's treatment of the Palestinians. The popular New Left slogan "question authority" epitomized the young radicals' attitude toward established institutions that men of Hook and Kristol's generation held dear. Angry at the young leftists, the neoconservatives turned on mainstream liberalism too, seeing it as too "permissive." By 1968 Kristol had a column in the business magazine *Fortune*; in 1970 he joined a lunch group with William F. Buckley that they called "the Boys Club"—in the process signaling their disdain for the spreading women's movement.

With *Commentary* and a new publication called *The Public Interest* to spread their ideas, the neoconservatives articulated a distinctive politics grounded in avid backing for the United States in the Cold War and for Israel in the Middle East, and attacks on the New Left at home. Seeing the postwar coalition between Jewish organizations and African American civil rights groups as no longer desirable, neoconservatives sought to end it. They reached out to gentile white conservatives who were delighted at the intellectual firepower they brought to fights against affirmative action, school busing, and other forms of proactive desegregation. Kristol, Podhoretz, and their fellows began developing a new way of framing conservatism that embraced classic nineteenth-century liberal ideals of freedom, above all market freedom, and discarded the biology-based racism and mourning for a lost golden age characteristic of traditionalist conservatives such as Richard Weaver and Russell Kirk. (The latter's disciples in time came to be called paleo-conservatives to signal their differences from neoconservatives.)

With the guidance of neoconservatives, longtime movement builders on the Right changed their rhetoric notably over the 1970s, not least in embracing calls for "color-blindness." William F. Buckley was among the old-timers who began framing conservatism as a defense of old-fashioned, pre–New Deal liberalism. By 1974 James Kilpatrick spoke of "contemporary Conservatives" as "old-fashioned 18th Century Liberals" who believed that "'equality' ought not to be achieved by state coercion." Discovering that color-blind, market-based arguments could now achieve nearly the same ends as their earlier defense of state-backed white power, conservatives dropped their now unpopular racialist arguments. The change in tactics was on display when James Buckley, William's younger brother, ran for the U.S. Senate as the Conservative Party of New York's candidate in 1970. He attacked those he called the "affirmative action shock troops" and pronounced their efforts "wrong, wrong, wrong." The policy, he said, went against "everything that the civil rights movement has sought to achieve." Condemning what he branded as "reverse discrimination," the senator declared that it "rewarded the untalented or lazy."

Clearly, the rhetorical turn had not lessened the underlying hostility. Indeed, even former segregationists could defend privilege with a new feeling of innocence by redefining it, no longer as an inherited racial prerogative but rather as an earned economic right to better housing, schools, and other goods. "I am getting to be like the Catholic convert," marveled Jack Kilpatrick, "who became more Catholic than the Pope." "If it is wrong to discriminate by reason of race or sex," he chastised an affirmative action supporter, "well, then, it is wrong to discriminate by reason of race or sex." The best defense being a good offense, Kilpatrick claimed "the egalitarians" were "worse racists—much worse racists—than the old Southern bigots." Appropriating civil rights language for such rhetorical jujitsu attacks was thus a calculated conservative strategy. In *Mandate for Leadership*, the Heritage Foundation later explained, "For twenty years, the most important battle in the civil rights field has been for control of language," particularly words such as "equality" and "opportunity." "The secret to victory, whether in court or in congress, has been to control the definition of these terms."

Even as conservatives trained their spokespersons to portray their cause in more appealing terms, however, the underlying chauvinism remained. It was unabashed in their reactions to the national liberation movements of the 1970s. While conservatives were criticizing U.S. civil rights measures in the name of color-blindness, they fought against color-blindness for Africa. They supported colonial governments practicing racial exclusion and segregation so as to keep blacks from power in southern Africa in particular. Discussing Zimbabwe in *National Review* in 1978, James Burnham saw nothing wrong in a situation in which "white votes will count more than black votes." Earlier in the decade, Burnham had proposed South African apartheid as a good model for U.S. race relations. Its "Bantustans," he wrote, offered a "more promising" way to handle black demands than "forced integration." Thus, the Right's color-blindness required neither a change of heart nor consistent application. Quite the contrary. Well after announcing his conversion, James Kilpatrick in 1984 privately chided one correspondent who criticized his support for the apartheid regime that if she were a white South African, she "would be repelled by the thought of surrendering every public institution to black domination" via the adoption of color-blind equal rights.

As challenges to established privileges mounted on the home front from other groups long denied fair treatment, beginning with women, movement conservatives again took the side of those privileged by prevailing law and practice. Antifeminism ran deep on the Right. Recent historians have exposed the male supremacy rife among conservative anti-Communists in the postwar period, who attacked professional women and homosexuals in government as examples of all that was wrong with the New Deal and Fair Deal. But in the formative era of conservative movement building leading up to the mid-1960s, feminism was less publicly visible and so drew little attention. That changed as the women's movement grew and won congressional passage of the Equal Rights Amendment in 1972 and the legalization of abortion in 1973. Phyllis Schlafly, an attorney by training and a long-term conservative activist, organized a countermovement as she discovered how many white middle- and working-class people were feeling anxiety about changes in family life, gender, and sexuality.

Numerous forces were altering American families. With the postwar economic boom coming to an end and new competition from abroad, U.S. businesses began restructuring. They eliminated more and more of the jobs that had enabled men with limited educations to earn enough to support their wives as full-time homemakers, and started cutting wages and benefits too. The new economy also demanded more education, which meant college tuition payments to equip kids for a decent living. By the 1970s, millions of families were feeling the pinch and fearing for their children's futures. Not only married women but also mothers of small children felt they had to get paying jobs to make ends meet. Divorce, meanwhile, had become more and more common. The women's movement was one response to the demise of the male-breadwinner family. Those who became feminists responded hopefully to the challenges of the era, turning them into an opportunity to promote women's development, more egalitarian relations between the sexes, and a fairer society with more fulfillment for all. Optimistic as they were, they sometimes failed to realize that they were challenging male privileges and gender norms built up over centuries, so some fear and anxiety was inevitable, especially among older people.

Schlafly's strategic genius was to realize that millions of middle-aged women saw danger, not promise, in independence. They had invested their lives in the expectation of being full-time housewives whose husbands would support them into old age, "til death do us part." From their perspective, the new autonomy—male and female—looked threatening. So, too, for many orthodox Catholics and evangelicals did the new cultural emphasis on sexual pleasure. It affronted their religious belief that the purpose of sex was procreation within marriage. And what of their sons' and daughters' futures in a world where the gender rules were no longer clear? Parents struggling to stay afloat in scary times were in no mood for risky experiments.

Seeing how enthusiastically some conservative white homemakers responded to a criticism of feminism, Schlafly in 1972 started a new organization called STOP ERA. Over the next decade, it encouraged housewives to feel threatened by the women's movement and the gender equity it sought. Feminism, Schlafly told homemakers, would undermine "the rights women already have," above all, "the right to be a housewife." "Why," she demanded, "should we lower ourselves to equal rights when we already have the status of special privilege?" The women's movement, she warned, would destroy the family and harm those who depended on it most: women and children. Other conservatives asserted that the women's movement, in the phrasing of *Human Events* magazine, was "wall-to-wall weirdos" and "loaded with lesbians." By portraying those seeking gender justice as the enemies of homemakers, conservatives engaged in a sleight of hand akin to their attribution of racial justice to a white liberal elite. It was a gross distortion, but effective. Seeing the political gain to be had, the GOP in 1980 reversed its forty-year support of the Equal Rights Amendment. As with civil rights, so with feminism: Conservatives correctly saw in the new

Phyllis Schlafly, a longtime activist in the Goldwater wing of the Republican Party, showed party leaders the galvanizing power of gender issues when she built a mass antifeminist movement against the Equal Rights Amendment. Shown here at a 1978 rally in the Illinois State Capitol rotunda, Schlafly persuaded many middle-aged white churchgoers, in particular, that the women's movement aimed to take away "the right to be a housewife." (Courtesy of Corbis)

movement a challenge to old hierarchies and an extension of New Deal principles and methods of reform into a new area. Their leaders exploited anxiety about family security without providing remedies that might actually help ease the strains on families.

In one notable instance, they killed a historic child care initiative for working families. Led by civil rights veteran Marian Wright Edelman, a broad-based liberal and feminist coalition persuaded Congress to pass the Comprehensive Child Development Act in 1971. It laid the groundwork for public, universally accessible child care that would have benefitted middle-class as well as poor families while enhancing children's learning capacity. Conservatives mobilized to defeat it. James Kilpatrick editorialized that the bill was "the boldest and most far-reaching scheme ever advanced for the Sovietization of American youth." *Human Events* screamed that "Big Brother Wants Your Children." "We thought it would become an entitlement that would explode in the future," recalled the American Conservative Union lobbyist leading the effort, so "we wanted to drive a stake through its heart." Illustrating how class elitism, racial chauvinism, and antifeminism reinforced one another, the conservative congressman John Ashbrook argued that one of the worst dangers of the child care plan was that "the socioeconomic and race mix of students would reach its greatest potential under this legislation." Patrick Buchanan, a Goldwater conservative who became a speechwriter for President Nixon, warned that "what we don't want is a national system of child-care centers" in which government "clowns" can issue guidelines on "what the racial make-up of each center ought to be."

Buchanan crafted a veto speech for President Nixon that aimed to kill the legislation while ingratiating Nixon with the Goldwater wing of the Republican Party. Denouncing the bill as a "radical piece of social legislation," Nixon said it threatened a "keystone of our civilization." Child rearing should be done by parents, not "communal approaches." Never after that veto did the U.S. government again support broad child care legislation. According to one of the law's proponents, "those attacks poisoned the well for early childhood programs for a long time—indeed, ever since." Thereafter, while wealthier families could purchase high-quality private attention for their children, middle-income and wage-earning families usually had to struggle to secure good child care arrangements.

At the same time that they were working to block child care provisions, conservatives also began organizing against legalized abortion, another prime goal of the women's movement. Seventeen states had already decriminalized abortion prior to the Supreme Court's *Roe v. Wade* decision in 1973, in deference to the counsel of the medical profession on the dangers of illegal abortion and to the nascent feminist movement's persuasive arguments that women needed the right to decide whether and when to bear children and should not have to risk their lives or undergo humiliation if they concluded they needed to terminate a pregnancy. In the view of many religious conservatives, however, *Roe v. Wade* seemed to give the imprimatur of federal authority to a practice they saw as sinful, and to sexual license more generally, by removing a potent deterrent to nonmarital intercourse. The orthodox correctly saw that sexual freedom for women and more egalitarian and flexible gender roles for both sexes would indeed change the traditional male-dominant family structure. The more feminists pushed for equality and autonomy for women, the angrier religious conservatives became over abortion as practice and as symbol.

The Catholic Church, already concerned about rising rates of divorce and birth control usage, responded to *Roe* by establishing a National Right to Life Committee to rally parishioners to fight abortion. Evangelicals debated longer on how to understand abortion but ultimately identified it, in the words of historian Scott Flipse, "as the most prominent symbol of moral disintegration and the breakdown of familial strength." That reading brought evangelicals together with Catholics as never before. Still, it took some work from conservative movement strategists to persuade Republican leaders to take up the issue. As New Right builder Paul Weyrich later complained, "the Republican Party is, in many parts of the country, an elitist social club which does not take kindly to association with the lower middle class, with precisely those people . . . most concerned with family issues." But as abortion showed the power to bring such voters out to the polls, party leaders came around. By 1980 the GOP became an arm of the antiabortion cause and home to mounting numbers of religious Right voters.

At the same time, the gay liberation movement was gaining momentum, and here, too, conservative leaders lined up in opposition. In 1977 the city council of Miami, Florida, issued the South's first human rights ordinance banning discrimination against gays and lesbians. Some southern Baptist leaders and their members were appalled. Among them was Anita Bryant, a former beauty pageant winner and spokesperson for the Florida Citrus Commission, known to millions from her widely aired television commercials proclaiming "breakfast without orange juice is like a day without sunshine." Bryant founded an organization called Save Our Children to collect signatures for repeal of the Miami human rights measure. As the name suggested, Bryant built on hateful stereotypes, even calling homosexuals "human garbage." Save Our Children spread fear that gays aimed to "recruit" children and could not be trusted. It worked. Voters repealed the ordinance.

Bryant's fight to preserve discrimination against homosexuals taught conservative leaders still another way to build their base among the millions of newly politicized conservative Christian voters that also accorded with their own values and prejudices. A year later, a California state senator named John Briggs proposed a measure to drive lesbians and gay men from school teaching. Although defeated, it made the antigay backlash a popular cause. Since 1974, more than fifty antigay ballot initiatives have succeeded. Seeing the potential to advance the larger conservative agenda, right-wing strategists such as Paul Weyrich of the Free Congress Foundation began in the 1980s to produce and mass market antigay tracts. They exploited fear of AIDS as "a gay plague" to turn voters against basic citizenship rights for gay men and lesbians. William F. Buckley in 1986 called for gay men with AIDs to be tattooed "on the buttocks, to prevent the victimization of other homosexuals" as he sought to defeat a bill to prohibit discrimination on the basis of sexual orientation. Rev. Jerry Falwell portrayed the illness as divine punishment for homosexuality. "You cannot shake your fist in God's face and get away with it," he told a national television audience in 1983. Such blame-the-victim thinking greatly delayed a national public health response to the AIDS crisis in the crucial first decade.

As the Republican Party and its religious right supporters inflamed homophobia for political advantage, they encouraged a climate of hatred that other conservatives, such as this man at a 1998 antigay rally in Columbia, Missouri, expressed more crudely. (Courtesy of Corbis)

In the early 1990s, contradicting long-standing conservative calls for states' rights, the American Family Association pushed a constitutional amendment to deny states the right to prohibit discrimination against lesbians and gay men. Begun toward the end of the 1980s and continuing today, this strategic drive for antigay laws and ballot initiatives, as one study puts it, "seeks to delegitimize not only gay people, but civil rights themselves." A primary tool for the Republicans to get religious conservative voters to the polls, the campaigns broadcast the falsehood that such rights, as one conservative slogan puts it, "are special rights"—just as Barry Goldwater had earlier condemned the Civil Rights Act as "special appeals for special welfare."

Discovering the mobilizing potential of conservative religious faith in turbulent times, conservatives began more systematically reaching out to unify and amplify what became known as the Religious Right. Some were deeply sincere churchgoers themselves, including Buckley, who attended mass regularly. "Conservatism," he maintained from early on, was "planted in a religious view of man." Yet just as they embraced a narrow and exclusive conception of liberty, so conservatives backed only certain types of religion—and sought to discredit others. The religious traditions with which they allied exalted orthodoxy and obedience, instilled feelings of superiority in believers, and promoted harsh judgment and stigma for those they deemed sinners, including both nonbelievers and people of other faiths. Back in 1950 Ernest van den Haag, a future ally of Buckley's on the *National Review* staff, had explained the instrumental value of religion this way: "Religious sanction is required—just as the police force is—for any society which wishes to be stable without being totalitarian." The conservative theorist Richard Weaver, for his part, described the public significance of belief in original sin as "a severe restraint upon democracy." Their enthusiasm was rewarded when early clerical allies such as Christian Crusade founder Billy James Hargis preached that the civil rights Freedom Summer of 1964 in Mississippi was a Communist plot and the Rev. Bob Jones Jr. campaigned for Goldwater under the slogan "Turn Back America."

In contrast, leading conservatives reviled then-popular faith traditions that urged followers to be humble, practice brotherhood, enact mercy, seek peace, and pursue justice. "Social gospel" Protestants, liberal Catholics, and Reform Jews had all played vital roles in labor reform and civil rights. Without their pressure on midwestern Republican power brokers in Congress such as Everett Dirksen of Illinois, the Civil Rights Act would never have passed, nor would many other progressive measures of the postwar era.

In 1979 the conservative strategists Paul Weyrich and Richard Viguerie expressly set out to construct a "reverse coalition" to contest the authority that such ecumenical liberals wielded in public life. Weyrich and Viguerie visited the Virginia fundamentalist Baptist minister and televangelist Jerry Falwell to urge him to form an organization to be called the Moral Majority. Weyrich soon boasted that thanks to "the new breed of religious leader" like Falwell, Catholics were "working with fundamentalist/evangelicals, for example, in the right-to-life movement rather than with liberal Protestants boycotting grapes with Cesar Chavez." Steering churches away from social justice causes like the farm workers' movement, Falwell's organization then harnessed the energy stirred by the fights against the ERA, abortion, and homosexuality to promote tax cuts for the wealthy, aggressive military action overseas, opposition to civil rights measures, and so on. The fact that long-standing segregationist Mississippians led in the development of Christian conservatism and church-based schools suggests motives other than divine inspiration. Two experts in survey research explained the political import of the values the Religious Right cultivates: "An enormous body of research has demonstrated that people who attach an uncommon importance to obedience and discipline tend to be harsh and judgmental, to be relatively unsympathetic and ungenerous, particularly in responding to others who are unfamiliar to them or different in background or belief or appear to deviate from conventional standards of morality." The Republican Right aimed well in targeting such voters.

By 1977 one study found over seventy million Americans describing themselves as "born-again" Christians. Many such conservative Protestants had been upset at the federal government at least since the Supreme Court stopped school prayer in 1962, and grew more so when agitated by clergy such as Falwell. Not all evangelicals moved to the Right; black evangelicals did not, for example, so race was a factor along with religion. But the majority of born-again whites became the most reliable conservative Republican voters, joined by growing numbers of Catholics, among whom a more conservative Vatican was enforcing antiabortion, antigay orthodoxy. Over the next two decades, combined movement, party, and church efforts persuaded millions of religiously active Americans who had once voted Democratic to stop. With more and more evangelical Protestants, Catholics, Mormons, and Orthodox Jews voting Republican, moreover, their houses of worship provided a potent organizing base for the GOP analogous to what CIO unions had been, in their heyday, for the Democrats.

At the same time the Republican Right was winning over religious conservatives, it was also gaining converts among corporations and wealthy Americans newly eager to change government policy. Most social scientists cite 1973 as the pivotal moment. That was when a deep recession set in, which by its end in 1975 proved to be the worst economic downturn since the Great Depression. It hit an economy already overheated by inflationary spending on Vietnam and stumbling in the face of mounting global competition. The result was the worst of both worlds of economic thinking: high inflation plus high unemployment, a condition dubbed "stagflation."

Some business leaders became persuaded that they needed to reverse the direction in which government had been headed, pushed by popular pressure to do more, first in the 1930s and 1940s, and then in the 1960s and 1970s. In particular, they wanted to stop—and even reverse—the growth of government regulation and citizen "entitlements" that came with President Johnson's Great Society, a series of programs intended to complete the New Deal. The progressive movements of the 1960s had won antidiscrimination laws, new protections for the environment, consumer product safety measures, workplace health and safety rules, and new government agencies to implement these commitments. In order to try to limit the impact of these reforms, which narrowed their freedom of operation and profit margins, business elites mobilized for political action and developed potent lobbying organizations such as the Business Roundtable and a revamped Chamber of Commerce.

One of those pushing greater business involvement in politics was the attorney and future Supreme Court justice Lewis Franklin Powell Jr. In a 1971 strategic memo that was later widely circulated in corporate circles, he suggested that the Chamber of Commerce enlist the help of the courts. "The judiciary," Powell noted, "may be the most important instrument for social, economic, and political change." He urged "business interests" to adopt "a more aggressive attitude" in shaping the courts and changing the culture and politics of the United States so as to uphold "free enterprise" against "the chorus of criticism" of their practices. It was coming, not just from the "extremists of the left," but "from perfectly respectable elements of society: from the college campus, the pulpit, the media, the intellectual and literary journals, the arts and sciences, and from politicians," who had all been criticizing the way big business operated. Persuaded that such action was to their advantage, powerful corporate interests set out to trim the sails of the New Deal state. Over the decade, the Chamber quadrupled its membership, tripled its budget, and became immensely influential in Washington. It was, as one pundit put it, "a revolt of the haves"—against the have-nots.

Such business leaders worked to change the terms of public debate by donating to media-savvy conservative think tanks. Most got their start in the early 1970s: first the Heritage Foundation, launched in 1973 with a half million dollars from beer magnate Adolph Coors (whose brewery was then being boycotted by Mexican Americans protesting discrimination), and in 1977 the Cato Institute and the Manhattan Institute for Policy Research. Those already established attracted far more generous funding, including the Hoover Institution, begun in 1919, and the American Enterprise Institute (AEI), founded in 1943. By 1979 the AEI had a staff of 160 and a budget of nearly $10 million. The more it pushed federal deregulation, the more corporate money the AEI drew. That expanding income, in turn, enabled it to reach voters and public officials through a television roundtable program, a weekly radio show aired by six hundred stations, op-ed articles in one hundred newspapers every few weeks, and fifteen staff scholars turning out conservative books and articles as a full-time job.

Mounting what one study described as "a sustained attack on the use of government money and regulation to solve social problems," the conservative think tanks called for "market solutions" to the nation's problems. As a *Business Week* editorial put the goal in 1974, "it will be a hard pill for many Americans to swallow—the idea of doing with less so that big business can have more." Hence the project needed to actively shape public opinion. Richard Viguerie, the conservative direct-mail expert, explained how the social issues and the corporate agenda worked together. "We talk about issues that people care about, like gun control, abortion, taxes, and crime. Yes, they're emotional issues, but that's better than talking about capital formation," a neutral-sounding phrase for the redistribution of money from working people to corporate investors. The issues that aroused strong feeling, in other words, helped build a following to advance the other, less popular, goals.

Seen against this history of a quarter century of alliance building to shore up privilege, Ronald Reagan's decision to launch his 1980 presidential bid from the Neshoba County Fair in Mississippi fits a larger pattern. It continued a well-honed strategy begun in 1964 when the Republican Right, in Goldwater's phrase, decided to "hunt where the ducks are." White supremacy and economic conservatism had long been mutually reinforcing commitments among rightward-leaning southern whites. Even those devoted to only one were seldom much troubled by the other. Conservatives thereafter looked to such white southerners as a pivotal voting block with which to gain power. Thanks to his appeals to the states' rights tradition, Reagan won white Mississippi voters by a landslide. His GOP became the undisputed home of those who never shed the biases that rationalized unfair advantages.

Ronald Reagan had a winning style and a better sense of humor than many movement builders on the Right ("a warmly ruthless man" was how one aide described him), but he was a thoroughgoing conservative. He had once Red-baited John F. Kennedy, writing to Richard Nixon in 1959: "Shouldn't one tag Mr. Kennedy's *bold new imaginative* program with its proper age? Under the tousled boyish hair cut it is still old Karl Marx." From then on, Reagan worked his way up the movement ladder, becoming conservatism's most popular electoral standard-bearer by the late 1960s. In his campaign for the California governorship in 1966, Reagan employed the movement's racialized populism by announcing his opposition to civil rights and open housing laws. Playing to racist stereotypes, he pledged that in the "Creative Society" for which he stood, there would be "no welfare benefits . . . for able-bodied persons who are too lazy to work." In case anyone missed the point, he noted that "many welfare recipients are members of minority groups." As governor, Reagan dismissed charges of police abuse of black and Latino citizens by announcing "the jungle is waiting to take over. The man with the badge helps to hold it back." After his victory at the polls, he cut funding for education, health, and welfare in California, though to his credit he opposed the antigay Briggs initiative. His 1980 presidential campaign tied antiwelfare, law-and-order commitments to conservative sexual and gender stances, and a vision of revived American power to police the wider world. Voters found Reagan appealing for varied reasons, of which the chief one was the weakness of the economy and the failure of the Carter administration to help those hurt by it. Reagan convincingly promised economic growth and patriotic strength; many who pulled the lever for him had little interest in the rest of the agenda.

Still, for conservative movement builders, the 1980 election was an epochal victory. Soon after moving into the White House, the new president spoke to a gala dinner of the nation's conservatives. In the audience were architects of such movement institutions as the *National Review*, the American Conservative Union, the Fund for a Conservative Majority, *Human Events*, *Conservative Digest*, and Young Americans for Freedom. Reagan exulted over "how far we have come" since Goldwater lost and the *National Review* was "ridiculed by the intellectual establishment." His own election signaled "a victory of ideas," said Reagan. But it was above all a triumph of divisive conservative movement strategy.

Reagan's base differed from the Republicanism that had prevailed until the 1960s. With the Sun Belt–based right wing of the party now dominant, GOP leaders felt little need for the East Coast "Rockefeller Republicans" who accepted the New Deal state and supported civil rights policies or even for the centrist Eisenhower Republicans. The most reliable voters now were hard-edged conservatives. "Few publications in Mississippi or America were more excited about Ronald Reagan's victory in 1980" than the magazine of the virulently racist white Citizens' Council, noted historian Joseph Crespino. "Whether it was Reagan's support for school prayer, his conservative positions on busing, welfare, women's rights, or the judiciary, the president's positions lined up remarkably well with those of the Citizen's Council."

USING POWER OVER GOVERNMENT, 1980 TO THE PRESENT

The inauguration of Ronald Reagan as the fortieth president indeed marked a new era, during which conservatives used their newfound power over government to try to roll back or at least limit and distort much of what it had done for ordinary citizens over the preceding fifty years. They particularly targeted efforts to undo inherited privileges and public harms and promote wider opportunity and inclusion through the use of government on the New Deal model. The new president had trumpeted moral issues in his campaign, such as support for school prayer and opposition to abortion. But once in office, he appointed no evangelicals to top positions. He focused on the economy and foreign policy, and buttressed business power in both realms. As one pundit put it, conservative leaders "may talk Christ, but they walk corporate." One of the first changes Reagan made in the White House was to hang up a portrait of Calvin Coolidge, the 1920s president famous for his insistence that "the chief business of Americans is business." The incoming president summed up his own ideology in his inaugural address: "Government is not the solution to our problem; government *is* the problem." He and the movement that brought him to the White House invited Americans to change their self-image from "citizen" to "taxpayer": from participants in the modern world's first democracy to suffering check-writers wanting, as the nation's new leader put it, "the government off our backs." "The minute any of you start to think of gov[ernmen]t as we, instead of as they," the president told his own appointees, "we will have begun to lose the fight . . . [to] drain [the] swamp."

The first priority of the Reagan administration was to cut taxes for corporations and the very wealthy. Reagan's concerns were those of the major investors in his party, also the prime beneficiaries of such cuts. Contrary to the myth that Reaganism was driven by popular demand, public opinion remained highly supportive of New Deal and even Great Society domestic policies. What political scientists do find is a lurch right on the part of the corporations and other wealthy donors with the power to drive the agendas of the two major political parties, and particularly the Republican Party. Reagan's 1981 tax cuts more than halved the marginal tax rates on corporate income, dropping them to the lowest level in four decades. The top tax rate for the richest Americans was cut from 70 percent in the 1970s to 28 percent in 1986, and the tax on unearned inherited wealth was also drastically reduced. To make up the shortfall in income, the Reagan administration cut social programs that served Americans in need, such as Aid to Families with Dependent Children, job training programs, housing supports, food stamps, and child nutrition and health programs. Working together, the president's tax, spending, and regulatory policies redistributed wealth and life chances up the economic ladder to a degree not seen since the business-dominated 1920s.

The president's tax cuts had another, insidious effect. They created a potent long-range stealth constraint on what Congress and those who followed him in the White House could even consider doing. As the government lost over $750 billion in tax income between 1981 and 1986, while engaging in the largest peacetime military buildup in history (another Reagan priority), the budget deficit surged to over $150 billion a year. By the time Reagan left office, the federal deficit had tripled to the historically unheard-of figure of $2.8 trillion, a debt that amounted to $11,000 for every American citizen. David Stockman, Reagan's budget director, later acknowledged it was a "fiscal catastrophe." But that catastrophe for the country cynically advanced a political goal on the Right. As one of the president's aides put Reagan's thinking, the deficit would "keep the liberals from new spending programs." By driving up the national debt so drastically, the Reagan administration controlled the political agenda even after leaving office.

By the end of the 1980s, the economists Barry Bluestone and Bennett Harrison described what conservative policy combined with deep economic change was producing. "The economic distance between rich and poor, between well paid and poorly paid, is higher today," they noted, "than at any point in the lifetimes of all but our most senior citizens, the veterans of the Great Depression." As real wages fell and one-third of working citizens earned less each year than the official poverty rate, the income of the top 1 percent nearly doubled. Rising inequality had complex causes, to be sure, including changes in the nature and operations of markets for labor. What is indisputable, however, is that the new Republicans, like the business interests that financed them so heavily, opposed the use of government to mitigate the impact of hostile markets on working people and so promoted policies that deepened the disparities. The Reagan administration further harmed the life chances of ordinary citizens by cutting the budgets of federal agencies responsible for ensuring workplace safety and consumer and environmental protection. To head such agencies, it appointed people who opposed their very missions. One of many examples was James G. Watt. His job as secretary of the interior was to safeguard the nation's natural resources. Yet as an arch defender of property rights, advocate of corporate use of federal land, and conservative Christian who believed the end of the world was coming, Watt called environmentalism "a left-wing cult."

The Reagan presidency proved most committed to advancing the goals of an economic elite, but it also worked to shore up other kinds of privilege by whittling away at gains made over preceding decades by the less powerful. Indeed, the varied parts of the conservative agenda worked together as the president, for example, blamed working women for male unemployment, and pushed more unpaid family labor onto women by cutting social services budgets. The Reagan White House aligned with the enemies of civil rights more generally, as black Americans understood; he had, after all, described the Voting Rights Act as "humiliating to the South." Having won less of the black vote than any Republican presidential candidate since the party's founding, Reagan in 1982 ended a more than decade-long bipartisan practice of refusing tax exemptions to segregated private schools. This gift to segregationists provoked outrage from Reagan's own Justice Department Civil Rights Division, one hundred of whose attorneys protested so loudly that the change was withdrawn. That was one of many ways in which the Reagan presidency tried to undo more than twenty years of bipartisan civil rights policy, in arenas from school desegregation to employment opportunity. Even some corporations balked when the Reagan administration tried to end affirmative action in federal contracts in the mid-1980s. Thanks to a strong defense led by women's organizations and civil rights supporters, the policies remained on the books, but with conservative Republicans in power there was little pressure to comply. "If the tax laws of the United States were enforced as slackly as the antidiscrimination laws currently are," one economist noted in 1986, "very few people would pay taxes."

The Reagan administration also sought to rewrite the rules of U.S. political economy in ways that would advance long-standing conservative aims. Attorney General Edwin Meese thus began to call for "original intent" jurisprudence in the nation's courts. Behind the reassuring language suggesting fealty to time-worn tradition was in fact an old radical dream of the Right's: to overthrow the tradition of judicial interpretation developed after 1938. The very phrase "original intent" came into its contemporary usage in the outraged mobilization of white supremacists against the *Brown v. Board of Education* decision. As the liberal Supreme Court justice Stephen Breyer has pointed out: "the Constitution originally and intentionally ignored" the majority of those most of us now recognize as part of "We the People." As Breyer explained, "literalism has a tendency to undermine the Constitution's efforts to create a framework for democratic government." Constraining democratic government was precisely what conservatives had sought from the time they first joined together to build a movement. Since 1980 their allies in the White House have remade the judiciary with appointments of Supreme Court justices such as Antonin Scalia, Clarence Thomas, Samuel Alito, and John Roberts (to say nothing of hundreds of lower-level judges) whose philosophy systematically favors big business and the very wealthy and hurts those long disadvantaged by class, race, or gender.

After Reagan left office, the Republican Right further marginalized the centrists who once led their party. The administration of George Herbert Walker Bush was less ideological, but it too paid homage to the Religious Right and the other conservative interests who more and more dominated the GOP base. In his two terms in office, Democratic president Bill Clinton revived inclusive policies, yet, trapped by the debt Reagan left, found himself governing on terms the Right had set. His main policy achievements were deficit reduction, trade liberalization in the form of the North American Free Trade Alliance, and a welfare "reform" that ended Aid to Families with Dependent Children.

Still, never did movement conservatives gain a tighter grip on the GOP or on more branches of government and institutions in civil society than during the presidency of George W. Bush. The forty-third president promised voters "compassionate conservatism" in his 2000 campaign. But what Americans actually got was the most aggressively partisan administration in modern U.S. history, in both domestic and foreign policy.

As was true of Reagan, Bush's number-one concern after inauguration was to cut taxes on the richest Americans. Bush once joked to a wealthy audience he described as "the haves and have-mores" that "some people call you the elite. I call you my base." Bush's 2001 tax act sharply cut income tax rates on "the haves and have-mores" and inheritance taxes on vast estates. Further cuts in 2003 shielded dividend income and capital gains. Bush's cuts outpaced Reagan's in magnitude. The very rich, with average annual incomes over $2 million, enjoyed windfalls of over $80,000 per year. Meanwhile, as a result of decreased government revenue and increased military spending, the Bush administration amassed a national debt of over $8 trillion by 2006. That amounted to $28,000 per citizen, a burden President Bush left to the nation's children and grandchildren to pay. He also sought to privatize Social Security, one of the most successful achievements of the New Deal, which had drastically cut poverty among the elderly. He failed in that, because the program remained so popular that resistance was widespread. But inequality in Bush-era America reached levels not seen for generations.

As Americans lost economic security, social mobility also diminished. In the country once known for the "American dream" of success as a reward for hard work and talent, rates of mobility fell below those of ten European nations. Even Britain, against whose class-ridden "Old World" society American colonists had revolted in the 1770s, by 2007 outpaced the United States in rates of escape from the lowest fifth of the income spectrum. Back in the Gilded Age of the late nineteenth century, many ordinary Americans found it scandalous that John D. Rockefeller, the country's richest man, had an income seven thousand times larger than the per capita average. Midway through Bush's second term, one of the nation's leading hedge fund managers brought home in a single year more than thirty-eight thousand times the average income. And he was just one of many lightly taxed billionaires atop an economic pyramid steeper than the country had ever known before.

While the Bush administration showed no interest in remedying the stunning inequality and diminishing opportunity over which it presided, it also stood out from previous presidencies for its extremism on other fronts. It overthrew generations of U.S. military policy and violated international law on torture with practices that undermined America's reputation across the world. Bringing the story told in this essay full circle, in June 2006 Bush nominated for the Fifth Circuit U.S. Court of Appeals a Mississippi state court judge who had ruled in favor of a white employee who called a black coworker "a good ole nigger." As the nation's newspaper of record summarized in its editorial, the problems went beyond racism—"Judge Southwick's judicial record also shows the usual pattern of President Bush's judicial nominees: insensitivity toward workers, consumers, and people injured by corporations." Meanwhile, the conservative movement elevated as spokespersons the likes of the radio talk show host Rush Limbaugh and the pundit Ann Coulter, who debased mainstream public debate. Coulter called Senator John Edwards a "faggot" and Al Gore a "total fag." She did so as a guest on platforms that leading conservative organizations provided to her, after she had already used the racial slur "raghead" for Arab Middle Easterners and argued that the way to stop terrorism was to "invade their countries, kill their leaders, and convert them to Christianity." Cynicism metastasized in the Republican Party as its corporate funders hired and profited from the undocumented immigrant workers whom so many of its candidates vilified to win election. As the conservative strategist and former Bush advisor David Frum noted in 2004 in *National Review*, "there's no issue where the beliefs and interests of the party rank-and-file diverge more radically from the beliefs and interests of the party's leaders."

In every arena, it seemed by the end of Bush's second term, the conservative contempt for government that led Reagan to call it a swamp undermined competence in running it. The most horrifying example was the laggardly response to Hurricane Katrina, which turned a devastating storm into a social catastrophe. Bush had appointed his 2000 campaign manager to head the Federal Emergency Management Agency, a responsibility about which the new head knew nothing, and the unqualified staff he chose undermined effective management of the disaster as it unfolded. Rooted in cynicism toward the fundamental responsibilities of governance, such cronyism drove Bush administration decisionmaking in virtually every realm, from the partisan firing of U.S. district attorneys to failed oversight of the student loan and housing finance industries, to the choices made in the occupation of Iraq that resulted in what many experts now view as the greatest strategic fiasco in American foreign policy history. The president had followed the counsel of the Heritage Foundation, a right-wing think tank that advised him back in 2001 to "make appointment decisions based on loyalty first and expertise second." By 2007 there had been what one journalist summarized as "corruption, incompetence, and contracting or cronyism scandals" in eight different cabinet departments. "People whose ideology says that government is always the problem, never the solution," explained the economist and *New York Times* columnist Paul Krugman, "see no point in governing well. So they use political power to reward their friends, rather than find people who will actually do their jobs."

No wonder that by 2008, a CBS News/*New York Times* poll found that 75 percent of Americans—three in four—believed the country had "pretty seriously gotten off on the wrong track." Not since that question was first posed in 1983 had more people disapproved of the country's direction. As the conservative British business magazine *The Economist* admitted: "The Republicans have failed the most important test of any political movement—wielding power successfully. They have botched a war. They have splurged on spending. And they have alienated a huge section of the population." As a result, their popularity sank to a forty-year low, according to their own pollsters.

CONCLUSION: "IDEAS HAVE CONSEQUENCES"

Over the quarter century after 1980, as conservatives gained a degree of power unimaginable to the movement's founders in the 1950s, they had an enormous impact on America. By their deliberately divisive waging of what some Republican leaders called a "cultural war" to turn out their base for elections, they poisoned public debate and produced unprecedented partisan enmity. They used the power accrued through such tactics to advance a policy agenda that enhanced the profits and power of big business and the wealthiest Americans and whittled away at policies to promote fairness and inclusion that had been won through years of struggle by working people, African Americans and Latinos, women, and lesbians and gay men. Conservatives disdained such victories for equity along with the model of government that made them possible. Whereas most Americans had savored the greater economic security they gained from New Deal measures such as Social Security, unemployment insurance, and civil rights at work, conservatives belittled these and, in the nostalgic words of columnist George F. Will, longed for bygone times "when Americans savored freedom's uncertainties and considered 'security' an unworthy goal for a free people."

Conservatives' core promise was that they would shrink "big government." But in fact, they never really limited the size of the federal government; what they changed was what it did and for whom. From Reagan forward, they sought to eviscerate the kinds of programs that helped ordinary citizens, such as student loans, unemployment compensation, and food stamps for low-income families. At the same time, they vastly expanded the military's capacity for aggressive action abroad, the government's monitoring of private life in areas from sexuality to Internet usage, and the prison system. Indeed, in the conservative era, the United States locked up a greater share of its population than almost any other nation in the world—including many brutal dictatorships. As for federal money, the top recipients of it in the age of conservative ascendency seemed to be those who needed it least. For example, few have denounced the federal government as vociferously as Newt Gingrich, the Georgia Republican congressman who coauthored the Contract with America, yet the wealthy county he represented on the eve of it ranked third among all suburban counties in the country in the amount of federal dollars it garnered in 2002. Per capita, residents of Cobb County, Georgia, received $4,000 more than those of New York City. In that, it was a stark symbol of the Republican Right in Congress, which excoriated the federal government while pocketing out-sized shares of its revenue.

Most pernicious for American culture over the long term, conservative power has created a self-reinforcing spiral of public distrust as a mis-shapen government offers less and less to ordinary citizens. "Through its power over the government it professes to hate, the right has put itself in a position to create a government that is ever more deserving of hatred," journalist Barbara Ehrenreich has astutely observed. "The less government does for us, the easier it is to believe the right's antigovernment propaganda; and the more we believe it, the less likely we are to vote for anyone who might use government to actually improve our lives." The result is debili-tating cynicism, neglected infrastructure and education, and festering un-met needs.

And, having gotten near-total possession of the party of Abraham Lin-coln, conservatives turned it into a haven of neo-Confederacy. They have made the Republican Party stand for the exact opposite of the values on which it was founded, those Lincoln called "the better angels of our nature." The party that saved the Union and ended human bondage in the United States is now home to those who exalt the South of slavery and Jim Crow. Why do they do it? To attract the votes of the whites most hostile to blacks and to the federal government that ended these systems of oppression. From 1960, when John F. Kennedy first commented on "that Confederate uniform that [Barry Goldwater] has been wearing in the South," GOP leaders began bowing to the icons of the slaveholders' rebellion. To take just a few examples: in 1981 sixteen prominent Republican U.S. senators recommended M. E. Bradford to Ronald Reagan as an "impeccable" scholar to head the National Endowment for the Humanities. Describing himself as an "unrepentant Southerner," Bradford had compared Lincoln to Hitler and denounced eman-cipation of the enslaved as a blow to "liberty." George W. Bush got ahead in Texas politics by befriending the Museum of the Confederacy, the United Daughters of the Confederacy, and the Sons of Confederate Veterans. Lead-ing Republican elected officials—including Phil Gramm, Dick Armey, Trent Lott, and John Ashcroft—gave friendly interviews to *Southern Partisan*. That arch-Confederate journal features articles such as "John C. Calhoun: A States-man for the 21st Century," a tribute to the states' rights advocate who declared slavery "a positive good." Republican public officials in several southern states ushered in that new century with campaigns for Confederate History and Heritage Month, a pointed insult to Black History Month.

Cartoonist Kevin Siers of the Charlotte [North Carolina] Observer *mocked President George W. Bush for pandering to the southern white voters most hostile to African Americans during the 2000 primaries. Bush was among those who turned the party of Lincoln into a promoter of the Confederacy in the years after Barry Goldwater won over the Deep South in 1964. (© North America Syndicate)*

Having won so many elections using people of color as a foil, it was perhaps unsurprising that the GOP included not a single African American among its 247-person-strong congressional delegation. So homogeneous had the Republican leadership become that comedian David Letterman joked that their 2008 presidential candidate lineup looked like "guys waiting to tee off at a restricted country club." No wonder, then, that young people began to reject the party in droves: from a high of 37 percent at the close of the Reagan era, the proportion who identify as Republican dropped to 25 percent by the close of the Bush era.

As illustrated here, the conservative movement was the main transmission belt carrying the spirit of the slaveholders into the Grand Old Party, from the founding of *National Review* in 1955 though the election of Ronald Reagan in 1980 and the 2000–2008 administration of George W. Bush. "The Confederacy," as James Kilpatrick wrote back in the early 1960s when its promoters were more honest, "was first of all, and still is . . . a state of mind." "Running through this state of mind," he explained, "is this inescapable awareness: the consciousness of the Negro." White race consciousness was—and is—integral to the "heritage" neo-Confederates celebrate and to which so many Republicans pander. Since the 1970s, conservative leaders have thus played a two-faced game, singing hosannas to "color-blindness" in some situations, while whistling Dixie in others.

Texan president Lyndon Johnson, in contrast, tried with courage and candor to persuade white southerners to reject such appeals to the morally wrong and nationally disastrous elements of their history. He called on his fellow southerners to share the best of their culture with the country, not the worst, as he urged them "not to heed those who would come waving the tattered and discredited banners of the past, who seek to stir old hostilities and kindle old hatreds, who preach battle between neighbors and bitterness between states." "Men cannot live with a lie," Johnson warned, "and not be stained by it." He was right. The unsavory record amassed by those who ignored that truth may help explain why the administration of George W. Bush was so fanatically devoted to secrecy, and why it closed off presidential records to citizens and researchers to a degree never seen before in American history. There was, indeed, much to hide.

There is a sharp irony in all this. Conservatives presented themselves as the country's best hope—in Ronald Reagan's words, as "creators of the future." Yet their philosophy was actually one of profound pessimism about the human capacity to use democratic institutions to better our world. Their dream was to return America to the kind of political economy and culture that prevailed in the business-dominated 1920s and even the Gilded

Age. Unable to win voters to this vision in its purer form in the 1950s, conservative leaders learned that they gained more followers when they deliberately cultivated fear and stirred hostility between people of different backgrounds, when they framed the world as a menacing place full of threats that required tough protectors. Whenever popular hopes arose for a fairer America, conservatives elected to shore up the power of the privileged; they actively worked to turn their listeners against the pleas for justice and inclusion. Faced with the proverbial question "Which side are you on?" they never hesitated. They always, by instinct and ideology, took the side of those advantaged by tradition. Time and again, conservative movement builders fought the forces of hope and democratic progress who sought "a more perfect union." They chose, instead, to uphold a tradition that protected slavery, suppressed labor, fought women's suffrage, defended segregation, advocated colonialism, flouted human rights, and belittled gender justice.

Does all this mean that those against whom the conservatives pitted themselves were flawless? Of course not. Liberals and progressives can be fairly criticized for plenty in their history, and, in fact, historians have done so at great length over the years and no doubt will continue to. But as Franklin Roosevelt eloquently put the core ethical difference: "Governments can err, Presidents do make mistakes, but the immortal Dante tells us that Divine Justice weighs the sins of the cold-blooded and of the warm-hearted on a different scale. Better the occasional faults of a government living in a spirit of charity, than the consistent omissions of a government frozen in the ice of its own indifference." In a founding tract of the conservative movement, Richard Weaver proclaimed that ideas have consequences. They certainly do. And that is why the most conservative presidential administration in modern U.S. history became the most unpopular ever recorded as it wound to a close, leaving behind a terrible mess for others to fix.

DOCUMENTS

1

FRANK MEYER, "WHAT IS CONSERVATISM?" (1966)

Frank Meyer was a key figure in the postwar conservative movement. A shrewd strategist, he orchestrated the fusion that brought militant anti-Communists, libertarians, and social traditionalists to see their common ground in conservatism. In this essay, he situates the movement historically. Why does he believe the election of Franklin Roosevelt led to a "revolutionary transformation"? What exactly was so threatening and subversive, in the conservative view? Do you agree that the New Deal was akin to Communism and Nazism? Why did conservatism start to gain ground in the late 1950s?

This essay is concerned with conservatism as a political, social, and intellectual movement—not as a cast of mind or a temperamental inclination. Such a movement arises historically when the unity and balance of a civilization are riven by revolutionary transformations of previously accepted norms of polity, society, and thought. Conservatism comes into being at such times as a movement of consciousness and action directed to recovering the tradition of the civilization. This is the essence of conservatism in all the forms it has assumed in different civilizations and under differing circumstances. . . .

In any era the problem of conservatism is to find the way to restore the tradition of the civilization and apply it in a new situation. But this means that conservatism is by its nature two-sided. It must at one and the same time be reactionary and presentist. It cannot content itself with appealing to the past. The very circumstances that call conscious conservatism into being create an irrevocable break with the past. . . . But while conservatism is not and cannot be naked reaction, neither can its concern with contemporary circumstances lead it, if it is to be true to itself, to be content with the status quo, with serving as a "moderating wing" within the existing situation. For that situation is the result of a revolutionary break with the tradition of the civilization, and to "conserve" it is to accept the radical break with tradition that conservatism exists to overcome. . . .

It is easy to show that contemporary American conservatism is not a replica of nineteenth-century European conservatism; while it resembles it in some ways, it also resembles nineteenth-century European liberalism in its commitment to individual liberty and its corollary commitment to an economic system free of state control. . . . [The] claim of the contemporary American conservative movement to the title conservative does not have to be based upon a surface resemblance to the conservative movement of another period. It is based upon its commitment to the recovery of a tradition, the tradition of Western civilization and the American republic, which has been subjected to a revolutionary attack in the years since 1932.

The crystallization in the past dozen years or so of an American conservative movement is a delayed reaction to the revolutionary transformation of America that began with the election of Franklin Roosevelt in 1932. That revolution itself has been a gentler, more humane, bloodless expression in the United States of the revolutionary wave that has swept the globe in the twentieth century. Its grimmest, most total manifestations have been the phenomena of Communism and Nazism. In rather peculiar forms in late years it has expressed itself in the so-called nationalism typified by Nasser, Nkrumah, and Sukarno; in Western Europe it has taken the forms of the socialism of England or that of Scandinavia. Everywhere, however open or masked, it represents an aggrandizement of the power of the state over the lives of individual persons. Always that aggrandizement is cloaked in a rhetoric and a program putatively directed to and putatively concerned for "the masses."

The American form of that revolution differs little in its essentials from Western European democratic socialism. But, by an ironic twist of history, it has become known as "liberalism." (So far is it removed from the classical liberalism of the nineteenth century, with its overriding concern for individual liberty and the limitation of the state, that clear discourse requires some mode of differentiation; and I shall for that reason, through the rest of this essay, refer to this twentieth-century American development as Liberalism, with a capital L, reserving the lower case for classical liberalism.) Ushered in by the election in 1932, so thorough was the victory of Liberalism that for many years afterwards it met with no concerted resistance, in either the intellectual or political spheres. . . . Only in recent years has there emerged a consistent, cohesive conservative movement, based upon a broad consensus principle, challenging Liberal assumptions and Liberal power all along the line. . . .

Source: Frank S. Meyer, "Conservatism," in *Left, Right, and Center: Essays on Liberalism and Conservatism in the United States*, ed. Robert A. Goldwin. Chicago: Rand McNally & Company, 1966. (Courtesy of Eugene B. Meyer)

2

BARRY GOLDWATER, "I SENSE HERE A REALIGNMENT OF SOUTHERN CONSERVATIVE DEMOCRATS" (1953)

In this journal entry, U.S. Senator Barry Goldwater (R-Arizona) bemoans the state of the Republican Party as he also envisions a future regional and ideological realignment of the two major parties that would bring together opponents of the "New Dealers and Fair Dealers" across party lines. Do you find his characterization of New Dealers and Fair Dealers accurate? Why does he look in particular to southern Democrats for hope? What did it mean, concretely, in American politics in the 1950s to advocate states' rights and the exclusion of the federal government from "the affairs of business"? Who is Goldwater referring to when he says "the dictates of the strongest minority groups" are influencing the decisions of "the New Deal and Fair Deal folks"? With what decisions in the 1940s and early 1950s would he take issue?

I am in my office. It is just about sundown. It's been a hot, muggy spring day, and as I look out to the northwest I can see the Washington Monument, and the low hanging clouds, and I am thinking about events that have transpired since I arrived here and what, if anything, I can begin to conclude from these experiences.

One thing giving me concern is an obvious lack of unity within the Republican Party. By this I don't mean lack of purpose rather a lack of unity along the lines that the Democratic Party displays so well in the Senate. They have discipline; we don't. We seem to lack aggressive, strong leadership willing to develop issues which are so clearly with us, and then bring them out on the floor. There is a lack of interest on the floor from the Republicans; there are very few members of our party on the floor during debate or during discussion. I don't know what it is. Perhaps it is the fact that we haven't been in power for twenty years and have forgotten the organization that is needed to get things done, and it's most important we get organized for next year, 1954. . . .

Now there is a group of people in both parties that we like to refer to as New Dealers or Fair Dealers. They are neither regular Democrats nor regular Republicans, and we've got them in both parties. These are people who, by long association with the New Deal and the Fair Deal, have become inculcated with their ideas and principles to the point that they feel the federal government should have the power over everything, that the federal government should dominate the states, it should dominate business, it should control the economy and the unions and control the life of this country. I suspect that if I told any one of these men that, they would probably challenge me, but nevertheless, their actions speak louder than their thinking and in their expression. Now on the other side, you have members of both parties, particularly among the Southern Democrats, who believe in states rights and who believe that the federal government should be out of the state and local government picture entirely, and out of the affairs of business as well.

I sense here a realignment of Southern conservative Democrats with Democrats and Republicans of the West and Middle West. The New Deal and the Fair Deal folks are coming from the eastern seaboard, and it is alarming to me to see how far they have gone. They are controlled by the dictates of the labor unions[;] the dictates of the stronger minority groups are felt in almost every decision they make, in almost every debate they enter. This thinking is a far cry from that of the Western senator and the Southern senator who believe in the free enterprise system, who believe in the freedom of the individual and the freedom of the states. After only four months, I am beginning to see a cleavage that is new, but nevertheless, I think it is going to develop as one of the major issues in the future and that will be the federal government against the states and individuals, and it should be an interesting one to pursue. . . .

Source: Journal entry (March 12, 1953), as appears in John W. Dean and Barry M. Goldwater Jr., *Pure Goldwater* (New York: Palgrave Macmillan), 94–96, reprinted from the Barry M. Goldwater Collection held by the Arizona Historical Foundation at Arizona State University in Tempe. (Courtesy of the Arizona Historical Foundation)

3

RICHARD M. WEAVER, "INTEGRATION IS COMMUNIZATION" (1957)

The conservative movement and the civil rights movement both took off in the heyday of the Cold War Red scare. In this excerpt from a review essay, University of Chicago professor Richard Weaver, a leading conservative intellectual who wrote the foundational tract *Ideas Have Consequences* (1948), maintains that the civil rights movement is a Communist cause antagonistic to American institutions. On what grounds does he do so? What does the document reveal about conservative thinking on race? How does Weaver's devotion to the rights of property affect his response to African Americans' quest for equal citizenship?

The Supreme Court's extraordinary dictate to the public schools promises to keep race relations inflamed for an indefinite period. It is therefore to be expected that there will be a continuing spate of books from "liberal" sources, filled with self-righteousness and preaching the funeral of what is pejoratively called "discrimination." . . .

Herein lies the clue to much that confronts us today. The Communists are skilled enough in warfare to know that their goal can be approached by different ways. . . . [T]he Communist tactic most aggressively used in this country now is . . . "racial collectivism." This phase of the leveling or obliterating process can now be presented with a great deal of moral unction. Moreover, it has the tactical advantage of undermining our historic constitutional structure.

In every part of the United States the common people, who do not wear the blinkers that some politicians prefer to don, have understood this for a good long while. To them Communism has always signalized its advent by an ostensibly free and natural but actually self-conscious and

tendentious racial mingling. This is the way the American public has intu-
itively spotted the emergence of Communism. And its reaction, despite the
stream of propaganda and wishful editorializing from many sectors of the
press, has been about 90 per cent in favor of our traditional American society and mores.

The common people often perceive elemental things which the over-
educated cannot see. That they have been right in identifying this as the
opening tactic of Communism in this country now seems beyond question.
We can observe in a number of areas how "racial collectivism" is being used
as a crowbar to pry loose rights over private property. There was a time
when ownership of property gave the owner the right to say to whom he
would and would not sell and rent. But now, with the outlawing of restrictive covenants by the Supreme Court (especially in *Shelley v. Kraemer*),
this right has been invaded, if not effectually taken away. There was a time
when owners had complete discretion as to whom they would and would
not hire to work in their private businesses. Now that right is invaded by
various kinds of FEPC laws, which tell him that he cannot consider differences of race in selecting his employees. There was a time when private educational institutions had the right to set up any standards they chose for the
admission of students. Now at least one state has a law which forbids any
institution even to accept applications with data relating to the race and religion of the student applying. . . . One must have a pretty sophistical education not to see in this a steady and indeed now far advanced eroding of
rights over private property following a Communist racial theory. In most
of the process the Supreme Court has been, as Mr. Frederic Nelson suggests in a contemporary article, the "running dog" of the Kremlin.

"Integration" and "Communization" are, after all, pretty closely synonymous. In the light of what is happening today, the first may be little
more than a euphemism for the second. It does not take many steps to get
from the "integrating" of facilities to the "communizing" of facilities, if the
impulse is there.

. . . Moscow is piping the tune; the American professoriate is beating
time; and we are beginning to dance to it.

While this surrender goes on, the Liberal publicists encourage it by
representing every concession as a gain and every evacuation as a victory.
We can expect no end to such demoralization until they and their followers calm down enough to see the truth of three propositions. 1) Integration
is not an end in itself. 2) Forcible integration would ignore the truth that
equals are not identicals. 3) In a free society, associations for educational,
cultural, social, and business purposes have a right to protect their integrity

against political fanaticism. The alternative to this is the destruction of free society and the replacement of its functions by government, which is the Marxist dream.

Source: Richard M. Weaver, "Integration Is Communization," *National Review* (July 13, 1957), 67. (© 1957 by National Review, Inc., 215 Lexington Avenue; New York, NY 10016. Reprinted by permission)

4

"OUR POSITION ON STATES' RIGHTS IS THE SAME AS YOUR OWN": LETTER FROM WILLIAM F. BUCKLEY JR. TO W. J. SIMMONS (SEPTEMBER 10, 1958); LETTER FROM W. J. SIMMONS TO J. P. McFADDEN (SEPTEMBER 5, 1958)

William F. Buckley Jr. was put in contact with William J. Simmons of the southern white Citizens' Councils by James Jackson Kilpatrick so that he could promote *National Review* to the organization's 65,000-member mailing list. Simmons also pledged to endorse *National Review* in his editorials. The Citizens' Councils, in the words of civil rights movement scholar Charles M. Payne, "pursu[ed] the agenda of the Ku Klux Klan with the demeanor of the Rotary." Its logo contained a Confederate flag and an American flag with the words "states rights" and "racial integrity." Why was Buckley comfortable allying with such a group? What did a stand for "political decentralization" mean in practice in 1958? What new insight into the conservative movement does the mutual appreciation of the two leaders across the Mason-Dixon line provide?

LETTER FROM WILLIAM F. BUCKLEY JR. TO W. J. SIMMONS (SEPTEMBER 10, 1958)

Dear Mr. Simmons:

I am so very grateful to you for making available your list. It is a generous gesture indeed, which I take advantage of only because I feel that our position on states' rights is the same as your own and that we are therefore, as far as political decentralization is concerned, pursuing the same ends.

Thank you so very much again for your kindness; and do drop in when you come to town.

Yours sincerely,
Wm. F. Buckley, Jr.

LETTER FROM W. J. SIMMONS TO J. P. McFADDEN, ASSISTANT TO THE PUBLISHER (SEPTEMBER 5, 1958)

Dear Mr. McFadden:

Confirming our phone conversation this morning, we are sending you a mailing list of our paid subscribers. These will be on plain white 3 inch tape in 4 inch rolls.

You should receive the list by the end of next week. It will consist of 7 or 8 rolls.

Since we feel that National Review is making a highly significant and material contribution to the cause of political and social sanity, we are happy to provide this list with our compliments.

Since you say you have not seen our paper, I am enclosing copies of the last couple of issues. You may be interested in the TV-radio story in the June paper. It represents an approach that I feel our side needs to concentrate on.

The next time you are in the South, come to see us.

Sincerely,
W. J. Simmons

Source: William F. Buckley, Jr. to W. J. Simmons, September 10, 1958, and W. J. Simmons to J. P. McFadden, September 5, 1958, box 6, William F. Buckley, Jr. Papers, 1951–2002, Manuscripts and Archives, Yale University, New Haven, CT. (Courtesy of the William F. Buckley Jr. Papers, Manuscripts and Archives, Yale University Library)

5

YOUNG AMERICANS FOR FREEDOM, "KING WAS A COLLECTIVIST" (1968)

Young Americans for Freedom (YAF) was the leading conservative youth group for decades after its 1960 founding at the estate of William F. Buckley in Sharon, Connecticut. YAF trained young conservatives who went on to staff movement institutions such as the Heritage Foundation and the American Conservative Union and to play important roles in the Republican Party and the presidential administrations of Ronald Reagan, George H. W. Bush, and George W. Bush. This editorial was the official YAF response to the assassination of Martin Luther King Jr. Why did they respond as they did? Given this history of hostility to Rev. King when he was alive, why do you think conservatives today so often quote the line from his "I Have a Dream" speech in which he says he hopes that someday his "children will live in a nation where they will not be judged by the color of their skin but by the content of their character"?

Martin Luther King, Jr., whatever his shortcomings, represented a moderate force in the civil rights movement. While Dr. King was by no means moderate in an absolute sense, he represented a deterrent to the growing influence of those who openly advocate violence. Dr. King was a symbol to many people who thought he could solve their problems. And now that symbol is gone.

The entire communications media—radio and television, newspapers and magazines, paid unqualified tribute to Dr. King. No segment of the media, no unit of any segment, deviated from the prevailing tone of praise, unrestricted in quantity or expression. Although one had the impression newsmen all received identical scripts to read, the truth is that intelligent newsmen were swept in by the hysteria. The days following Dr. King's death were unreal, and a sad commentary on the alleged diversity of the American scene.

Much of the mourning was, and there is no better word, artificial. One suspects that if the New York Stock Exchange remained opened, trading would have proceeded at a healthy pace. If students had been given the option of attending schools where schools were closed the day of the funeral, they would have attended. . . .

The problem of the conservative: to reconcile his shock at the assassination with the necessity to maintain a perspective, for both himself and those around him, about what Dr. King stood for, and what effects he had on America. . . .

In the Montgomery bus boycott, Dr. King used the power of the market. It is not the Liberal, but the free market advocate, who believes in consumer sovereignty. Dr. King boycotted a bus company to cause it to give equal service to Negro customers. Business should be responsive to demand: that is the test of the market. If King were market-oriented, his next step might have been to introduce competition by starting another bus company. But King was a collectivist.

Dr. King helped secure legislation which, in the name of civil rights, destroyed both human and civil rights. Unconstitutional legislation has given the federal government dictatorial powers. King was not radical enough, in that radical means going to the root of the problem. Government action cannot do that.

The most recent example is the federal open housing bill, passed largely due to King's assassination. The bill, unconstitutional and dictatorial, makes a mockery of the human right to possess and exchange property. Like other King-inspired legislation, it will do little to solve the problem, since housing discrimination is sustained by a lack of purchasing power among Negroes, and their inability to influence that market. Discriminating against Negroes in housing does not yet cause economic hardship and disincentive for the discriminator.

Like other King-inspired legislation, the latest bill will aggravate racial problems by further antagonizing whites, both bigots and those that can be reached. Meanwhile, the legislation will provide further rationale for rioting, by providing unfulfillable promises for the Negro. . . .

Dr. King did not deal with the problems of discrimination and poverty. The former is a matter of education and persuasion, not the force of government, which aggravates the problem. King inspired Negroes wherever he preached, but he antagonized whites, especially those who needed to be reached.

Dr. King could never really deal with poverty, because he did not recognize that the best cure for poverty was operation of the market. King advocated a guaranteed annual income, which would be financed by further taxing of society's productive [citizens]. But a guaranteed annual income is the best way to colonize, not liberate the American Negro. It gives him security, *not* opportunity.

When the Negroes looted stores in cities across the nation, it was said that this was a poor tribute to Dr. King's memory. The sad fact, as has been pointed out in articles in this magazine, is that Dr. King advocated precisely what the looters did, except that he advocated the government do it. King provided the rationale: that society owes the Negro, that income should be redistributed, and that private property need not be respected, in theory, law, or practice. . . .

If Dr. King was unable to confront American problems, what did he confront? The answer is authority. King frequently marched in defiance of laws and rulings, often passed for public safety. Perhaps his motives were sincere, but the results of Dr. King's years of lawlessness were skepticism and disregard for the law among many Negroes.

If the law can be disregarded, and if a lawbreaker can receive a Nobel Peace Prize and White House recognition, then why should the law be respected by the man in the street? If the government can loot by force, then why should people, conditioned to handouts by Dr. King's philosophy, use the intermediary of government? Why not loot directly?

The tragedy is that the stupid legislation continues, and government refuses to seek solutions to poverty and race relations within the private sector. . . .

Martin Luther King's assassination should spotlight the American crisis, not conceal it. We cannot condemn Memphis, as some impetuously condemned Dallas, or as President Johnson's silly Kerner Commission condemned white racism. We must deal with the problems at hand . . . for Dr. King rests in peace, unlike the American city.

Source: Editorial, "Martin Luther King, Jr., RIP," *The New Guard* [The Magazine of Young Americans for Freedom, Inc.], vol. 8, no. 5 (May 1968), 3–4.

6

WILLIAM F. BUCKLEY JR., "LINDA'S CRUSADE" (MAY 21, 1968)

The conservative movement disapproved of the entire student New Left of the 1960s, from civil rights and antiwar and campus activism to feminism and gay liberation, and it tapped the anger of many older white Americans at the youthful protestors to build its own ranks. In this newspaper column, William F. Buckley Jr. expresses the outrage many religious traditionalists, in particular, felt about how young people were transforming the sexual ethos of America with their embrace of erotic pleasure and practices such as living together in committed relationships outside marriage. Here, Buckley reveals the double standard that blamed women, in particular, for nonmarital sex, showing a discomfort that would help drive the antiabortion movement and opposition to feminism, while he also displays the signature humor that helped make him famous. How might the reactions of college students and their parents to this column have differed? Why is Buckley so much harsher to the female partner than the male?

New York, April 28—It is now a national story that Miss Linda LeClair, twenty, of Barnard College, has been living off campus in New York with Mr. Peter Behr, 22, of Columbia, and that a general story on such practices by the *New York Times* flushed out the cohabitation and put the authorities of Barnard College on the spot. Complications came swift and fast. Dozens upon dozens of Miss LeClair's classmates stepped forward to admit that their living arrangements were similarly loose-minded, and that therefore it would be unfair to penalize Miss LeClair simply because she happened to be the one who was caught, a defensive doctrine which is not exactly airtight.

The authorities, visibly disconcerted, demonstrated from the outset a total lack of conviction about the significance of Miss LeClair's sexual habits, and decided instead to focus on her having lied in the college form she had filled out giving the required details on where she was domiciled. All of a sudden, all of Barnard was rising in indignation over the false entry in the form, which is rather like being indignant at Iago because he was rude to Desdemona. And then, to make opera bouffe of the whole thing, after meeting solemnly to consider the disposition of the LeClair case, the authorities voted to deprive her of access to the school cafeteria, which was a joke enough for a public unfamiliar with the school cafeteria, but for those who are forced to patronize it, it was apparently something in the nature of black humor.

Miss LeClair's parents were finally consulted, and it transpires that they, being of the older generation of course, disapprove their daughter's habits, and have gone so far as to cease to send her money. Mr. Behr, who is a draft evader, is apparently unable to take up the slack; so that perhaps the indomitable Miss LeClair will list herself as an unemployed concubine and apply for relief from the City, which has never been known to deny relief to anyone who applies for it: and that should settle the economic exigencies of the matter.

As for the future, we learn from Miss LeClair that it is her intention to continue to live with Mr. Behr after he is let out of prison, to which he expects to repair in consequence of his violation of the statute law if not the moral law. And they will then found a colony where couples can live and bear and raise children, without getting married. Miss LeClair, in other words, desires to abrogate the institution of marriage, which is apparently okay by Barnard, now that she has ceased to lie about it.

The commentary on the case in the urban press is of course more interesting than the delinquency of this pathetic little girl, so gluttonous for sex and publicity. My favorite is Mr. Max Lerner's, ever on his avant garde. Surveying the story, he concludes, "In moral terms, while it says that the sexual code is no longer there, it fails to deal with the question of truthfulness . . ." So much for a code that developed over three thousand years of Judaeo-Christian experience—shot down, in a subordinate phrase, by Mr. Max Lerner.

There isn't anyone around who seems prepared to say to Miss LeClair: Look, it is wrong to do what you have done. Wrong because sexual promiscuity is an assault on an institution that is central to the survival of the hardiest Western ideal: the family. In an age in which the *Playboy* philosophy is taken seriously, as a windy testimonial to the sovereign right of all human appetites, it isn't surprising that the LeClairs of this world should multiply like rabbits, whose morals they imitate. But the fact that everybody does it—even Liberace, as Noel Coward assures us—doesn't make it the right thing to do, and doesn't authorize the wishful conclusion of Mr. Lerner that, like God, the sexual code is dead.

Perhaps the sexual code *is* dead. Question: Should we regret it? Or should we take the position that that which is "no longer there" is no longer missed? . . .

One wonders whether, if Miss LeClair were plopped in the middle of Columbia's Union Theological Seminary, a single seminarian would trouble to argue with her, as Christ did the woman at Jacob's well, that her ways are mistaken?

Source: William F. Buckley Jr., "Linda's Crusade," *National Review* (May 21, 1968), 518. (© 1968 by National Review, Inc., 215 Lexington Avenue; New York, NY 10016. Reprinted by permission)

PHYLLIS SCHLAFLY, "WHAT'S WRONG WITH 'EQUAL RIGHTS' FOR WOMEN?" (FEBRUARY 1972)

Phyllis Schlafly had been active in building the Republican Right for two decades before the fight against the Equal Rights Amendment brought her to national attention. In 1964 she produced a biography of Barry Goldwater called *A Choice Not an Echo*, which became a conservative bestseller. In this document, Schlafly argues that feminism will hurt home-makers, and that the ERA in particular must be defeated. How accurate is her portrayal of the women's movement? How does she link antifeminism to other conservative com-mitments? If you were persuaded by her case against femi-nism, what other positions might you be accepting in the process? Which women would be most likely to share her views?

What's Wrong With "Equal Rights" for Women? Of all the classes of peo-ple who ever lived, the American woman is the most privileged. We have the most rights and rewards, and the fewest duties. Our unique status is the result of a fortunate combination of circumstances.

1. We have the immense good fortune to live in a civilization which respects the family as the basic unit of society. This respect is part and par-cel of our laws and our customs. It is based on the fact of life—which no legislation or agitation can erase—that women have babies and men don't.

If you don't like this fundamental difference, you will have to take up your complaint with God because He created us this way. The fact that women, not men, have babies is not the fault of selfish and domineering men, or of the establishment, or of any clique of conspirators who want to oppress women. It's simply the way God made us.

Our Judeo-Christian civilization has developed the law and custom that, since women must bear the physical consequences of the sex act, men must be required to bear the other consequences and pay in other ways. These laws and customs decree that a man must carry his share by physical protection and financial support of his children and of the woman who bears his children, and also by a code of behavior which benefits and protects both the woman and the children.

THE GREATEST ACHIEVEMENT OF WOMEN'S RIGHTS

This is accomplished by the institution of the family. Our respect for the family as the basic unit of society, which is ingrained in the laws and customs of our Judeo-Christian civilization, is the greatest single achievement in the entire history of women's rights. It assures a woman the most precious and important right of all—the right to keep her own baby and to be supported and protected in the enjoyment of watching her baby grow and develop. . . .

Do we want financial security? We are fortunate to have the great legacy of Moses, the Ten Commandments, especially this one: "Honor thy father and thy mother that thy days may be long upon the land." Children are a woman's best social security—her best guarantee of social benefits such as old age pension, unemployment compensation, workman's compensation, and sick leave. The family gives a woman the physical, financial and emotional security of the home—for all her life.

THE FINANCIAL BENEFITS OF CHIVALRY

2. The second reason why American women are a privileged group is that we are the beneficiaries of a tradition of special respect for women which dates from the Christian Age of Chivalry. The honor and respect paid to Mary, the Mother of Christ, resulted in all women, in effect, being put on a pedestal. . . .

In other civilizations, such as the African and the American Indian, the men strut around wearing feathers and beads and hunting and fishing (great sport for men!), while the women do all the hard, tiresome drudgery including the tilling of the soil (if any is done), the hewing of wood, the making of fires, the carrying of water, as well as the cooking, sewing and caring for babies.

This is not the American way because we were lucky enough to inherit the traditions of the Age of Chivalry. In America, a man's first significant purchase is a diamond for his bride, and the largest financial investment of his life is a home for her to live in. American husbands work hours of overtime to buy a fur piece or other finery to keep their wives in fashion, and to pay premiums on their life insurance policies to provide for her comfort when she is a widow (benefits in which he can never share).

THE REAL LIBERATION OF WOMEN

3. The third reason why American women are so well off is that the great American free enterprise system has produced remarkable inventors who have lifted the backbreaking "women's work" from our shoulders. . . .

The real liberation of women from the backbreaking drudgery of centuries is the American free enterprise system which stimulated inventive geniuses to pursue their talents—and we all reap the profits. The great heroes of women's liberation are not the straggly-haired women on television talk shows and picket lines, but Thomas Edison who brought the miracle of electricity to our homes to give light and to run all those labor-saving devices—the equivalent, perhaps, of a half-dozen household servants for every middle-class American woman. Or Elias Howe who gave us the sewing machine which resulted in such an abundance of readymade clothing. Or Clarence Birdseye who invented the process for freezing foods. Or Henry Ford, who mass-produced the automobile so that it is within the price-range of every American, man or woman.

THE FRAUD OF THE EQUAL RIGHTS AMENDMENT

In the last couple of years, a noisy movement has sprung up agitating for "women's rights." Suddenly, everywhere we are afflicted with aggressive females on television talk shows yapping about how mistreated American women are, suggesting that marriage has put us in some kind of "slavery," that housework is menial and degrading, and—perish the thought—that women are discriminated against. New "women's liberation" organizations are popping up, agitating and demonstrating, serving demands on public officials, getting wide press coverage always, and purporting to speak for some 100,000,000 American women.

It's time to set the record straight. The claim that American women are downtrodden and unfairly treated is the fraud of the century. The truth is that American women never had it so good. Why should we lower ourselves to "equal rights" when we already have the status of special privilege? . . .

WOMEN'S LIBBERS DO NOT SPEAK FOR US

The "women's lib" movement is not an honest effort to secure better jobs for women who want or need to work outside the home. This is just the superficial sweet-talk to win broad support for a radical "movement." Women's lib is a total assault on the role of the American woman as wife and mother, and on the family as the basic unit of society.

Women's libbers are trying to make wives and mothers unhappy with their career, make them feel that they are "second-class citizens" and "abject slaves." Women's libbers are promoting free sex instead of the "slavery" of marriage. They are promoting Federal "day-care centers" for babies instead of homes. They are promoting abortions instead of families. . . .

Modern technology and opportunity have not discovered any nobler or more satisfying or more creative career for a woman than marriage and motherhood. The wonderful advantage that American women have is that we can have all the rewards of that number-one career, and still moonlight with a second one to suit our intellectual, cultural or financial tastes or needs.

And why should the men acquiesce in a system which gives preferential rights and lighter duties to women? In return, the men get the pearl of great price: a happy home, a faithful wife, and children they adore.

If the women's libbers want to reject marriage and motherhood, it's a free country and that is their choice. But let's not permit these women's libbers to get away with pretending to speak for the rest of us. Let's not permit this tiny minority to degrade the role that most women prefer. Let's not let these women's libbers deprive wives and mothers of the rights we now possess.

Tell your Senators NOW that you want them to vote NO on the Equal Rights Amendment. Tell your television and radio stations that you want equal time to present the case FOR marriage and motherhood.

Source: Phyllis Schlafly, "What's Wrong with 'Equal Rights' for Women?" *The Phyllis Schlafly Report* 5, no. 7 (February 1972): 1–4. (Courtesy of Phyllis Schlafly)

8

"JEFFERSON DAVIS'S DESCENDENTS . . . ARE BECOMING INVOLVED WITH THE REPUBLICAN PARTY": *SOUTHERN PARTISAN* INTERVIEW WITH TRENT LOTT (1984)

Trent Lott was one of the many conservative southern whites who left the Democratic Party over its support of civil rights. A protégé of the veteran Mississippi segregationist William M. Colmer, Lott won election to Congress as a Republican in 1972. By 1980, a year in which he also oversaw Ronald Reagan's Mississippi presidential campaign, he rose to the position of minority whip of the U.S. House of Representatives. In 1988 he won election to the U.S. Senate, and in 1995 was named Senate Majority Leader. He served as one of the top Republican leaders in the Senate in various capacities until a 2002 scandal exposed his long-standing segregationist sympathies and led to a temporary loss of position and power. How does Lott reach out to unrepentant white supremacists in this interview with the magazine *Southern Partisan*? How accurate was his characterization of Democrats? Why do you think the Republican Party looked to Trent Lott for leadership? What kind of "religious people" do you think Lott hoped to get active in politics and why? In what ways has the growing power of southerners such as Lott altered the party of Lincoln?

Partisan: At the convention of the Sons of Confederate Veterans in Biloxi, Mississippi you made the statement that "the spirit of Jefferson Davis lives in the 1984 Republican Platform." What did you mean by that?

Lott: I think that a lot of the fundamental principles that Jefferson Davis believed in are very important today to people all across the country, and they apply to the Republican Party. It is the more conservative party. It is the party more concerned about not having government dominance. It is the party that believes the least government is the best government, the party that is closest to the grass roots.

. . . The Republican Party still believes that the states have a specified role under the Constitution.

After the War between the States, a lot of Southerners identified with the Democrat[ic] Party because of the radical Republicans we had at that time, particularly in the Senate. The South was wedded to that party for years and years and years. But we have seen the Republican Party become more conservative and more oriented toward the traditional family values, the religious values that we hold dear in the South. And the Democratic Party has been going in the other direction. As a result of that, more and more of the South's sons, Jefferson Davis' descendents, direct or indirect, are becoming involved in the Republican Party. The platform we had in Dallas, the 1984 Republican platform, all the ideas we supported there—from tax policy, to foreign policy; from individual rights, to neighborhood security—are things that Jefferson Davis and his people believed in. . . .

The Democratic Party just basically does not stand for the things we believe in as Southerners. For us to continue to be wedded to it because of events that took place after the War between the States, the War of Aggression, and because our fathers or grandfathers were identified with that Party, is a terrible mistake. We have to begin at the grass roots, by electing supervisors, state legislators and governors who won't pay lip service to a national party that Southerners really don't agree with. Now the Democrats are for big government. They are for higher taxes. They are for weakening the national defense of this country. They are for rolling over and playing dead when it comes to confronting the Communists all over the world. And we've got to realize that the South is going to have to be a part of the Republican Party, and I think maybe 1984 will be another step in that direction. . . .

Partisan: That's a good point. Let me raise an issue that was very much in the news on the presidential front. The question of religion and politics, the separation of church and state. Of course it goes back to the platform. Do you think that issue cut in a positive or negative way for the president's campaign?

Lott: I think it was a totally bogus issue for Democrats to be raising and the press too, quite frankly. They were perpetuating the biggest double standard I have ever seen. . . .

I've made speeches all over the South, all over the country, and particularly in my own state, saying, "Look, if the religious people don't get involved in politics, it's going to be run by others." And during the late 50's and 60's and 70's that's exactly what happened to the federal government. It was taken over by the people who held extreme liberal views, views that in my opinion were inconsistent with the traditions that we have always believed in in this country. They moved in the direction of socialism, and we are trying to take it back. . . .

Richard T. Hines conducted this *Partisan* interview. He is a Senior Executive with the Reagan administration, a former member of the South Carolina House of Representatives and Assistant Editor of the *Southern Partisan*.

Source: "A Partisan Conversation with Trent Lott," interview by Richard T. Hines, *Southern Partisan* 4, no. 4 (Fall 1984). (Courtesy of *Southern Partisan* magazine, www.southernpartisan.net)

9

ELIZABETH BIRCH, "AN OPEN LETTER TO THE CHRISTIAN COALITION" (1995)

Led by conservative activists, the Republican Party targeted right-wing religious voters along with recalcitrant white southerners. As the previous document showed, there was much overlap in the two groups, but the Religious Right was a broader, national cause that grew as it organized against the reforms won by the feminist and lesbian and gay movements, in particular. Conservative activists sought to amplify their interpretations of the Bible and build church-based electoral power in the late 1970s by creating such organizations as the Moral Majority, the Religious Roundtable, and the Christian Coalition. Founded by Pat Robertson and led by Ralph Reed in the 1990s, the Christian Coalition mobilized such religious conservatives to vote Republican, often using incendiary direct mail that alleged grave threats to the nation from the gay rights movement. In 1995, Elizabeth Birch, director of the nation's largest policy organization for lesbians and gay men, asked Reed for permission to speak directly to a Christian Coalition conference in hopes of breaking through the stereotypes to "our common humanity." He said no. Why do you think he refused direct communication? How persuasive is Birch's case for common ground? Why did conservative Republicans focus so much attention on such a small minority of the population? How do you explain the fury the Christian Coalition summoned against gays and lesbians? How was it similar to or different from the hostility that the conservative movement had earlier directed against black civil rights activists and feminists?

Dear Members of the Christian Coalition:

An open letter was not my first choice as a way of reaching you. I would have preferred speaking to all of you directly, and in a setting where you would be most comfortable.

That was my motivation some weeks ago when I asked your executive director, Ralph Reed, for the opportunity to address the Christian Coalition's "Road to Victory" conference. It is still my motivation today. And it is supported by a single, strong belief that the time has come for us to speak to each other rather than past each other.

It took Mr. Reed very little time to reject my request. Perhaps he misunderstood my motivation. But I can assure you that what has driven my request is this: I believe in the power of the word and the value of honest communication. During my years of work as a litigator at a major corporation, I was often amazed at what simple, fresh, and truthful conversation could accomplish. And what is true in the corporate setting is also true, I'm convinced, in our communities. If we could learn to speak and listen to each other with integrity, the consequences might shock us.

Although your podium was not available to me, I am grateful for those who have come today and will give me the benefit of the doubt and be willing to consider what I have to say. I will be pleased if you are able to hear me without prejudging either the message or the messenger. And I will be hopeful, most of all, if you respond by joining me in finding new ways to speak with honesty not only *about* one another, but also *to* one another.

If I am confident in anything at all, it is this: Our communities have more in common than we care to imagine. This is not to deny the many differences. But out of our sheer humanity comes some common ground. Although the stereotype would have us believe otherwise, there are many conservative Americans within the nation's gay and lesbian communities. What's more, there are hundreds of thousands of Christians among us—Christians of all traditions, including those represented in the Christian Coalition. And, like it or not, we are part of your family. And you are part of our community. We are neighbors and colleagues, business associates and friends. More intimately still, you are fathers of sons who are gay and mothers of daughters who are lesbians. I know many of your children very, very well. I work with them. I worry with them. And I rejoice that they are part of our community.

Part of what I want you to know is that many of your children who are gay and lesbian are gifted and strong. Some are famous. Most of them are not. But many are heroic in the way they have conquered barriers to their own self-respect and the courage with which they've set out to serve a higher good. All were created by God. And you have every right to be proud of each of them.

I begin by noting the worthiness of gays and lesbians in your family and in our community for a reason: It's hard to communicate with people we do not respect. And the character of prejudice, of stereotype, of demagoguery, is to tear down the respect others might otherwise enjoy in public, even the respect they would hold for themselves in private. By taking away respectability, rhetorically as well as legally, we justify the belief that they are not quite human, not quite worthy, not quite deserving of our time, of our attention, of our concern.

And that is, sadly, what many of your children and colleagues and neighbors who are gay and lesbian have feared is the intent of the Christian Coalition. If it were true, of course, it would be not only regrettable, but terribly hypocritical. It would not be worthy of the true ideals and values based in love at the core of what we call Christian.

The reason I have launched this conversation is to ask you to join me in a common demonstration that this is not true. I make my appeal as an individual, Elizabeth Birch, and also as the executive director of the Human Rights Campaign Fund, America's largest policy organization for gay men and lesbian women.

This is such a basic appeal to human communication and common decency that I do not even know how to distinguish between what is personal and what is professional. But my appeal is sincere. I am convinced that if we cannot find ways to respect one another as human beings, and therefore to respect one another's rights, we will do great damage not only to each other, but also to those we say we represent.

I recognize that it is not easy for us to speak charitably to each other. I have read fund-raising letters in which people like me are assigned labels which summon up the ugliest of dehumanizing stereotypes. Anonymous writers have hidden under the title of "Concerned Christian" to condemn me with the fires of God and to call on all of you to deny me an equal opportunity to participate in the whole range of American life. I have heard of political agendas calling not merely for the defeat of those I represent, but for our eradication.

Such expressions of hatred do not—cannot—beget a spirit of trust. Nor do they pass the test of either truthfulness or courage. They bear false witness in boldface type. And I believe that they must embarrass those who, like me, heard of another gospel—even the simple Gospel taught me as a child in Sunday School.

I would not ask you, as members of a Christian group, or as supporters of a conservative political cause, to set aside either your basic beliefs or
your historic commitments. The churches which many of you represent—
Baptist, for example, and Pentecostal—were also the churches I attended as
a young woman. In those days, I heard sermons about justice and sang songs
about forgiveness. My greatest hope is not that you will give up your faith,
but that it will work among all of us.

Neither of us should forsake our fundamental convictions. But we
could hold those convictions with a humility that allows room for the lives
of others. Neither of us may be the sole possessors of truth on every given
issue. And we could express our convictions in words that are—if not af-
fectionate, and if not even kind then at least decent, civil, humane. We need
not demonize each other simply because we disagree. . . .

Many of us in this community have a long history with the church. . . .

For some, the deepest agony of life is not that they risk physical abuse
or that they will never gain their civil rights, but that they have felt the
judgment of an institution on which they have staked their lives: the
church. What they long for most is what they once believed was theirs as a
birthright: the knowledge that they are God's children, and that they can
come home.

And it is not only those of us who are gay or lesbian who have suffered on the doorstep of some congregations. Parents, fearing what others
at church might whisper, choose to deny the reality that their son is gay or
their daughter is a lesbian. Brothers and sisters suffer an unhealthy, and unwarranted, and un-Christian shame. They bear a burden that cripples their
faith, based on a fear that cripples us all.

This means, I think, that we are still a long way from realizing the ideal
of America as a land of hope and promise, from achieving the goal of religion as a healing force that unites us, from discovering that human beings
are, simply by virtue of being human beings, deserving of respect and common decency.

And so, I have come today—in person, bearing this letter, and in writing, to those who will only receive it—to make three simple, sincere appeals to those of you who are members of the Christian Coalition.

The first appeal is this: Please make integrity a watchword for the campaigns you launch. We all struggle to be people of integrity, especially when
we campaign for funds. But the fact that we are tempted by money is no
excuse. We need to commit ourselves to a higher moral ground.

I do not know when the first direct-mail letter was issued in your
name that defamed gay men and abused gay women, that described us as

less than human and certainly unworthy of trust. Neither do I know when people discovered that the richest return came from letters that depicted gays and lesbians with intentionally dishonest images. But I do know—and I must believe that you know too—that this is dishonest, this is wrong.

I can hardly imagine that a money machine is being operated in your name, spinning your exaggerations as if they were truths and that you do not see it. But perhaps you do not. In which case, I ask that you hear my second appeal: I ask that, as individuals, you talk to those of us who are gay or lesbian, rather than succumb to the temptation to either avoid us at all cost, as if we are not a part of your community, or to rant at us, as if we are not worthy of quiet conversation.

We are, all of us and those we represent, human beings. As Americans, you will have your political candidates; we will have ours. But we could, both of us, ask that our candidates speak the truth to establish their right to leadership, rather than abuse the truth in the interest of one evening's headline. We may work for different outcomes in the elections, but we can engage in an ethic of basic respect and decency.

Finally, I appeal to you as people who passionately uphold the value of the family. You have brothers and sons who have not heard a word of family affection since the day they summoned the courage to tell the simple truth. You have sisters and daughters who have given up believing that you mean it when you say, "The family is the basic unit of society," or even, "God loves you, and so do I."

Above all the other hopes with which I've come to you hovers this one: that some member of Christian Coalition will call some member of the Human Rights Campaign Fund and say, "It's been a long time, son," or "I'm missing you, my daughter," and before the conversation ends, someone will hear the heartfelt words, "Come home. Let's talk to each other."

In that hope, I appeal to each of you.

Source: Elizabeth Birch, "Out of Our Sheer Humanity Comes Common Ground," reprinted in Harriet Sigerman, ed., *The Columbia Documentary History of American Women Since 1941* (New York: Columbia University Press, 2003). (Permission granted by the Human Rights Campaign, Washington, DC)

SELECTED READINGS

Allitt, Patrick. *Catholic Intellectuals and Conservative Politics in America, 1950–1985*. Ithaca, NY: Cornell University Press, 1993.

Anderson, Carol. *Eyes Off the Prize: The United Nations and the African American Struggle for Human Rights, 1944–1955*. Cambridge: Cambridge University Press, 2003.

Anderson, Martin. *Revolution: The Reagan Legacy*. Stanford, CA: Hoover Institution Press, 1990.

Applebome, Peter. *Dixie Rising: How the South Is Shaping American Values, Politics, and Culture*. New York: Harcourt Brace, 1996.

Babbitt, Irving. *Democracy and Leadership*. Indianapolis, IN: Liberty Fund, 1979.

Babbitt, Irving, with a new introduction by Claes Ryn. *Rousseau and Romanticism*. New Brunswick, NJ: Kessinger, 2004.

Bastiat, Frederic. *The Law*. Ivington-on-Hudson, NY: Filiquarian Publishing, 1998.

Belloc, Hilaire. *The Servile State*. Indianapolis, IN: Liberty Fund, 1977.

Berman, William C. *America's Right Turn: From Nixon to Bush*. Baltimore: Johns Hopkins University Press, 1994.

Billingsley, Kenneth Lloyd. *Hollywood Party: How Communism Seduced the American Film Industry in the 1930s and 1940s*. Rocklin, CA: Prima Lifestyles, 1998.

Bjerre-Poulsen, Niels. *Right Face: Organizing the American Conservative Movement, 1945–1965*. Copenhagen: Museum Tusculanum Press, 2002.

Black, Merle, and Earl Black. *The Rise of Southern Republicans*. Cambridge, MA: Belknap Press, 2003.

Bloom, Allan. *The Closing of the American Mind*. New York: Simon & Schuster, 1987.

Bork, Robert H. *Slouching Towards Gomorrah: Modern Liberalism and American Decline*. New York: HarperCollins, 1996.

———. *The Tempting of America: The Political Seduction of the Law*. New York: Free Press, 1990.

Bozell, L. Brent. *The Warren Revolution: Reflections on a Consensus Society*. Chicago: Crown, 1966.

Brennan, Mary C. *Turning Right in the Sixties: The Conservative Capture of the GOP.* Chapel Hill: University of North Carolina Press, 1995.

Buchanan, Patrick J. *Where the Right Went Wrong: How Neoconservatives Subverted the Reagan Revolution and Hijacked the Bush Presidency.* New York: St. Martin's Griffin, 2005.

Buckley, William F., Jr. *The Jeweler's Eye: A Book of Irresistible Political Reflections.* New York: G. P. Putnam's Sons, 1968.

———. *Miles Gone By: A Literary Autobiography.* Washington, DC: Regnery, 2004.

———. *Up From Liberalism.* New York: Hillman Periodicals, 1959.

Carter, Dan T. *The Politics of Rage: George Wallace, the Origins of the New Conservatism, and the Transformation of American Politics.* Baton Rouge: Louisiana State University Press, 1995.

Chamberlain, John. *Farewell to Reform: The Rise, Life and Decay of the Progressive Mind in America.* Chicago: Quadrangle Books, 1965.

Chamberlin, William Henry. *America's Second Crusade.* Chicago: Regnery, 1950.

———. *Confessions of an Individualist.* New York: Macmillan, 1940.

Chambers, Whittaker. *Witness.* Washington, DC: Regnery, 1980.

Chodorov, Frank. *Out of Step: The Autobiography of an Individualist.* New York: Devin-Adair, 1962.

Clendinen, Dudley, and Adam Nagourney. *Out for Good: The Struggle to Build a Gay Rights Movement in America.* New York: Simon & Schuster, 1999.

Cohen, Lizabeth. *Making a New Deal: Industrial Workers in Chicago, 1919–1939.* New York: Cambridge University Press, 1990.

Collins, Robert M. *Transforming America: Politics and Culture During the Reagan Years.* New York: Columbia University Press, 2006.

Courtois, Stephene, Nicholas Werth, Jean-Louis Panne, Abdrezej Paczkowski, Karel Bartosek, and Jean-Louis Margolin, eds. *The Black Book of Communism: Crimes, Terror, Repression.* Cambridge, MA: Harvard University Press, 1999.

Cram, Ralph Adams. *My Life in Architecture.* New York: Little, Brown, 1937.

Crespino, Joseph. *In Search of Another Country: Mississippi and the Conservative Counterrevolution.* Princeton, NJ: Princeton University Press, 2007.

Critchlow, Donald T. *The Conservative Ascendency: How the GOP Right Made Political History.* Cambridge, MA: Harvard University Press, 2007.

———. *Intended Consequences: Birth Control, Abortion, and the Federal Government in Modern America.* New York: Oxford University Press, 1999.

———. *Phyllis Schlafly and Grassroots Conservatism: A Woman's Crusade.* Princeton, NJ: Princeton University Press, 2005.

Critchlow, Donald T., and Agnieszka Critchlow, eds. *Enemies of the State: Personal Stories from the Gulag.* Chicago: Ivan R. Dee, 2002.

Crocker, George N. *Roosevelt's Road to Russia.* Chicago: Regnery, 1959.

Crunden, Robert M., ed. *The Superfluous Men: Conservative Critics of American Culture, 1900–1945.* Wilmington, DE: Intercollegiate Studies Institute, 1999.

Curtis, George M., III, and James J. Thompson Jr., eds. *The Southern Essays of Richard M. Weaver.* Indianapolis, IN: Liberty Fund, 1987.

Dawley, Alan. *Changing the World: American Progressives in War and Revolution.* Princeton, NJ: Princeton University Press, 2003.

Dennis, Lawrence. *The Coming American Fascism.* New York: Noontide Press, 1993 (orginally published 1936).

Dennis, Lawrence, and Maximillian St. George. *The Trial on Trial.* New York: Institute for Historical Review, 1945.

Diggins, John Patrick. *Ronald Reagan: Fate, Freedom and the Making of History.* New York: W. W. Norton, 2007.

Doherty, Brian. *Radicals for Capitalism: A Freewheeling History of the Modern American Libertarian Movement.* New York: Public Affairs, 2007.

Easton, Nina J. *Gang of Five: Leaders at the Center of the Conservative Ascendency.* New York: Simon & Schuster, 2000.

Ebenstein, Alan. *Friedrich Hayek: A Biography.* New York: Palgrave Macmillan, 2001.

Edsall, Thomas Byrne. *The New Politics of Inequality.* New York: W. W. Norton, 1984.

Edsall, Thomas Byrne, with Mary Edsall. *Chain Reaction: The Impact of Race, Rights, and Taxes on American Politics.* New York: W. W. Norton, 1992.

Edwards, Lee. *The Conservative Revolution: The Movement That Remade America.* New York: Free Press, 1999.

Ehrenreich, Barbara. *The Hearts of Men: American Dreams and the Flight From Commitment.* Garden City, NY: Anchor Press, 1983.

Ehrman, John. *The Eighties: America in the Age of Reagan.* New Haven, CT: Yale University Press, 2005.

———. *The Rise of Neoconservatism: Intellectuals and Foreign Affairs, 1945–1994.* New Haven, CT: Yale University Press, 1995.

Evans, M. Stanton. *Blacklisted by History: The Untold Story of Senator Joe McCarthy and His Fight Against America's Enemies.* New York: Crown Forum, 2007.

Evans, Thomas W. *The Education of Ronald Reagan: The General Electric Years and the Untold Story of His Conversion to Conservatism.* New York: Columbia University Press, 2006.

Everitt, David. *A Shadow of Red: Communism and the Blacklist in Radio and Television.* Chicago: Ivan R. Dee, 2007.

Faludi, Susan. *Backlash: The Undeclared War Against American Women.* New York: Crown, 1991.

Ferguson, Thomas, and Joel Rogers. *Right Turn: The Decline of the Democrats and the Future of American Politics.* New York: Hill & Wang, 1986.

Feulner, Edwin J., Jr. *Intellectual Pilgrims: The Fiftieth Anniversary of the Mont Pelerin Society.* Washington, DC: Self-published, 1999.

Flipse, Scott. "Below-the-Belt Politics: Protestant Evangelicals, Abortion, and the Foundation of the Religious Right, 1960–1975." In *The Conservative Sixties*, edited by David Farber and Jeff Roche. New York: Peter Lang, 2003.

Flynn, John T. *The Road Ahead: America's Creeping Revolution.* New York: Devin-Adair, 1949.

———. *While You Slept: Our Tragedy in Asia and Who Made It.* New York: Dodd Mead, 1951.

Francis, Samuel. *Beautiful Losers: Essays on the Failure of American Conservatism.* Columbia: University of Missouri Press, 1993.

Fried, Richard M. *Nightmare in Red: The McCarthy Era in Perspective.* New York: Oxford University Press, 1990.

Friedman, Milton. *Capitalism and Freedom.* Chicago: University of Chicago Press, 1962.

Friedman, Milton, and Rose Friedman. *Two Lucky People: Memoirs.* Chicago: University of Chicago Press, 1999.

Friedman, Murray. *The Neoconservative Revolution: Jewish Intellectuals and the Shaping of Public Policy.* Cambridge: Cambridge University Press, 2005.

Frohnen, Bruce, Jeremy Beer, and Jeffrey O. Nelson, eds. *American Conservatism: An Encyclopedia.* Wilmington, DE: Intercollegiate Studies Institute, 1996.

Frum, David. *Dead Right.* New York: Basic Books, 1994.

Fukuyama, Francis. *America at the Crossroads: Democracy, Power and the Neoconservative Legacy.* New Haven, CT: Yale University Press, 2006.

Gaddis, John Lewis. *The Cold War: A New History.* New York: Penguin, 2006.

———. *Strategies of Containment: A Critical Appraisal of American National Security Policy During the Cold War,* rev. and expanded ed. New York: Oxford University Press, 2005.

———. *Surprise, Security and the American Experience.* Cambridge, MA: Harvard University Press, 2004.

Gallagher, John, and Chris Bull. *Perfect Enemies: The Religious Right, the Gay Movement, and the Politics of the 1990s.* New York: Crown, 1996.

Garfinkle, Adam. *Telltale Hearts: The Origins and Impact of the Vietnam Anti-War Movement.* New York: Palgrave Macmillan, 1997.

Goldberg, Robert Alan. *Barry Goldwater.* New Haven, CT: Yale University Press, 1995.

Goldwater, Barry M. *The Conscience of a Conservative.* Shepherdsville, KY: Hillman Books, 1960.

———. *With No Apologies: The Personal and Political Memoirs of Barry Goldwater.* New York: Morrow, 1979.

Gordon, Linda. *Woman's Body, Woman's Right: Birth Control in America,* rev. ed. New York: Penguin, 1990.

Gottfried, Paul Edward. *The Search for Historical Meaning: Hegel and the Postwar American Right.* DeKalb: Northern Illinois University Press, 1986.

Gottfried, Paul, and Thomas Fleming. *The Conservative Movement.* Boston: Twayne, 1988.

Hamby, Alonzo L. *For the Survival of Democracy: Franklin Roosevelt and the World Crisis of the 1930s.* New York: Free Press, 2004.

Hayek, Friedrich A. *The Constitution of Liberty.* Chicago: University of Chicago Press, 1960.

———. *The Road to Serfdom.* Chicago: University of Chicago Press, 1944.

Haynes, John E. *Red Scare or Red Menace? American Communism and Anticommunism in the Cold War Era.* Chicago: Ivan R. Dee, 1996.

Haynes, John Earl, and Harvey Klehr. *In Denial: Historians, Communism and Espionage.* San Francisco: Encounter Books, 2003.

———. *Venona: Decoding Soviet Espionage in America.* New Haven, CT: Yale University Press, 1999.

Hayward, Steven F. *The Age of Reagan: The Fall of the Old Liberal Order, 1964–1980.* New York: Prima Lifestyles, 2001.

Heineman, Kenneth J. *God Is a Conservative: Religion, Politics and Morality in Contemporary America.* New York: New York University Press, 1998.

Herman, Arthur. *Joseph McCarthy: Reexamining the Life and Legacy of America's Most Hated Senator.* New York: Free Press, 2000.

Himmelstein, Jerome L. *To the Right: The Transformation of American Conservatism.* Berkeley: University of California Press, 1990.

Hodgson, Godfey. *The World Turned Right Side Up: A History of the Conservative Ascendency in America.* New York: Houghton Mifflin, 1996.

Hoeveler, J. David, Jr. *Watch on the Right: Conservative Intellectuals in the Reagan Era.* Madison: University of Wisconsin Press, 1991.

Johnson, David K. *The Lavender Scare: The Cold War Persecution of Gays and Lesbians in the Federal Government.* Chicago: University of Chicago Press, 2004.

Keller, Morton. *In Defense of Yesterday: James M. Beck and the Politics of Conservatism, 1861–1936.* New York: Coward-McCann, 1958.

Kelly, Daniel. *James Burnham and the Struggle for the World: A Life.* Wilmington, DE: ISI Books, 2002.

Kengor, Paul. *The Crusader: Ronald Reagan and the Fall of Communism.* New York: Harper Perennial, 2007.

Kilpatrick, James Jackson. *The Sovereign States.* Chicago: Regnery, 1957.

Kirk, Russell. *The Conservative Mind: From Burke to Santayana.* Chicago: Regnery, 1953.

———. *The Sword of Imagination: Memoirs of a Half-Century of Literary Conflict.* Grand Rapids, MI: Eerdmans, 1995.

Kirkpatrick, Jeane J. *Making War to Keep Peace.* New York: Harper, 2007.

Klatch, Rebecca E. *A Generation Divided: The New Left, the New Right, and the 1960s.* Berkeley: University of California Press, 1999.

Klehr, Harvey, John Earl Haynes, and Fridrikh Igorevich Firsov. *The Secret World of American Communism.* New Haven, CT: Yale University Press, 1995.

Kotz, Nick. *Judgement Days: Lyndon Baines Johnson, Martin Luther King, Jr., and the Laws That Changed America.* Boston: Houghton Mifflin, 2005.

Kristol, Irving. *Neoconservatism: The Autobiography of an Idea: Selected Essays, 1949–1995.* New York: Free Press, 1995.

Kruse, Kevin. *White Flight: Atlanta and the Making of Modern Conservatism*. Princeton, NJ: Princeton University Press, 2005.

Lassiter, Matthew. *The Silent Majority: Suburban Politics in the Sunbelt South*. Princeton, NJ: Princeton University Press, 2006.

Layman, Geoffrey. *The Great Divide: Religious and Cultural Conflict in American Party Politics*. New York: Columbia University Press, 2001.

Leffler, Melvyn. *A Preponderance of Power: National Security, the Truman Administration and the Cold War*. Stanford, CA: Stanford University Press, 1993.

Lettow, Paul. *Ronald Reagan and His Quest to Abolish Nuclear Weapons*. New York: Random House, 2005.

Lewis, George. *The White South and the Red Menace: Segregationists, Anticommunism, and Massive Resistance, 1945–1965*. Gainesville: University Press of Florida, 2004.

Lichtenstein, Nelson. *State of the Union: A Century of American Labor*. Princeton, NJ: Princeton University Press, 2002.

Link, William A. *Righteous Warrior: Jesse Helms and the Rise of Modern Conservatism*. New York: Macmillan, 2008.

MacLean, Nancy. *Freedom Is Not Enough: The Opening of the American Workplace*. Cambridge, MA: Harvard University Press, 2006.

Mann, James. *Rise of the Vulcans: The History of Bush's War Cabinet*. New York: Viking, 2004.

Marlin, George J. *The American Catholic Voter: 200 Years of Political Impact*. South Bend, IN: St. Augustine's Press, 2004.

McAllister, Ted V. *Revolt Against Modernity: Leo Strauss, Eric Voegelin, and the Search for a Postliberal Order*. Lawrence: University Press of Kansas, 1996.

McGirr, Lisa. *Suburban Warriors: The Origins of the New American Right*. Princeton, NJ: Princeton University Press, 2001.

Melich, Tanya. *The Republican War Against Women: An Insider's Report From Behind the Lines*. New York: Bantam Books, 1996.

Meyer, Frank S. *In Defense of Freedom and Related Essays*. Indianapolis, IN: Liberty Fund, 1996.

———, ed. *What Is Conservatism?* Chicago: Holt, Rinehart, and Winston, 1964.

Micklethwait, John, and Adrian Wooldridge. *The Right Nation: Conservative Power in America*. New York: Penguin, 2004.

Middendorf, J. William, II. *A Glorious Disaster: Barry Goldwater's Presidential Campaign and the Origins of the Conservative Movement*. New York: Basic Books, 2006.

Miles, Michael. *The Odyssey of the American Right*. New York: Oxford University Press, 1980.

Morgan, Kimberly. "A Child of the Sixties: The Great Society, the New Right, and the Politics of Federal Child Care." *Journal of Policy History* 13 (2001): 215–250.

Morley, Felix. *For the Record*. South Bend, IN: Regnery, 1979.

Moser, John E. *Right Turn: John T. Flynn and the Transformation of American Liberalism*. New York: New York University Press, 2005.

Murray, Charles. *Losing Ground: American Social Policy, 1950–1980*. New York: Basic Books, 1984.

Nash, George H. *The Conservative Intellectual Movement in America Since 1945*. New York: Basic Books, 1976 (third ed., 2006).

Nock, Albert Jay. *Memoirs of a Superfluous Man*. Tampa, FL: Hallberg, 1994.

———. *Our Enemy the State*. San Francisco: Fox & Wilkes, 1995.

Ortega y Gasset, José. *The Revolt of the Masses*. New York: W. W. Norton, 1932.

Panichas, George, ed. *The Critical Legacy of Irving Babbitt*. Wilmington, DE: ISI Books, 1999.

———. *The Essential Russell Kirk: Selected Essays*. Wilmington, DE: ISI Books, 2007.

Patterson, James T. *Congressional Conservatism and the New Deal: The Growth of the Conservative Coalition in Congress, 1933–1939*. Lexington: University of Kentucky Press, 1967.

———. *Mr. Republican: A Biography of Robert A. Taft*. Boston: Houghton Mifflin, 1972.

Perlstein, Rick. *Before the Storm: Barry Goldwater and the Unmaking of the American Consensus*. New York: Hill and Wang, 2001.

Person, James E., Jr. *Russell Kirk: A Critical Biography of a Conservative Mind*. Lanham, MD: Madison Books, 1999.

Podhoretz, Norman. *Breaking Ranks: A Political Memoir*. New York: Harper Colophon, 1979.

———. *Making It*. New York: Random House, 1967.

———. *My Love Affair With America: The Cautionary Tale of a Cheerful Conservative*. New York: Free Press, 2000.

Radosh, Ronald, and Allis Radosh. *Red Star Over Hollywood: The Film Colony's Long Romance With the Left*. San Francisco: Encounter Books, 2003.

Raimando, Justin. *An Enemy of the State: The Life of Murray N. Rothbard*. Amherst, NY: Prometheus, 2000.

———. *Reclaiming the American Right: The Lost Legacy of the Conservative Movement*. Burlingame, CA: Intercollegiate Studies Institute, 1993.

Rand, Ayn. *Atlas Shrugged*. New York: Signet, 1957.

Reagan, Ronald. *An American Life: The Autobiography*. New York: Simon & Schuster, 1990.

———. *The Reagan Diaries,* ed. Douglas Brinkley. New York: HarperCollins, 2007.

Regnery, Alfred S. *Upstream: The Ascendance of American Conservatism*. New York: Simon & Schuster, 2008.

Regnery, Henry. *A Few Reasonable Words: Selected Writings*. Wilmington, DE: Intercollegiate Studies Institute, 1996.

———. *Memoirs of a Dissident Publisher*. Chicago: Harcourt Brace Jovanovich, 1985.

———. *Perfect Sowing: Reflections of a Bookman*. Wilmington, DE: Intercollegiate Studies Institute, 1999.

Ribuffo, Leo P. *The Old Christian Right: The Protestant Far Right from the Great Depression to the Cold War*. Philadelphia: Temple University Press, 1983.

Roberts, Paul Craig. *The Supply-Side Revolution: An Insider's Account of Policymaking in Washington*. Cambridge, MA: Harvard University Press, 1984.

Rodgers, Marion Elizabeth. *Mencken: The American Iconoclast*. New York: Oxford University Press, 2005.

Romerstein, Herbert, and Eric Breindel. *The Venona Secrets: Exposing Soviet Espionage and America's Traitors*. Washington, DC: Regnery, 2000.

Rothbard, Murray N. *For a New Liberty: The Libertarian Manifesto*. New York: Collier Books, 1978.

Rusher, William A. *The Making of a New Majority Party*. Ottawa, IL: Green Hill, 1975.

———. *The Rise of the Right*. New York: William Morrow, 1984.

Russello, Gerald J. *The Postmodern Imagination of Russell Kirk*. Columbia: University of Missouri Press, 2007.

Ryn, Claes G. *America the Virtuous: The Crisis of Democracy and the Quest for Empire*. New Brunswick, NJ: Transaction, 2003.

Schlafly, Phyllis. *A Choice Not an Echo*. Alton, IL: Pere Marquette Press, 1964.

———. *Feminist Fantasies*. Dallas, TX: Spence, 2003.

Schneider, Gregory L. *Cadres for Conservatism: Young Americans for Freedom and the Rise of the Contemporary Right*. New York: New York University Press, 1999.

———, ed. *Conservatism in America since 1930: A Reader*. New York: New York University Press, 2003.

Schoenwald, Jonathan M. *A Time for Choosing: The Rise of Modern American Conservatism*. New York: Oxford University Press, 2001.

Schrecker, Ellen. *Many Are the Crimes: McCarthyism in America*. Boston: Little, Brown, 1998.

Schulman, Bruce J. *The Seventies: The Great Shift in American Culture, Society, and Politics*. New York: Free Press, 2001.

Schweizer, Peter. *Reagan's War: The Epic Story of His Forty-Year Struggle and Triumph Over Communism*. New York: Doubleday, 2002.

Scotchie, Joseph. *Barbarians in the Saddle: An Intellectual Biography of Richard Weaver*. New Brunswick, NJ: Transaction, 1997.

———. *The Paleoconservatives: New Voices of the Old Right*. New Brunswick, NJ: Transaction, 1999.

Shafer, Byron E., and Richard Johnston. *The End of Southern Exceptionalism: Class, Race and Partisan Change in the Postwar South*. Cambridge, MA: Harvard University Press, 2006.

Shirley, Craig. *Reagan's Revolution: The Untold Story of the Campaign That Started It All*. Nashville, TN: Nelson Current, 2004.

Shlaes, Amity. *The Forgotten Man: A New History of the Great Depression*. New York: HarperCollins, 2007.

Skinner, Kiron K., Annelise Anderson, and Martin Anderson, eds. *Reagan in His Own Hand: The Writings of Ronald Reagan That Reveal His Revolutionary Vision for America*. New York: Simon & Schuster, 2001.

Smant, Kevin J. *Principles and Heresies: Frank S. Meyer and the Shaping of the American Conservative Movement*. Wilmington, DE: Intercollegiate Studies Institute, 2002.

Smith, Ted, III. *In Defense of Tradition: Collected Shorter Writings of Richard M. Weaver, 1929–1963*. Indianapolis, IN: Liberty Fund, 2000.

———, ed. *Steps Towards Restoration: The Consequences of Richard Weaver's Ideas*. Wilmington, DE: Intercollegiate Studies Institute, 1998.

Sniderman, Paul M., and Thomas Piazza. *The Scar of Race*. Cambridge, MA: Belknap Press, 1993.

Spencer, Herbert. *The Man Versus the State*. Indianapolis, IN: Liberty Fund, 1982.

Storrs, Landon R. Y. "Attacking the Washington 'Femmocracy': Antifeminism in the Cold War Campaign Against 'Communists in Government.'" *Feminist Studies* 33 (Spring 2007).

Tanenhaus, Sam. *Whittaker Chambers: A Biography*. New York: Random House, 1995.

Thomas, Clarence. *My Grandfather's Son: A Memoir*. New York: HarperCollins, 2007.

Tuccille, Jerome. *It Usually Begins With Ayn Rand*. San Francisco: Fox & Wilkes, 1997.

Twelve Southerners. *I'll Take My Stand: The South and the Agrarian Tradition*. Baton Rouge: Louisiana State University Press, 1977.

Tyrrell, R. Emmett, Jr. *The Conservative Crack-Up*. New York: Simon & Schuster, 1992.

Van Mises, Ludwig. *Liberalism: The Classical Tradition*. Indianapolis, IN: Liberty Fund, 2005.

Vargas, Zaragosa. *Labor Rights Are Civil Rights: Mexican American Workers in Twentieth-Century America*. Princeton, NJ: Princeton University Press, 2005.

Viguerie, Richard A. *The New Right: We're Ready to Lead*. Falls Church, VA: Viguerie Co., 1980.

Viguerie, Richard A., and David Franke. *America's Right Turn: How Conservatives Used New and Alternative Media to Take Power*. Chicago: Bonus Books, 2004.

Weaver, Richard M. *Ideas Have Consequences*. Chicago: University of Chicago Press, 1948.

———. *The Southern Tradition at Bay: A History of Postbellum Thought*. New Rochelle, NY: Arlington House, 1968.

———. "Up From Liberalism." *Modern Age* (Winter 1958–1959): 21–32.

Weinstein, Allen. *Perjury: The Hiss-Chambers Case*. New York: Knopf, 1976.

Weinstein, Allen, and Alexander Vassiliev. *The Haunted Wood: Soviet Espionage in America—The Stalin Era*. New York: Random House, 1999.

Wilentz, Sean. *The Age of Reagan: A History, 1974–2008*. New York: HarperCollins, 2008.

Will, George. *Suddenly: The American Ideal at Home and Abroad, 1986–1990*. New York: Free Press, 1990.

Wills, Garry. *A Necessary Evil: A History of American Distrust of Government*. New York: Simon & Schuster, 1999.

Wilson, Clyde N., ed. *A Defender of Southern Conservatism: M.E. Bradford and His Achievements*. Columbia: University of Missouri Press, 1999.

Woods, Jeff. *Black Struggle, Red Scare: Segregation and Anti-Communism in the South, 1948–1968*. Baton Rouge: Louisiana State University Press, 2004.

Young, Fred D. *Richard Weaver, 1910–1963: A Life of the Mind*. Columbia: University of Missouri Press, 1995.

INDEX

racial mixing and, 155; Republican Party as defender of, 5, 21. *See also* King, Martin Luther

Civil Rights Act of 1964, 77–82, 126; conservatives mobilization against, 142; Goldwater on, 26, 83–86

civil unions, 52

Civitas Humana (Roepke), 67

Clinton, Bill, 50; challenges in office, 50–52; NAFTA and, 166

Clinton, Hillary, 50

cohabitation, 193–95

Cold War, viii; conservatism influenced by, 55; conservative debate over, 10–11; questions arising from, 12; SALT agreements and, 87–98

collectivism, 190. *See also* liberalism

college students: W. Buckley, commentary on sexual code of, 193–95; as Vietnam War protesters, 30

Commentary magazine, 150

Committee for a Sane Nuclear Policy, 71

Common Sense (Paine), 3–4

Communism, 106; civil rights and, 138; conservatives focused on, 14, 22, 63–64; Hayek on dangers of, 11; *How Communists Negotiate*, 19; individual liberty threat from, 76; integration as tactic of, 184; libertarian v. conservative views of, 63–64; Meyer comparing Roosevelt policies to, 178; *National Review*'s campaign against, 127; Pegler on, 138; "racial collectivism" and, 183; religion and, 107; spies for, 13; *You Can Trust the Communists (to Be Communists)*, 19. *See also* anti-Communist movement; collectivism; socialism

Communist spies. *See* spies

Comprehensive Child Development Act, 155

Confederate States of America, 124. *See also* neo-Confederates

Congress of Industrial Organizations (CIO), 131

Connor, Eugene "Bull," 141

The Conscience of a Conservative (Goldwater), 4, 23–24

conscription, 65

conservatism, vii; American individualism, 3; anti-Communist movement as part of foundation of, 10; Cold War influencing, 55; distrust of centralized government, 3–4; economic freedom/political freedom linked, 4; equal opportunity, 5; European liberalism and, 178; free markets, 4; Goldwater as sword of, 61; Kirk on, 12; liberalism and, 56, 178; Meyer on, 177–79; New Deal and, 1; post–World War II gains of, 55; as reaction to New Deal, 1; revitalization during 1970s, 40; revival of, after Nixon's resignation, 36; as social movement, viii; strong national defense, 6; tide of history supporting, 110; traditional family values, 5; two-sided nature of, 177; voter self-identification with, 2; welfare reform, 4–5; wisdom of history, 6–7

The Conservative Affirmation (Kendall), 127

"Conservative Manifesto," 133–34

The Conservative Mind (Kirk), 12, 127

conservatives: accomplishments of, 56; African Americans and, 138; American Conservative Union, 109; *Brown v. Board of Education* opposed by, 135; W. Buckley as founder, 126–27; G. W. Bush and,

ABOUT THE AUTHORS

Donald T. Critchlow is professor of history at St. Louis University. He is the author and editor of many books including, most recently, *The Conservative Ascendancy: How the GOP Right Made Political History* (2008) and *Phyllis Schlafly and Grassroots Conservatism* (2005). Among his other books are *Intended Consequences: Birth Control, Abortion, and the Federal Government* (1999, 2001), *Studebaker: The Life and Death of an American Corporation* (1997), and *The Brookings Institution: Expertise and the Public Interest in a Democratic Society* (1989). He serves as editor of the *Journal of Policy History* and is currently working on a book on Hollywood politics.

Nancy MacLean is professor of history and African American studies at Northwestern University. She is the author of *Behind the Mask of Chivalry: The Making of the Second Ku Klux Klan* (1994), which received the Frank L. and Harriet C. Owsley Prize for a distinguished book in southern history, the James A. Rawley Prize for a distinguished book on the history of race relations, and the Hans Rosenhaupt Book Award for a distinguished book of broad humanistic significance; and of *Freedom Is Not Enough: The Opening of the American Workplace* (2006), which received numerous honors including the Philip Taft Labor History Award, the Allan Sharlin Book Award for the best book in social science history, and the Willard Hurst Prize for best book in socio-legal history. Her most recent book is *The American Women's Movement, 1945–2000: A Brief History with Documents* (2008).